CATERING
SERVICE

BAR-B-Q
HOT SAUSAGE

JOHN DeMERS

FOLLOW THE SMOKE

14,783 MILES OF GREAT

TEXAS
BARBECUE

PLACES, PEOPLE, SECRETS AND RECIPES!

b

bright sky press

bright sky press

2365 Rice Boulevard, Suite 202,
Houston, Texas 77005

Copyright © 2008 John DeMers

10   9   8   7   6   5   4   3   2   1

Library of Congress Cataloging-in Publication Data

DeMers, John, 1952-
Follow the smoke : 14,783 miles of great Texas barbecue / by John DeMers.
p. cm.
ISBN: 978-1-933979-22-9 (softcover : alk. paper) 1. Barbecue cookery—Texas—
Guidebooks. 2. Restaurants—Texas—Guidebooks. I. Title.

TX840.B3D46 2008
641.7'6—dc22

2008019382

Book and cover design by
Tutu Somerville and Cregan Design
Edited by Kristine Krueger
Photography by John DeMers

Printed in China through Asia Pacific Offset

ACKNOWLEDGMENTS

TO RESEARCH AND WRITE any book like this, an author needs many sources holding many differing opinions. Happily, I was granted all this and more by the following people in cities and towns across Texas, some speaking in an official capacity and others just because I asked them:

Christian Fletcher and the Wallace Guest House in Marble Falls; Beth Krauss in Austin, along with Kerri Holden at the Four Seasons Hotel; Nancy Liles in Abilene; Linda Sweatt in Odessa; Brenda Kissko in Midland; Patti Salter in Port Arthur; Stephanie Molina and Ashley Jennings in Beaumont; Diane Brandon in Arlington; Jim Aanstoos and Jason Ford in Taylor; Margaret Jackson in Irving; Veleisa Patton, Ariana Hajibashi-Martin and the Hotel Palomar in Dallas; Mel and Lisa Polk of the Gruene Outpost River Lodge in Gruene; Paul Anderson of the North East Texas Tourism Council; Gus Gustafson in Pittsburg; Mayor J.D. Baumgardner and Teresia Wims in Mount Vernon; Micki Wright in Texarkana; Mercy Rushing in Mineola; Mike Koston in Kilgore; Amie Hacker, Kimberley Lemley, Patti Young and Christopher Semtner in Corpus Christi, along with Nils Stolzlechner of the Omni Corpus Christi Hotel; David and Laura Denham of Pelican Bay Resort in Fulton; Lee and Tom Lowrie of the Jefferson Street Bed & Breakfast in Irving; Pat Adams in Mount Pleasant; Evelynn Bailey in San Antonio, along with Skip James and Edna Villanueva of the Westin Riverwalk; Judy Young in New Braunfels; Teo Rojas and Nancy Millar in McAllen; Keith Hackland and Cheryl Rodriguez of the Alamo Inn in Alamo; Gloria Dick and Pifas Silva in El Paso, along with that city's Camino Real Hotel.

On the Bright Sky Press side of the fence, kudos and gratitude are due to publisher Rue Judd, editor Kristine Krueger, and all-around publicist and planner Leslie Little, along with Ellen Cregan and Tutu Somerville at Cregan Design, who made my words and photos alike look beautiful.

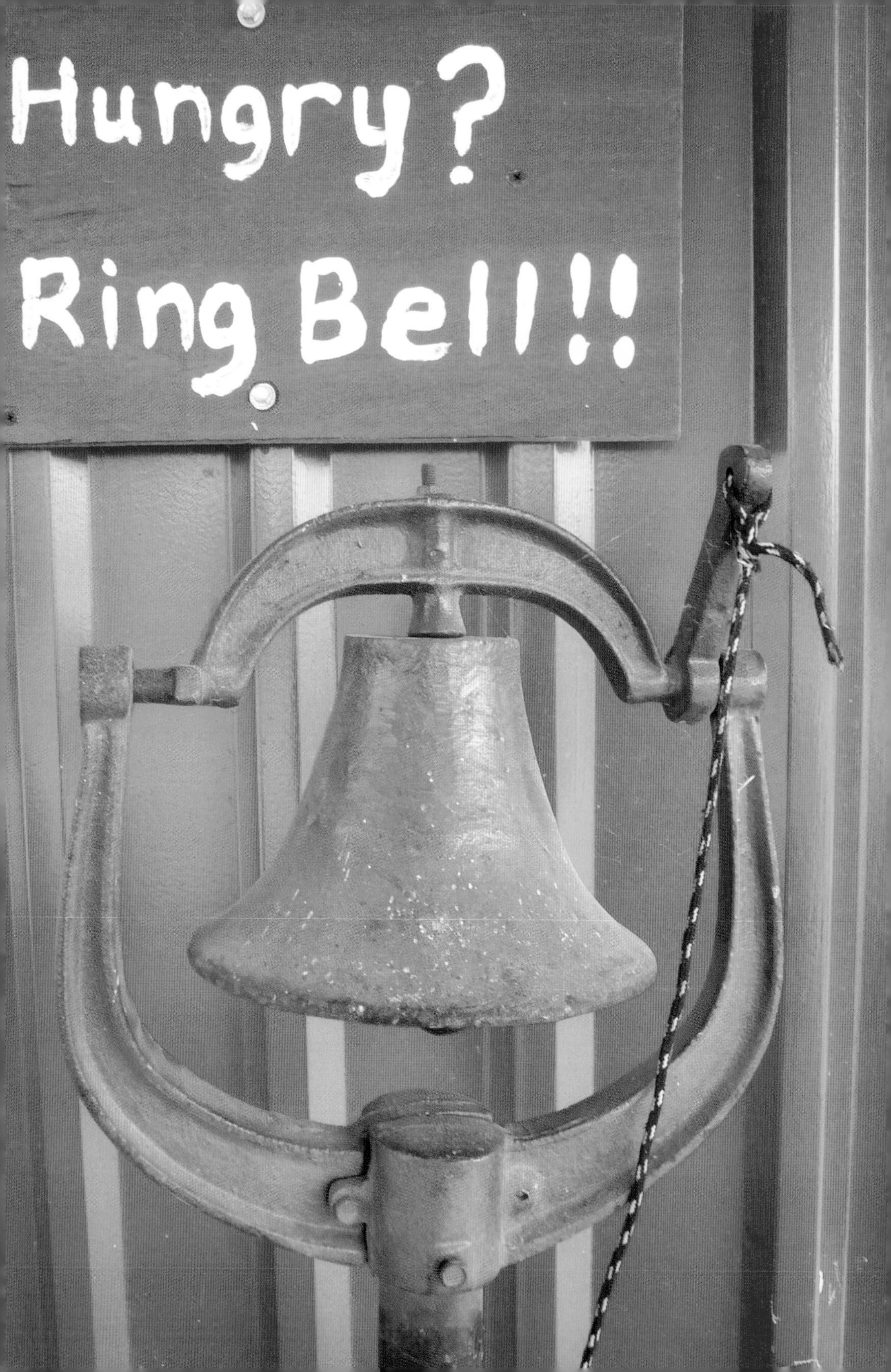
Hungry?
Ring Bell!!

TABLE OF CONTENTS

FOREWORD
BY TOM PERINI
PERINI RANCH STEAKHOUSE

I ALWAYS SAY: If you want to turn a wedding, family reunion or any other happy Texas occasion into a shouting match or a fistfight, just ask somebody what kind of wood they use.

Here in Texas, asking folks how they cook barbecue is like inquiring a bit too closely about their politics or their religion. It's a *lot* like that, actually—politics because a lot more votes have been "bought" with barbecue here than ever could be with hard cash, and religion because barbecue is a faith statement and, for many, a doctrine...like something Moses might have dragged down off that mountaintop. The funny thing is, many of the earliest settlers came to Texas in the 1800s to escape religious persecution and even religious wars in Europe. To hear the ancestors of these immigrants argue about barbecue today, you might not think we've come very far.

Beginning in the 1960s, I learned to cook barbecue around my family's cattle ranch from members of two great traditions: the Germans who made central Texas in their own image, and the African-Americans who lived everywhere in Texas after slavery ended on that day all true Texans know as Juneteenth. Both barbecue traditions are different, as are so many others spread around this huge state filled with different land types and weather patterns; and both barbecue traditions, done right, can be delicious. I learned them both—my goal was to master them, since I figured I owed my generous teachers nothing less—and set about sharing them with the world. Believe me, it's been one heck of a journey.

In addition to operating Perini Ranch Steakhouse in Buffalo Gap (pop. 463) just outside Abilene since the 1980s, I have been lucky enough to cater barbecue events all over the United States...you know, not just in fellow Wild West states like Oklahoma and Colorado but in very different places with very different taste buds: Washington, D.C. (yep, politics again) and California. Suffice it to say that, even in California, we didn't serve a lot of tofu or alfalfa sprouts! Even more amazingly, with support from industry groups like the Beef Council, we've been able to take our style of Texas barbecue to many of the far-flung corners of the globe. Just picture a typical Texas barbecue, but *then* picture it in Japan, Poland or Russia. We really turned some heads with our kind of food. No doubt about it.

I am well aware there are barbecue traditions beyond the borders of our Lone Star State, and (within reason) I respect those styles and the people who believe in them as *their* religion. Generally, barbecue means pork everywhere but Texas, from the slabs of ribs served in Kansas City to the pulled pork that stretches eastward from Memphis to the Carolinas, with tasty stops in Arkansas, Alabama and Georgia. Like I said, I'm not here to tell anybody the barbecue they grew up eating and loving isn't any good. I've tasted it, and it *is* good. What I am trying to do is invite you deep into the heart of Texas barbecue, to take you by the hand and lead you to the people and places who express everything that matters—ethnicity, generational respect, geographic uniqueness—by what they throw on, under and around an old-fashioned barbecue pit.

I think we can all agree on one definition, at least: Barbecue means slow-cooking, nothing more and nothing less, always has and always will. If you cook a steak quickly over a hot mesquite fire (as we do at the steakhouse), that's absolutely wonderful—but it's not barbecue. If you invite friends over to your home, gather in your backyard or by your pool and start flaming up burgers or hot dogs, that's wonderful too—but that's not barbecue either.

That's all I'm going to say right now. Barbecue means slow-cooking. I'll let John DeMers say the rest in the pages of this book, based on his ridiculous amount of driving around Texas and his death-defying willingness to eat more barbecue on any given day than mere mortals around him. I'm not prepared at this time to issue any more ultimatums. At my stage in life, I don't particularly want to be starting any fistfights.

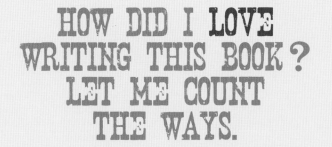

HOW DID I LOVE WRITING THIS BOOK? LET ME COUNT THE WAYS.

FIRST, starting with the obvious, I got to eat lots of terrific Texas barbecue. Yes, sometimes the regimen seemed overwhelming, especially on those days of six or even eight places in a stretch of almost uninterrupted eating. Pretending that you're hungry enough to appreciate the fine points of each pit master's smoked brisket, to evaluate the subtleties of this or that smoked sausage, or even to notice the differences from one slice of pecan pie to the other required acting skills worthy of an Oscar. By the same token, no one who didn't secretly desire to taste every bit of Texas barbecue ever produced—and who didn't secretly suspect he *could*—would propose such a book. Most of the meals devoured (or picked at) during this research were devoured or picked at with the owner looking on, usually discussing why each item was prepared the way it was, and what mother, grandmother, aunt or uncle gave him (or in some cases, her) the recipe. Such conversation about Texas barbecue is the ultimate side dish—the ultimate window into the heart and soul of a cooking tradition that speaks more directly than any other to native Texans, adopted Texans, homesick Texans and wannabe Texans.

    SECOND, I got to meet and visit with some terrific Texas people. There is no single theme, other than the willingness to work incredibly hard for incredibly modest rewards, that connects all the makers of Texas barbecue. They certainly aren't all the same race, color or creed, the major subsets being African-American, Hispanic, Middle European and cowboy. They don't all belong to the same socioeconomic level, as some still run tiny shacks on forgotten highways while others have grown into multiunit operators, sometimes fielding concepts removed from their barbecue roots. And while "barbecueing" (as it's incorrectly known in America) is a predominantly male hobby, the people who produce Texas barbecue as their job are by no means all men. Particularly in the African-American and Hispanic cultures, hardworking women regularly turn up as creators of successful barbecue places.

    THIRD, I got to see some terrific Texas countryside. By now it's a familiar notion that the Lone Star State is like a "whole other country." And like a country (as opposed to any typical state), Texas encompasses almost every land form, soil type and climate that exists in the Western Hemisphere. It is a joy to drive and drive and drive—the only thing I did more than eat, as the mileage in the book's subtitle makes plain—in a place that rewards the effort with beauty. Of course, some parts of Texas are more dramatic than others, from the long, lonely (off-season) beaches of the Gulf Coast to the eye-popping theatricality of Big Bend National Park, the nation's least visited by virtue of its sheer distance from anywhere. Still, the people of every Texas region love their hills and forests, lakes and streams, or their impossibly open vistas filled with absolutely nothing. Texans love Texas—the mythology, naturally, and the shared sense of birthright, but also the history, culture and topography of the specific region they call home. With apologies to all the airports that get frenzied businesspeople from one meeting to the next, the only real way to see the grandeur of Texas is at ground level.

FINALLY, with awareness of a notion that many will deny or at least dislike, I came to understand an American original under attack, one that most assuredly is something of a dinosaur. No, I don't mean barbecue itself (already a part of nearly every national menu), but the small, family-owned, mom-and-pop barbecue joint. While I felt no compulsion to punish families for success—homegrown concepts that have sprouted multiple locations deserve our respect—I felt a special fondness for the "little guy" doing what he does against extraordinary odds. We seldom talked politics with our...well, at least with *my* mouth full...yet it was clear that the complexity of today's chain-dominated restaurant industry against the backdrop of government regulations makes nearly all veterans wistful for simpler, better times. When a chain can "research and develop" some new rendition of Thai-Chipotle Buffalo Wings and roll them out with a national TV campaign for $5.99 a pop, the purveyors of small-scale, hands-on Texas barbecue understand they are fighting what almost certainly is a losing battle.

THIS BOOK IS ABOUT *ALL* THAT: a unique food prepared by unique people in one of the world's unique places—always haunted by the shadow of culture's tendency to wipe uniqueness off the face of the Earth. We don't understand it, this culture says. We can't control it, engineer it or mass-produce it for a profit to show stockholders, therefore it has to go. With the turning of this generation of Texas barbecue masters into the next, I worry how these smallest of the small entrepreneurs will fare. As many have noted over the centuries, however, Texas is a rather strange place. I hope Texas is strange enough to value forever the contributions these tireless men and women have made to everything we are.

A SHORT HISTORY
OF SMOKE

NO CULTURAL DESCRIPTION OF TEXAS, from pop journalism
to scholarly treatise, can afford to ignore the thing called barbecue.
Starting with the most obvious and anecdotal evidence, few things on
Earth unite Texans with each other (and when necessary, *against* all
others) more than these simple notions of what constitutes its single
most famous food.

Texans cringe at the very idea that other parts of America consider themselves blessed with, or even important to, the true history of
barbecue—the worst offenders being Memphis, Kansas City and that
amorphous mass of undiluted Southernism known as "the Carolinas."
Yet we join barbecue practitioners in all those areas whenever we hear
anyone going to a mere outdoor grilling party and claiming they're
going to a "barbecue." "Say it ain't so," we whisper amongst ourselves.
Because, of course, it *ain't*.

While the uninitiated may think barbecue—like country music,
NASCAR or super-sweet iced tea—helps unite Texas with the rest of the
Deep South (with the rest of the former Confederacy, if you will), nothing could be further from the truth. Barbecue is the great divider of
Southern cultural identity. And in the case of Texas, Lone Star barbecue
is not only preferred passionately within its borders but actually confirms to Texans their essential self-notions of vastness, diversity and
dominance. We gaze out at those other types of barbecue and, if we're
feeling honest, might see something worth lifting to our lips. But in
those traditions, we recognize nothing of the many-splendored-thing
that is Texas barbecue—a tradition equally beloved here (and claimed
with equal fervor) by trail-riding white cowboys, German and Czech
butchers, Hispanic horsemen and African slaves. Each of these groups
has an indelible barbecue tradition within this vast Spanish territory,
which, after tumultuous events that gave the countryside its mythology,
became Texas.

Oddly, considering all this pride of place, virtually no Texan
believes barbecue was *invented* here—and we're quick to tell you some
variation, real or fanciful, of the origins of the word itself. These days
many know "barbacoa" as a specific form of Hispanic barbecue in South
Texas; but there was a time when the word meant the whole, well,
enchilada. Those who've sampled Jamaican "jerk pork," created by runaway slaves as a way to preserve meat while on the run from British

14

soldiers (and, incidentally, bearing the same linguistic roots as Texas "beef jerky"), are on the right path.

Scholars tell us the word *barbicu* (meaning "sacred fire pit," as well it should) was first used among the Taino Indians of the Caribbean. It was not a cooking style per se, but a makeshift grill resting on sticks. Originally, the Tainos and other Caribbean populations dug a pit to house this makeshift structure, topped it with a whole pig or goat, then covered the entire affair with coal and maguey leaves. This *barbicu* was then set afire, creating a steady, low level of heat and considerable smoke. If these Indians were lucky, by morning their meal was done. There is no record, however, of Tainos obsessively setting their alarm clocks to ring every hour on the hour to check on their meat's progress—as more than a few Texans do with their beef brisket today.

Over time, both the word and the technique were absorbed into the three main languages of Caribbean colonialism: Spanish, French and English. Though it turns up, logically, as *barbacoa* in Spanish, it ends up something like *barbecue* in both French and English. The French, in fact, are involved in one of barbecue etymology's greatest

inaccuracies...the silly notion that the word started out French for "from beard to tail." Since there is no evidence of Frenchmen ever calling this food by any name *other* than the one born of Taino, this at best is putting the egg before the chicken. The French, we believe, should be satisfied with their crucial role in our other favorite related word. A different Caribbean tribe, the Arawaks, called that same wooden grill a *buccan*, which the French adjusted slightly into *boucan*. It didn't take long for wild Europeans who lived as outcasts in the islands, slow-cooking whatever meat they could steal, to become known by their preferred cooking method—as *boucaniers*. That's, of course, buccaneers to you and me.

The link between the "great houses" of the Caribbean and the "plantations" of the Deep South is simple, cruel and clear—slavery. Many preferred foods, cooking methods and other cultural definers made it into the South on the backs of African slaves who'd spent time working on those hot and disease-ridden islands. Students of such things find evidence of so much that is Southern—yes, even *white* Southern—in the tragic odyssey of blacks onto these shores as property rather than people. States with the strongest barbecue tradition are, not surprisingly, states with the strongest slave tradition...or else they are urban areas to which African-Americans migrated once slavery *was* abolished. Even places far removed from Memphis and Kansas City showcase this phenomenon, explaining the delicious pork barbecue served for generations from Chicago's South Side to New York's Harlem.

Texas was a slave state in the years leading up to the Civil War, and no less a figure than Sam Houston owned slaves, though he argued loudly for emancipation, and both educated and freed his slaves long before the official proclamation celebrated as Juneteenth in Texas and 28 other states. Particularly in East Texas, where the soil and climate were most appropriate for plantation-style crops and, therefore, plantation-style labor, slavery took hold as a fact of Texas life, with the same preference for pulled pork and pork ribs identified with African-Americans everywhere. Yet, while this type of barbecue was the be-all and end-all in other parts of the so-called Barbecue Belt (again, you might as well call it the Slave Belt), in Texas, with its unique geography and unique history, this was only the beginning.

An utterly different style of barbecue entered Texas by "crossing the border"—except that in those earliest days, there *was* no border. Texas was part of Spain's holdings in the New World, connecting this state and places like New Mexico, Arizona and California to a colonial powerhouse reaching down through Mexico to the southern tip of the Americas. Driven by dreams of gold under the magical banner *El Dorado*, the Spanish marched through and brought every civilization they met under their control. And while they were smart enough to pick up a taste for chocolate and vanilla from the Aztecs, they were also smart enough to bring along pigs and a nifty way to cook them. So the notion of *barbacoa* became Spanish, long after the Tainos of the Caribbean had been dispersed, destroyed and forgotten.

Over the centuries, the cost of maintaining such colonies so far from Mother Spain spiraled upward, while the local sense of being "Spaniards" spiraled downward. A series of independence movements in Mexico finally separated that huge land (including the part of it known as Tejas) from its often-corrupt European overseers. In a sense, Mexico's independence movements echoed the same hopes and dreams heard in 1776 in the 13 British colonies to the north. In a more important sense, they foreshadowed a difficult time when Mexico would hear the same arguments fired back from upstarts claiming a unique identity and a unique right to be free in Texas.

In Texas, therefore—and arguably *only* in Texas—barbecue spoke Spanish before it spoke English. Across the vast and arid plains of the far south, the region just above the Rio Grande, what must have been the state's first "lonesome cowboys" did what lonesome cowboys still do in the movies. They rode the range, herded the cattle that became their stock and trade, and helped blaze the long, dusty cattle trails north that someday would bring their product to an eager market. It was cows not pigs that these independent *vaqueros* herded day and night, through blazing heat in summer and murderous winds in winter. And it was cows not pigs that they turned to when they were hungry, adopting and adapting the cultural heritage of Spanish-Mexican *barbacoa* to suit the expanses of the Texas range.

Whenever the debate over immigration heats up in Washington, we should remember that Texas history is one *long* debate over immigration, with quite a few heroes and far more villains. But immigration—good times and bad, visionary or imbecilic—has been the force that defines Texas more profoundly than any and all others.

Over time, the ideas of Texas barbecue would expand far beyond the Hispanic universe straddling the border...when there finally came to *be* a border to straddle. And while the pork-smoking African-Americans of East Texas would remain a delicious "lost world," a cut-off Shangri-la of the Pig, the beef-centric barbecue of Spanish cowboys merged smoothly with the smoking techniques raised to an art by the German and Czech butchers of Central Texas. Again and again, immi-

gration gave force and focus to the ongoing process of becoming Texan—and, eventually, of becoming American.

An entire collection of now-forgotten European wars and religious persecutions sent wave after wave of men, women and children to a place they'd barely heard of. Ironically, European politics and religion being the topsy-turvy things they were, many groups ended up sharing towns and farmlands in Texas with the very people they'd run away *from*. This would become one of America's first great challenges, and arguably one of its greatest triumphs—the ability to mold a new identity from ancient fears and hatreds. As part of this process, while many Texas towns held onto the richness of their own cultures, their own churches and, happily for us, their own favorite foods, they did so within the larger picture frame of building a better territory, republic, state and nation.

The result, as we'll savor region by region in the pages that follow, is Texas as we know it today: a place where any citizen can list his or her must-have "national dishes" as Czech kolaches, German spaetzle, Mexican enchiladas…and perhaps most of all, that unique style of cooking meat created by Indians in the Caribbean, annexed by conquering Europeans, and brought in from different directions by African slaves and cowboys who spoke nothing but Spanish.

THE
CENTER

THE COUNTY LINE AUSTIN

ADDRESS: 3345 BEE CAVE ROAD, AUSTIN,
PLUS OTHER LOCATIONS
PHONE: (512) 327-1742
ESTABLISHED: 1975
OWNERS: SKEETER MILLER, ED NORTON, RANDY GOSS
BEST BITES: FRIED CHICKEN AND CHIPOTLE POPPERS,
HOMEMADE BREAD, BUFFALO CHICKEN BITE CAESAR
SALAD, BEEF BRISKET, BABY BACK PORK RIBS, GARLIC
MASHED RED-SKIN POTATOES, BREAD PUDDING, BROWNIES
PAYMENT: CREDIT CARDS

Like most people who tell you their name is "Skeeter," the ruddy, blond-locked public face of The County Line started out in life as somebody else.

Don Miller was a serious young man with a serious baseball talent who found himself going to college on a scholarship in Arkansas. Now, though, to hear Skeeter tell it, he never *really* found himself until he decided he'd rather work his own way through school in Austin than get a free ride anywhere else. That's how he ended up stooped and steaming night after night as the dishwasher of a barbecue joint with a decidedly checkered past.

During Prohibition, the first of several locations now packing them in as The County Line was a bar/café/procurement zone for the movers and shakers of Texas politics. They could drink alcohol here, of course, and meet with anyone wishing to influence them who was too shady to show up at the Capitol—which meant shady, indeed. There was also the matter of women, who would turn up nightly in this ramshackle building on a hill. The women appeared here for love or money, and that meant lawmakers were breaking the law.

"The cool thing about being up on this hill," Skeeter relates, from a time before he was born, "was that they kept a guy down on the main road looking for the cops. Whenever they'd turn in hoping to make a bust, the lookout would shoot his gun in the air. By the time the cops could make it up here, the politicians and the women had all managed to scatter."

Texas politicians and police officers still find their way to this old rock-and-wood structure on the hill, as they do to other County Line locations around Austin, San Antonio, El Paso, Albuquerque, Houston, Edmond and Oklahoma City. This time, though, they just eat barbecue.

You get the feeling, sitting with Skeeter at a table piled high with food, that he and his partners have asked themselves a different question over the past 30 years. As that college kid washing dishes became a manager and finally an owner, you picture conversations based not only on the typical Texas barbecue query—"What would be traditional?"—but on the one closest to Skeeter's heart—"What would be really cool?" That's why, for instance, while some barbecue joints serve only iced tea and others offer a few beers, The County Line's signature beverage is the almighty margarita. It's as though the same spirit that inspired Kinky Friedman's gubernatorial campaign slogan is behind this place's menu: "Why the Hell Not?"

"In the old days, most of the barbecue places had sawdust on the floor," says Skeeter. "They had butcher paper they put the meat on, and they made you walk through a line to get your food. We wanted to create something upscale, a big place in a unique setting." And as for whether a margarita really "goes" with barbecue…"When we opened, we just had 'em, and people never stopped ordering 'em. Hell, I'd drink a margarita in a Chinese place if they'd let me."

When Skeeter says "upscale," he means having table service, cloth napkins and real utensils, not having a fancy, quiet atmosphere or snooty French-accented waiters. The County Line is big-time fun, as though the old building never forgot the wild times it saw during Prohibition.

The menu features that Holy Trinity of Texas meats (brisket, ribs, sausage) along

milder taste than hickory. So...lots of time, lots of labor, lots of care, all invested each day by people who've worked there a very long time and know what they're doing. It's a chain-restaurant operator's *worst* nightmare.

"That's the thing about the barbecue business," Skeeter says, refilling his margarita glass from the shaker. "If you wanna do it right, you gotta baby that thing for 18 hours. Who the hell wants to be in that kinda business? That's why nobody's bought us. It's too damn hard. You gotta love it, and be a little bit crazy."

THE IRON WORKS BARBECUE, AUSTIN

ADDRESS: 100 RED RIVER STREET, AUSTIN
PHONE: (512) 478-4855
ESTABLISHED: 1978
OWNER: CHARLOTTE FINCH
BEST BITES: BEEF RIBS, BEEF BRISKET, IWB HOT SAUSAGE, BEANS, SPICY BARBECUE SAUCE, CHILI, PEACH OR BLACKBERRY COBBLER
PAYMENT: CREDIT CARDS

Roland Cantu keeps turning three decades of Austin barbecue history in his mind and can't get past a single basic theme. "We haven't really changed much," he says, settling into a rustic wooden booth as the day's lunch crowd builds around him. "We've stayed the same. We really don't try to make it new and improved. Every day, you want to get better. But once you've set the bar so high, how are you going to get better?"

The Iron Works has been doing what it does—the same, according to Cantu— since 1978. Yet the place is what it is, and is called what it's called, because of the story that came before the first brisket or ribs were ever smoked here. To this day, a huge amount of the décor harks back to the building's earlier life, as F. Weigl Iron Works. Whether you're one of the 225 people seated downstairs or the 40 on the

with the Holy Trinity of Texas sides (potato salad, coleslaw, beans), but there the resemblance to a traditional limited list grinds to a halt. In their pursuit of the next "really cool thing," Skeeter and his partners have cobbled together a vast collection of foods people simply love to eat. There are terrific appetizers, from super onion rings to batter-fried jalapeños stuffed with chicken, two cheeses and red and green chipotles.

At the other end of your feast, there are gargantuan desserts light years removed from the typical banana pudding. The standouts are homemade bread pudding blanketed in Jack Daniel's sauce and a Kahlúa pecan brownie.

While fielding multiple locations has allowed The County Line some efficiencies of scale, you get the feeling the owners resist such things daily at every turn. No location looks anything like any other, Skeeter boasts, which means that operational problems must be worked out differently in each new place.

Still, the main thing The County Line refuses to make "efficient" is barbecue itself. The meats are slow-cooked hour after hour over green oak, which Skeeter says throws off a lot of smoke but with a upstairs patio, Roland and Iron Works owner Charlotte Finch want you to live and breathe another time with every bite. Best of all, you won't be alone.

"We've had people coming here for 30 years," says Roland, an Austin native who's worked here as a manager for nearly a decade. "And they order the same thing every time. We lose customers when they pass away or when they move someplace else—that's about the only reasons. And there's always new people coming in."

Ironworker Fortunat Weigl Sr., his wife, Anna, and their sons, Lee and Herbert, were "new people" here once. They were among the many who came to America for opportunity at the start of the 20th century, passing through Ellis Island before steaming south to Galveston. They came to Texas, says the legend, because the parents had read Wild West stories to their sons all the way over on the *S.S. Breslau* and decided the free spirit of these cowboys was just the thing for them. A train carried the family from the Galveston dock to Austin, where Fortunat did his best to support his family as a construction worker.

As with so many immigrants, special skills admired in the Old Country got forgotten during the crossing, with only the chance at hard labor remaining. All the same, when a Swiss wood-carver took on a project in San Marcos, he was smart enough to ask Fortunat to create the iron wall figures he had in mind. Peter Mansbedel even advanced Fortunat enough to buy what he needed: a few tools, a sack of coal and some flat iron. The total came to $75.38. From that advance, F. Weigl Iron Works was born in 1922.

As business grew, so did thoughts of a new and bigger workspace. And when the family's original lease ran out, the search took on greater urgency, leading them to a supremely cheap plot of abandoned land on Red River Street. Weigl and sons created the building that now serves barbecue from materials left over from construction of the Texas State Capitol. In one of the worst bits of timing ever, the Weigls had just gotten their Iron Works up and running when one of the most horrific floods in Austin's history struck. The building was devastated, as were the Weigls, with no jobs and no time to have built up a cash reserve.

How they responded to this disaster, though, probably reflects their memories of those tough and resilient Wild West cowboys: They cut pieces of floorboard from their building and shoveled huge piles of dank mud into the basement. Today, the disaster is recalled by license plates covering the holes the Weigls dug, as well as by markings on the walls seven feet up, each carrying the notation "Flood Stage, June 5, 1935."

Lee and Herbert continued to run the business after their father's death in 1973, but by 1977 they were ready to retire. By then, the old-world skills and patience required to create their style of ornamental works had faded from the American skill set, along with the deep appreciation that set the family's pieces in the State Capitol, at Texas A&M and in the homes of show-business greats Bob Hope, Jack Benny and Lucille Ball. The stage was set for another generation of celebrities with names like Kevin Costner, Leonardo DiCaprio, Bob Dylan and Jay

Leno. These would come to this tumble-down corner in a tangle of trees searching not for iron but for barbecue.

"I think Leno started it, really," says Roland. "He came here to eat when he was just a standup comic and he was playing this club downtown. Then, every so often, a star would come in, and I'd ask him how he'd heard of us. I mean, it makes you wonder sometimes, right? And almost every one of them says something like, 'Jay Leno told me I had to eat here.' Jay has mentioned us on *The Tonight Show*, too, telling anybody coming to Texas, 'Tell my friends at The Iron Works I said hello.' "

STUBB'S, AUSTIN

ADDRESS: 801 RED RIVER STREET, AUSTIN

PHONE: (512) 480-8341

ESTABLISHED: 1995

OWNERS: JEFF WAUGHTAL AND CHARLES ATTAL

BEST BITES: BEEF BRISKET, SMOKED TURKEY BREAST, MASHED YAMS, COLLARD GREENS, BLACKBERRY COBBLER, BANANA PUDDING, PECAN PIE

PAYMENT: CREDIT CARDS

Ask anybody around Austin about the barbecue produced today in the place that's C.B. Stubblefield's legacy and you're likely to hear: "Oh, that's mostly a music venue." Just don't try saying such a thing to executive chef Margaret Vera.

"I'm the only food person in management here," laughs Margaret, a sixth-generation Texan who grew up in Houston and once ran her own restaurant in Austin. "I'm the one who always looks at people working and asks, 'What are those guys doing?' Everybody kinda makes fun of me and says, 'That's a sound check.' From the very beginning, there's been music here. C.B. Stubblefield always had a feeling for music, for blues and R&B especially, and he made sure music was on the menu of every barbecue place he ever owned."

The public perception of Stubb's as a music venue is helped along by the fact that it mostly is one. The place produces 70 to 75 outdoor concerts in its "back-yard" each year, many shows reaching the open area's capacity of 2,400. In addition, Stubb's plays host to between three and five indoor performances a week, filling a

dusty-looking downstairs auditorium for about 400. Music being the diverse thing it is, Stubb's can feel like quite a different place night to night, depending on whether the music is traditional blues or jazz, rock or punk, or something exotically ethnic. The barbecue doesn't change, of course, but the crowd and its ordering patterns do.

"For some shows," says Margaret, "people are perfectly happy to wait two hours to get a table here in the dining rooms. Other shows, everybody just wants to drink beer and eat a chopped beef sandwich standing up outside."

Everything at Stubb's is about keeping one man's barbecue legacy alive—for fun and profit. Virtually every wall is decorated with an oversized black-and-white portrait of the man himself, always wearing his signature cowboy hat pitched back on his forehead and nearly always bent over something producing smoke. For many walking into Stubb's, the face on all the walls is strangely familiar, thanks to the line of canned foods the company once produced for supermarkets and its current line of barbecue sauces and rubs. Still, as Margaret points out more than once, if the place called Stubb's seems all about C.B. Stubblefield's face, it's even more profoundly about his story.

Stubb was born in tiny Navasota, pretty much in the woods northwest of Houston, an area with a strong African-American barbecue tradition. Early on, Stubb developed a felicity with the language, particularly for quotable quotes, perhaps as a method of getting attention among 11 siblings. In one of the quotes seen most often on Stubb's products today, he dealt definitively with his view of tradition: "God born me a black man and I plan to stay that-a-way."

Almost in response, when Stubb went off to fight for his country in the Korean War, he was assigned to the 96th Field Artillery Battalion, the last all-black unit in the U.S. Army. Though he started out as a gunner and a tank driver, the young man discovered his true calling as a mess sergeant on the front lines. Essentially, he spent the Korean War cooking for 10,000-plus at a time. Were Stubb alive today, feeding those 2,400 out back for a concert would seem like small potatoes.

Back home in Texas, Stubb learned how to barbecue from the legendary Amos Gamel, and he also attacked his craft from the other end—enrolling in welding school to learn how to produce barbecue pits.

The result of this double-edged mastery was an initial restaurant-music club in Lubbock, opened in 1968 and operated to some acclaim for 17 years. Somewhere along the way, the not-so-shy word "Legendary" crept into the place's name, but nobody seemed to think it was far off the mark. Still, Stubb's most quotable quote came to stay during those years, remaining a slogan for his commercial lines and connecting past to present: "Ladies and gentlemen, I'm a cook."

Stubb started his retail food company with several partners, including Texas musician Joe Ely, in 1991. Presumably the idea was to merchandise the quality of Stubb's tradition without making the man work so hard every day. As Margaret tells it today, the only person not overjoyed with this arrangement was Stubb himself.

At his insistence, the partnership found a restaurant location in downtown Austin and renovated the original building created by Mexican stonemasons in the 1850s. Music was part and parcel to this "new" Stubb's since opening night in 1995, Joe Ely and his band serving as the first entertainment. Later acts have included Willie Nelson, George Strait and Pat Green. Sadly, C.B. Stubblefield passed away at age 64, just as his name was about to achieve its highest visibility ever.

"The outdoor shows really drive the eating and drinking," Margaret explains, setting a plate of smoked brisket, ribs, sausage and turkey in front of a visitor, along with a welcome rainbow of soul-food sides like mashed yams and smothered collard greens. "Even though we're a music venue, people still have the choice of eating anyplace else in town before they come. What they want from us is the full barbecue and live music experience. And until you've had a chopped beef sandwich and a Lone Star in our backyard, you don't really understand what that is."

THE GREEN MESQUITE BARBEQUE & MORE AUSTIN

....

ADDRESS: 1400 BARTON SPRINGS ROAD, AUSTIN, PLUS TWO OTHER LOCATIONS
PHONE: (512) 479-0485
ESTABLISHED: 1956, BECOMING GREEN MESQUITE IN 1988
OWNER: TOM DAVIS
BEST BITES: 4 MEAT BBQ PLATE, CHICKEN-FRIED STEAK, BIG CATFISH PLATE, POTATO SALAD, FRIED OKRA, PEACH COBBLER, PECAN PIE, BLUEBERRY PIE
PAYMENT: CREDIT CARDS

Since South Austin's appropriately funky Green Mesquite started life as a burger joint called Dunks, serving crowds after the old Austin Senators' semipro baseball games, you shouldn't be surprised to find that good burgers are still on the menu.

Yet over the years as a barbecue place, Green Mesquite has not only taken on all the basics of the Texas genre, but a fair number of surprises as well. How many other barbecue joints, for instance, use their front window to proclaim "Excellent Coffee"?

Operating as Jerry Jacobs Pit Barbecue System beginning in the mid-1950s, the place Austin now embraces has made a habit of the care required for things like brisket. As far back as Jerry's time, that drill required 16 hours over low wood heat. However, as local historians recall, some days it was less what was being served at Jerry Jacobs than the people being served. True to barbecue's multiracial roots, Jerry's was one of the few public places in town at the time that happily served both black and white customers.

"We consider ourselves very South Austin," general manager Deedee Anderson says today, as though she and her entire staff fervently believe that explains everything. "We do what we do, and we try to do it the best we can. We just want to keep the funky flair about it, instead of going all corporate and sterile."

In its current incarnation as Green Mesquite, a few things have changed since the old days as Jerry Jacobs, or the even older days as Dunks. Most importantly, a fire devastated the dining room in 1999 and forced owner Tom Davis to rebuild a good bit, in the process removing the unexpected step down when customers first entered from the street. "That was the fun part," giggles Deedee, "watching people come in."

The whole building ended up looking and feeling more stable, after some iffy times in the course of construction. "For a while, we were afraid the whole thing was going to collapse around us like a matchbox."

These days, the man in charge of working the pit is director of operations Joe Reese. He has learned to work the Ole Hickory rotisserie smoker like a master, relying on the mesquite mentioned in the place's name for heat, smoke and flavor. Brisket goes in for 12 to 16 hours, depending on the size of the pieces and how many are being cooked. Either way, a thermostat keeps the heat low and slow, even for those few hours at night between the last guy's departure and the first guy's arrival.

Joe and his smoker turn out all three of the meats in the combo that is Green Mesquite's biggest seller: the 3 Meat BBQ Plate of brisket, either all-beef sausage or pork spareribs, and turkey breast. For those who can't quite handle the "either," there's an efficient, problem-solving 4 Meat BBQ Plate.

Green Mesquite realized quickly it had to do the Big Three of barbecue side dishes: potato salad, coleslaw and beans. Still, customers kept asking for more, so the kitchen staff searched for things that would be good without requiring too much extra labor. Corn on the cob was easy, for instance, as were green beans. Jambalaya was added as a tasty way to use up leftover chicken and sausage, while they introduced crispy Deep South fried okra more or less because they could. And as long as they had a fryer going, why not offer chicken-fried steak?

New dishes kept turning up as questions, and regulars looking for variety loved the fact that the answer always seemed to be yes. Eventually "Green Mesquite Barbeque" found itself adding "& More" to its painted and neon signs.

"We're a fast-service restaurant," Deedee says by way of definition. "We have table service instead of a cafeteria line, and we have a little more variety on our menu. Just because one person in the family is having barbecue doesn't mean everybody has to."

Joe thinks about all that variety for a moment, then focuses again on the Main Event: "Barbecue is a different kind of animal because of the way you cook it. When you first start out in this business, it's just so hard to figure. You have to cook it way ahead of time, and you have to sell everything you cook. Do we want to be a barbecue legend someday? Sure. But we'd at least love for everybody to know we're here."

ARTZ RIB HOUSE
AUSTIN

....

ADDRESS: 2330 S. LAMAR BOULEVARD, AUSTIN
PHONE: (512) 442-8283
ESTABLISHED: 1986, THIS LOCATION IN 1992
OWNER: ART BLONDIN
BEST BITES: PORK RIBS, SMOKED SAUSAGE, SOUP OF THE DAY, SAUSAGE TORTILLA WRAP, SOUTH AUSTIN CHEESE STEAK TACOS, COLESLAW, SWEET POTATO PECAN PIE
PAYMENT: CREDIT CARDS

Listening to him talk about his two favorite things, eating barbecue and playing country music, it seems like the people of Art Blondin's native Vermont should have long ago given him two simple words of advice: *Austin, Texas.* As it was, it took him years to make his way south from the Green Mountain State, famous for producing only one Ben and one Jerry, with results that couldn't have been more predictable or more delicious.

"We came down to look at a possible restaurant and bar deal," Art reports matter-of-factly. "They left. I stayed."

Twenty-seven years after arriving in Austin—"any 27 years you don't have to shovel snow are 27 good years, if you ask me"—Art thinks back to those early days. He spent most of his time playing with

various bands and driving all over central Texas looking for gigs. All that driving required, of course, lots of stops for barbecue. He had tasted the stuff here and there before, though he was disturbed (as any future Texan should be) that some Vermonters thought "barbecue" was throwing burgers on a grill. Fascinated by this American culinary artifact, as well as by the quasi-religious devotion to detail of its greatest practitioners, Art took his first baby steps toward becoming a Barbecue Guy.

"I had no real experience 'til I took over this little restaurant on 5th Street, just to do lunches and downtown delivery," he remembers. "The place had a nice brick smoker, so I started experimenting—you know, trial and error, plus reading everything about Texas barbecue I could get my hands on. I came up with a dry rub and a sauce. And then I heard about something called a 'rib-ticklin' barbecue cook-off.' There were four categories, and I took first place in all four. It shocked the heck out of me, but that was when I started getting serious about this. I thought: Maybe I can do something with this."

It didn't take long, on the heels of his surprising victory, for that downtown eatery—called Artz Caboose—to be called instead "that little place with the great ribs." The name Artz, by the way, combined Art for Art's sake, with that final flourish of a "z" honoring his better half, Zenobia Sutton. Still, the Caboose that Art established in 1986 was awfully small, especially as he morphed it from a simple lunch joint into a barbecue destination. His current location in ever-funky South Austin opened up in 1992, and Art was way past ready.

While establishing his reputation for ribs, Art has remained true to his musical calling. For one thing, he does his bit for the self-proclaimed Live Music Capital of the World by featuring live music in his restaurant every night. Genres, sounds, personalities and instruments come and go through the little corner Art assigns to performers, but they're always there... and always playing their stuff. For another thing, Art has kept up his own stuff, playing as a member of the Austin-based Jon Emery Band. The five-piece ensemble has performed locally and regionally, and has even carried their "hillbilly rock and roll" to Holland, France and Germany.

As the name Artz Rib House implies, Art serves plenty of traditional Texas brisket but concentrates on those ribs. He serves both pork (country-style or baby back) and beef ribs, subjecting them to the wonderful rub he perfected years ago and then to low-level heat from an all-mesquite fire. "I really like the flavor of mesquite," he explains. "It burns really hot, but I keep the temperature down to 200. The ribs get tender and stay moist that way."

Other interesting twists, which Art considers *pure* South Austin, include tortilla soup, nachos, a teriyaki cheeseburger from Artz Caboose days and something he calls cheese steak tacos, with a glancing nod to Philly before making a run for the border via grilled onions and lots of jalapeños. There's a grilled shrimp plate for healthy-choicers, and a grilled vegetable plate to satisfy the most militant of vegans. This *is* Austin, after all.

Speaking of which, Art has some mighty definite feelings about the shades of personality in his adopted town. Though immense economic development has come to Austin from a wide array of global technology directions, so have frazzling traffic, subdivisions that mask the once-lovely hillsides, and a loss of original outlaw identity. In South Austin, along his colorful stretch of Tex-Mex joints, gun shops, liquor stores and dusty antique dealers, Art seems to deal with modernity the best way there ever was—by pretending it isn't there.

"South Austin is a lot different from North Austin," he says. "Here it's more bubbas and old hippies, instead of yuppies and lawyers. I get really nervous if I have to go north of the river."

28

LAMBERTS DOWNTOWN BARBECUE, AUSTIN

ADDRESS: 401 W. 2ND STREET, AUSTIN
PHONE: (512) 494-1500
ESTABLISHED: 2006
OWNER: LOU LAMBERT
BEST BITES: FRIED GREEN TOMATOES, ROASTED GREEN CHILE QUESO, "SOUP ON THE CHALKBOARD," ACHIOTE- AND LIME-RUBBED FREE-RANGE CHICKEN, PESTO-RUBBED SAN ANGELO LAMB CHOPS, MAC AND THREE CHEESES, FRIED BLACKBERRY PIE
PAYMENT: CREDIT CARDS

Lou Lambert isn't the least bit afraid somebody might call his food "fancy barbecue" or, potentially even worse, "gourmet barbecue." As a chef trained in the French *cuisine classique* and formed by the likes of Wolfgang Puck, Lou uses such phrases himself from time to time. What's important to him is the way great flavors flow naturally from great ingredients—and from the tantalizing truth that his "new" ways with Texas classics are prob-ably the oldest ways of all. He's willing to bet his West Texas ranch upbringing on it.

"To me, fancy barbecue goes back to the very roots of barbecue," Lou says, enjoying his first-time visitor's reaction to the polished tables and suave lime-green banquettes filling a dining room that's as old-meets-new as his cooking.

"We're looking at barbecue as an art form. I've worked in New York and California, but what I really loved growing up in West Texas was barbecue. That doesn't mean we're painting plates and bastardizing everything. It just means we're using different rubs and different sauces to give our own interpretation to everything we serve here."

In addition, by bringing his New American chef's sensibility to a culinary form that probably needs it—thinking seasonally and locally, emphasizing organic produce and free-range meats— Lou is, wonder of wonders, cooking things in ways that produce flavors quite close to those enjoyed a century or more ago in the wilds of Texas.

These days, of course, with the high-volume food supply system we have in place, this method does mean somewhat higher prices, which is all the word "gourmet" means in a lot of cases. But in a long-ignored part of downtown Austin now reborn as a shopping district, with a chic W Hotel coming in and the new home of so-rustic-it's-hip PBS music show *Austin City Limits*, it's a safe bet nobody's counting their pennies from heaven.

The whole idea of Lamberts seems a delicious contradiction. While most barbecue joints in Texas are old and decrepit, few of them actually sport a history that's, well, *historic*. Lamberts occupies the 133-year-old Schneider Brothers building, as the painted words on the outside wall make clear, all lovingly restored by the city in 2002. And almost no barbecue joints in Texas can include in their physical description phrases like "Venetian plaster," "frosted tracery windows" or "plush old-style leather." Lamberts can, along with a lot of other impressive phrases supplied by the restaurant's interior design firms.

Still, to the serious eater in any crowd, such elegant verbiage pales in comparison to poetry like "broiled Gulf oysters with wood-charred tomatoes, apple-smoked bacon and spicy pesto butter" or "fried green tomatoes with lump crab salad, mizuna and Green Goddess dressing."

For once on a barbecue menu, a distinction is made between meats from the smoker and meats from the grill... such things as "brown sugar and coffee rubbed natural beef brisket" hailing slowly from the former and "mustard and brown sugar coated Niman Ranch rib eye with roasted garlic bulb" or even "wild Tasmanian salmon with broken charred tomato vinaigrette" emerging quickly from the latter. Despite an absence of hyphens that would surely help with meaning, we are powerless to resist the word cascades.

Sides are served family-style at Lamberts, no fewer than 12 items ranging from classic buttermilk potato salad for those who can't eat barbecue without it to Texas soul foods like green chile cheese grits and smoked bacon braised collard greens.

Lou calls himself a "purist" when it comes to the meat that's ever at the heart of a barbecue meal. All smoking is done over Hill Country oak, though time and temperature vary wildly depending on the type and cut of meat. No sauce gets "mopped" on during cooking, since Lou prefers using a dry rub created for each meat (or seafood) all by itself. Barbecue sauce does turn up, in the shape of three bottles on your table holding a traditional Texas tomato-based sauce, a spicy variation inspired by South Texas, and a mustard-based barbecue sauce borrowed from North Carolina or Memphis or somewhere else that isn't Texas.

Of all the courses in a restaurant meal, none needs to stroke more traditional chords than dessert. Even the wildest and most adventurous of diners wants something like apple pie à la mode when his or her meal nears its end. Lamberts meets those needs with old-fashioned peach cobbler with vanilla bean ice cream, but also with less traditional barbecue finales like fried blackberry pie and warm Carmelita with cajeta caramel.

Like most of the best dishes here, these desserts have started out familiar, then packed their bags to go traveling, some arriving at the place they began.

"We love Austin and we love what's happening downtown," says Lou, who made his name locally some years back with Liberty Catering, Liberty Pies and Lamberts on funky South Congress.

"We love the vitality of all the new retail coming in. I think we're so wildly popular because we're trying to be true to our Texas roots and true to our Austin roots. We have the new and the old, both from an aesthetic and a food point of view. We approach barbecue not just as a form of cooking. We are looking at barbecue as an event."

THE SALT LICK BAR-B-QUE, DRIFTWOOD

ADDRESS: 18300 FM 1826, DRIFTWOOD
PHONE: (512) 858-4959
ESTABLISHED: 1967
OWNER: SCOTT ROBERTS
BEST BITES: BEEF BRISKET, SMOKED SAUSAGE, POTATO SALAD, COLESLAW, PECAN PIE, PEACH OR BLACKBERRY COBBLER
PAYMENT: CASH

The barbecue joint—more like a barbecue *ranch*, really—that Scott Roberts' father and mother built by hand four decades ago doesn't seem so remote anymore. And thanks to Scott and some of his high-profile neighbors, it's feeling less remote all the time.

For several years, The Salt Lick hosted thousands for Sunday Faire, the swirling outdoor finale of the Texas Hill Country Wine and Food Festival, thus making the winding hill road to Driftwood a bit less intimidating to dyed-in-the-jeans Austinites. Wineries, too, have come to this section of the Hill Country, including the large one started by Houston-born Damian Mandola of Carrabba's fame, with

restaurant and cooking school and who-knows-what-else part of his plan. And finally, Scott himself is contributing to local growth—developing a residential section with 83 lots, virtually across the street.

"It's really growing, as you can see, both Driftwood and Dripping Springs," says Miriam Wilson, The Salt Lick's general manager and director of operations. "North Austin is pretty much full by this point. Now I think it's South Austin's turn. I think our being here for 40 years has proven itself, and each year our business keeps being stronger and stronger."

The scope and scale of an operation that can serve Texas barbecue to 800 people at one time (or 2,900 on a busy summer day), that has two other locations around Austin and two in Las Vegas, and that sells its sauce and other merchandise to customers around the world might amaze Scott's late father, Thurman Roberts. He'd seen the potential of a plot of ground that only deer seemed to cherish, making their way here to lick salt and other minerals off the property's rocks. Beginning in the mid-1960s, returning to the ranch where he was born and raised, Thurman started doing the one thing he loved best: cooking barbecue

with all the simple devotion he could muster.

Word got out about The Salt Lick, as word about good barbecue always does in Texas. At the beginning, selling right from his brick pit on weekends, Thurman watched his first customers sit on the ground to eat in the cooling shade of the trees. This sight inspired him to enclose a little porch that ran off the cooking area, large enough to hold no more than eight people. There was a time, Miriam says, that holding eight people seemed enough. And the volume of that time allowed a level of personal involvement on Thurman's and wife Hisako's part that, wonder of wonders, still attempts to be The Salt Lick way today.

"He built this pit by hand," Miriam says of the open brick area in sight of everyone who places an order. "He built these walls by hand." She glances down at the rustic surface supporting two overflowing platters of brisket, sausage, chicken and ribs. "He built this table, too. To this day, we cook completely over wood—no charcoal and no gas. We make our pie crusts from scratch every day. We make our potato salad and coleslaw right here, every day. And we never make anything in advance. When each pan runs out, we make a new one."

All of The Salt Lick's meats are slow-cooked—18 hours for the brisket that is the big seller, until each slice gets a bright red ring. The sausage is made special for the place, a pleasing blend of beef and pork that takes on major-league smoke. Still, if the meat is a festival of tradition, everything else feels surprisingly free to wander the globe, with strikingly delicious results. Most notable is the sweet-tangy barbecue sauce, different from any other by being sweeter in taste and lighter in consistency.

Many a food writer has declared this sauce "Asian style," yet Miriam clearly doesn't like the reference. "Asian style?" she responds, as though nothing so stupid has ever been expressed before. "Nope, I don't think so at all. You taste it, and you tell me if this"—she frowns—"is Asian style!"

Other quirky elements beloved to Salt Lick fans include the chopped-not-mashed potato salad, not quite served warm in the German manner but kissed with vinegar and spices and devoid of mayonnaise, and the coleslaw. The latter is also mayo-free, with only a light and tanged-up touch of vinegar. "It's more of a cabbage salad, probably," says Miriam. It more than probably is incredible.

Thurman Roberts passed away some years ago, but you get the feeling around The Salt Lick that he'd have been proud of the numerous new directions his son is going with the business. Completely understood them? Probably not, if other Texas barbecue families are any indication. But he'd have been proud to see new ideas (and new profits) gathering around an enterprise he surely never thought would open in Las Vegas or cater celebrity events in New York and California.

"This was his life, and he loved Driftwood," Miriam says. "Mrs. Roberts still comes into the restaurant. She's pretty active for 95."

BLACK'S BARBECUE LOCKHART

ADDRESS: 208 N. MAIN STREET, LOCKHART
PHONE: (512) 398-2712
ESTABLISHED: 1932
OWNERS: THE BLACK FAMILY
BEST BITES: BEEF BRISKET, SMOKED TURKEY, CREAMED CORN, FRUIT COBBLER
PAYMENT: CREDIT CARDS

With origins in 1932 and no purchase or family feud to restart the clock, Black's can stake its claim as Lockhart's oldest barbecue place owned by a single family. Yet one of Edgar Black Jr.'s sons is a CPA in town and the other is a lawyer in Austin. Working together, they insist they'll keep the old man out of jail, but their time for smoking meats is limited. With "Mr. Junior's" third attempt at retirement looking like a keeper at age 83, he has brought in management with real-live culinary training to keep the place going strong.

"As I tell most people," says Terry Black, the CPA, "my office is right across the street, so I get to work both sides of the street. We're looking at expanding our catering operation in the near future, and doing some shipping of meat when we get all the proper licensing. We might even look into opening a second location. We don't plan on closing this location or changing anything much that we're doing here. We've been in business for 75 years, and we're hoping to continue to be in business for at least another 75."

On this particular day, Terry is joined by his father at a table in the dining room. At different milestones in life's journey, neither has to go in the back to slice barbecue for the customers moving through the line. Terry gets up from the impromptu platter of smoked meats only once, to show a visitor around the pits and explain how this wall used to be here and that wall used to be there. It seems extraordinary that such time-crusted equipment had ever stood somewhere else, and the stuff looks heavy besides. But move it has over the decades, allowing the family and now its management team to make the most of the limited kitchen space.

Back at the table, Edgar is all about memories. You get the feeling he often is; and even if he's not, customers will ask him to be whenever he's in the dining room. From his childhood, he remembers his father struggling to farm near Delhi at the height of the Depression, and he remembers the day a family friend called on them with a proposition.

"I was just a little kid," says Edgar, "but this friend said to my dad, 'Edgar, if you will go to Lockhart and open up a little meat market, I've got all the cattle in the world and no market for them. I rent a building there that already has meat market equipment. If you'll do that, we'll be partners.' They shook hands on it right there, and they were partners in this business for more than 50 years."

Most customers in the early days wanted fresh meats, but as elsewhere around Lockhart and around Texas, the Blacks maintained a small "barbecue room" in the back. This is where cuts of meat that wouldn't sell got smoked as barbecue, while scraps trimmed from meats that *did* sell became sausage. Either way, without refrigeration, it was

a race to get meat cooked or dried before it started to spoil.

All these years later, the menu hasn't changed—the brisket and sausage are both excellent, outshone only by the smoked turkey breast that's rich in smoke flavor without being dry. The ordering line is pretty much a cafeteria now, with numerous side dishes (including today a creative salad made with corn roasted on the pit) and several flavors of cobbler. In the dining room, soft drinks and iced tea appear to be available free, but it turns out someone has to give you a cup with ice.

There are many components to the Black's Barbecue experience, and no one could be more amazed than Edgar.

"When my dad started," he says, "the only barbecue we sold was beef and sausage. Before we had all these sides, we furnished crackers, which was kinda unique. A lot of people from up north would say they never heard of serving crackers with barbecue, but that's just what we did. When you ordered your meat, our cooks would reach into these big 12-pound boxes and grab you some crackers with their hands, which, of course, would be a no-no today. And we used to always have sawdust on the floor, which gave the place a fresh and clean smell. But then the health department frowned on that, too."

Edgar glances down at his plate, then up with a wistful smile. "The secret is just hanging in there, through lean years and good years. I've heard people tell me how they were so burned out after three or four years in the restaurant business. By that time, I'd been in it 30 or 40 years. You know, these 75 years haven't always been easy. But they sure have been fun."

SMITTY'S MARKET LOCKHART

ADDRESS: 208 S. COMMERCE STREET, LOCKHART
PHONE: (512) 398-9344
ESTABLISHED: 1900
OWNER: NINA SCHMIDT SELLS
BEST BITES: BEEF BRISKET, PORK CHOPS, HOT RINGS, BEANS
PAYMENT: CREDIT CARDS

In one sense, Smitty's Market is the newest of the four barbecue destinations in Lockhart, and in another sense, it's the original. It was here, in 1900, that the Kreuz (pronounced "Krites") family opened their meat market and began the slow, unwitting evolution into barbecue joint. The Schmidts bought Kreuz Market in 1948 but decided to keep the name. And that worked fine until "Smitty" Schmidt died in 1989, leaving the market to his son Rick—and the building that housed it to his daughter Nina.

Ten years later, a bitter falling-out between the siblings not only made national headlines but led to Rick taking Kreuz Market to a huge new location and Nina operating the original space with many of the original recipes. She called this new/old venture Smitty's Market, in honor of her dad.

"My mom's not the evil sister portrayed in some of the press," says John Fullilove, slicing brisket for a hungry visitor as the smoke swirls around him. "She's been an elected official, the county clerk, around here for so long, she just couldn't be that bad. Here, we still cook the old-fashioned way, and we keep everything real simple. That means a lotta work and a lotta hours. We touch everything four or five times. And if anything is ever wrong, we know it's our fault. There really isn't anybody to blame."

One of the joys of eating at Smitty's is being in the space that started it all, including a photo-plastered wood-rich "hallway," where people still eat at dark, gnarled counters complete with chains that used to hold public knives. The health department stepped in on that tradition years ago, but with a heaping helping of Nina's collected antiques, most other traditions come through loud and clear.

Though all four Lockhart barbecue joints adhere to the traditional (and practical) notion of keeping the dining area separate from the meat-smoking area, Smitty's seems even more schizophrenic than the rest. Its dining area, the place customers order drinks and side dishes, is yellow-white with light—a mixture of what's hanging overhead and any sunlight pouring in through the windows. This side of the operation has its own entrance from a downtown street, looking for all the world like a grocery store that might hustle sandwiches at lunchtime.

Passing to the meat-smoking side, however, is a bit like heading under Paris with the Phantom of the Opera. While impeccably clean, as you start poking around, this side is all deep brown merging with black, the visual impact of brick, stone and wood subjected to more than a century of black smoke. The pit area is a kind of outpost, as though against encroaching savages, with John and his minions slicing every shape and size of dark-crusty meat and setting it out on butcher paper.

There's no specific menu at Smitty's, though presumably after 100-plus years, no one needs one. Customers choose between the fatter pieces of Angus beef sold as brisket or the leaner pieces offered as shoulder, cooked only 4 to 5 hours over post oak. "I was always told," explains John, "to buy a good piece of meat and put a hot fire to it."

Patrons fill in around those unusually thick and juicy beef slices with rings of Smitty's smoked beef-and-pork sausage. The place turns out as many as 15,000 of these per week, selling many cold for takeout and dropping others onto the pit to emerge as "hot rings."

Though pork also shows up in rib form, it appears all the more spectacularly as a $^1/_2$- to $^3/_4$-pound bone-in chop. This is meat that, more than any other good thing, is worth a special trip to Smitty's. Miraculously, the pit crew here has managed to find the perfect temperature and time, letting the pork absorb the maximum amount of smoke while losing the minimum amount of moisture. Many upscale steakhouses offer pork chops these days, but it's the rare one that cooks it any better than this.

"It's probably not economical if you sit down and put a pencil to it," says John, surveying the constant motion around the fire and smoke than envelops him. "I think barbecue will be around longer than all of us are going to be. It's an art form, and it's a passionate thing. You really don't even want to argue about it, since everybody can do it and everybody can do it better than the other guy. It's really about what you like and what you'll pay for. Simple's best, really. Simple is something you can do every day."

KREUZ MARKET LOCKHART

....

ADDRESS: 619 N. COLORADO STREET, LOCKHART
PHONE: (512) 398-2361
ESTABLISHED: 1900
OWNER: KEITH SCHMIDT
BEST BITES: SMOKED SAUSAGE, SHOULDER CLOD, PORK RIBS, WARM GERMAN POTATO SALAD, SAUERKRAUT
PAYMENT: CASH AND CHECKS

You don't usually make friends in the restaurant business by telling people "No." But high above the huge dining area of the new/old Kreuz Market hangs the Schmidt family's version of those fabled tablets from Mt. Sinai: "No Barbecue Sauce (Nothing to Hide)," reads the foundational document, written on wood instead of stone. "No Forks (They Are at the End of Your Arm). No Salads (Remember, No Forks). No Credit/Cards Also (Bank Doesn't Sell Barbecue). No Kidding (See Owner's Face)."

Formed from the nationally publicized "barbecue feud" between Rick Schmidt and his sister Nina, Kreuz Market opened as a larger-than-life, high-volume operation on the town's outskirts just about the time the Legislature was busy declaring Lockhart the Barbecue Capital of Texas. In terms of New York-based media, the confluence of these two colorful stories was too good to be true. Not only were Texans crazy enough to legislate a barbecue "capital," this big-city logic went, they were crazy enough to choose sides in a family feud over who had the best barbecue.

As often happens in such family feuds, a new generation now operates both Kreuz Market and Smitty's, the latter housed in the location the Kreuz family chose way back in 1900. Both sides, while calmer about the split than their parents had been, claim the original start date.

The new, 500-plus-seat Market is big and boisterous and successful and good. You enter through a vast wooden dining area surrounding by other vast wooden dining areas, find your way back to order meat on butcher paper from pit boss Roy Perez and his crew, then wander into yet another vast wooden dining area to pick out drinks and sides.

Despite the purist tradition of serving smoked meat all by itself, Kreuz has been compromising a bit. In fact, using chopped-up, near-caramelized scraps from their meats, Rick Schmidt's son Keith has kicked up both warm German potato salad and sauerkraut that's better than anybody back in Germany might dream of. Meat and these two sides, plus a bowl of pinto beans, a couple slices of tasteless white bread and a mountain of salty crackers...this is the part where true Texans figure they've died and gone to heaven.

"And people just love our pork ribs," Keith confesses and brags at the same time. "At the old place, we had such limited pit space. When we got over here, we had room to start playing around with pork, and we were pretty much right. The pork ribs walk out of here on their own."

Still, for all the pork ribs walking out, most days they can't keep up with the smoked sausage, all of which is made and hand-tied at Kreuz Market. It comes in two flavors, original and a newfangled variation that's caught on with customers in the past five years. With a name like "jalapeño cheese," how could it not?

Though beef brisket is a solid seller for the Schmidts, they have made a distinction that sits atop even their brisket— both on the menu and in daily sales. So-called "shoulder clod," part of the chuck and apt to be more tender and lean, out-sells the Texas favorite here by a significant margin. Maybe it's simply the fact that the words shoulder clod are followed by the word (Lean), or maybe, this being 21st-century America, you can't sell anything that carries the word (Fat) as part of its title. That, again displaying the family's love affair with parentheses, is exactly what the Kreuz Market menu calls beef brisket.

As elsewhere, barbecue is a 24-hour

operation within these walls. Being located in the Barbecue Capital of Texas, Rick and his workers are as likely to look up and see a packed tour bus pull into the parking lot as some little couple driving an Oldsmobile. This place was built with such visions in mind. Despite the old meat scales and dusty calendars and cute sayings lying about as though by accident, Kreuz Market was built to push 'em through—to get them their meat and sides, to hand them their pack of crackers and explain why no one should *ever* use barbecue sauce, and point them out toward the sprawl of tables.

"We've been in this new building about eight years," Keith says, "and the big thing is consistency. You want somebody who came to our old location 20 years ago to walk in, taste our food and say, 'That's what I remember.' That's really what this is about. If you change too much or try to get too fancy, you lose something. That's when you lose the soul you've accumulated over the generations."

CHISHOLM TRAIL BAR-B.Q. & HOT SAUSAGE LOCKHART

ADDRESS: 1323 S. COLORADO STREET, LOCKHART
PHONE: (512) 398-6027
ESTABLISHED: 1978
OWNER: FLOYD WILHELM
BEST BITES: BEEF BRISKET, SMOKED SAUSAGE, SMOKED CHICKEN, FRIED CATFISH, BROCCOLI SALAD, COLESLAW, FRIED OKRA
PAYMENT: CREDIT CARDS

Like Scarlett O'Hara's vow to never be hungry again, Floyd Wilhelm apparently took a similar oath involving his bass boat.

"The out-of-towners try the famous places first, but I bet I get 60 percent of the local business—because of our lower prices." He speaks from beneath his cap in a quiet near-mumble. "Money was pretty scarce back around '78." Floyd is clearly

survive, and eventually to succeed, was... something else. Where the Big Three of Lockhart barbecue reluctantly backed into side dishes and sauce, sensing the frowns of their mostly German ancestors every step of the way, Floyd leapt in with both feet. Sides go on and on along the Chisholm Trail steam table, some smothered, some merely heated up, some crisply deep-fried. If the old folks sought to keep the menu small and the process simple, Floyd sought to keep his customers happy.

To that end, at some point, he did the one thing the other guys in Lockhart would to this day consider unthinkable. After years of rejecting sales pitches for rotisserie-style cookers that "smoked" meat by electricity or gas, he finally agreed to try one from Fort Worth that drew its heat (and by definition, its smoke) solely from wood.

For the first week or two, Floyd's son Danny remembers, all the meat came out of this rotisserie with a weird, unpleasant taste. But once it was broken in, father and son both found the flavors wonderful, along with its ability to maintain more moisture (and therefore more weight) in the different cuts of meat. This benefited not only the restaurant's bottom line in the course of a year; it delivered a tender and moist product more in keeping with today's tastes than with the pre-refrigeration need to dry meat for preservation. As with all his other new touches, Floyd allowed himself to experiment because his need for a competitive edge outweighed his obsession with tradition.

"I don't know about the other ones in town," says Floyd, "but I'm really convinced. When we started out, all the meat was cooked on flat pits. That rotisserie was the best investment I ever made. You can put about 75 briskets on it, come in around midnight and put another log on, and by the time you come back in the morning, they're ready. Tender and juicy and delicious. There's different ways to make barbecue good, but if you do it right, people will buy it. It's a heck of a deal."

remembering it all, and not without discomfort. The scrimping. The going in at midnight to throw on a new piece of post oak. The many sacrifices. He grimaces. "When the checks started bouncing... well, that's when I had to sell my bass boat."

You might hear Floyd of Chisholm Trail called Lockhart's "new kid on the block." But what you'd expect from that description is hardly what you get. New kid he is, relatively speaking. Yet Floyd opened Chisholm Trail in 1978...after spending 18 years working at Black's. That adds up to nearly 50 years doing things the old-fashioned way, and thinking up a few new ways as well.

Chisholm Trail added the notion of a "salad bar" for sides, letting each customer self-serve three glories from the likes of crunchy-sweet broccoli salad and mustard-kissed homemade potato salad. On certain days of the week, Floyd kicks in fried catfish with hush puppies or Texas chicken-fried steak with cream gravy. And wackiest of all, his is the first and only barbecue joint in Lockhart to borrow fast food's concept of a drive-thru. The window almost always opens onto a line of cars, a cinematic stream of soccer moms and construction workers pulling in beneath the sign. It would seem, listening closely as he slices and serves, that Floyd Wilhelm is one Texan who knows his place in the barbecue universe.

After all, he knew what he was doing after 18 years with the "other guy." He could do all that. What he had to do to

CITY MARKET LULING

ADDRESS: 633 E. DAVIS STREET, LULING

PHONE: (830) 875-9019

ESTABLISHED: 1957

OWNER: WILLIE "BUDDY" ELLIS

BEST BITES: BEEF BRISKET, PORK RIBS, SAUSAGE, POTATO SALAD

PAYMENT: CASH

According to Joe Capello, Luling deserves better than it gets vis-à-vis Lockhart and all that stuff about it being the Barbecue Capital of Texas. Fact is, while Lockhart is closer to Austin and its feverish barbecue hunters, Luling at least gets to be closer to I-10. That means City Market's brand of barbecue can be more of an impulse buy than the larger, better-known destination to the north.

Joe insists their Lockhart-style items are every bit as good here, and he takes credit for competing just enough to inspire Lockhart to ease up on its Teutonic authoritarian ways, adding side dishes and sauce in all but one place—even the long-heretical pork ribs.

With the Barbecue Capital just a hop up the highway, it's been hard for Luling to establish itself in terms of smoke. Plus, Lockhart has four barbecue joints when Luling has only two—and according to some purists, only one. For that reason,

more attention gathers each June around the town's annual Watermelon Thump, surely the cleverest name for a food celebration this side of the Shrimp and Petroleum Festival across the Sabine River in Louisiana. The thousands who come to Luling before the Fourth of July eat their share of barbecue right along with their watermelon, and (speaking again for the purists) City Market is where most of them get it.

"First of all, the barbecue here is real good," says Joe, who started cleaning tables at City Market for the Ellis family while still a student in 1962, taking over its day-to-day operation as soon as he got out of the service in 1969. "When you get away from this area here, you just don't see people eating their meat off butcher paper and you don't see the barbecue pits with smoke everywhere."

Unlike many Texas barbecue joints with roots as groceries or markets, the overall layout of City Market hasn't changed much. While clearly functioning as a restaurant to its public, to the Ellis family that started the business down the block in 1957, it's still a matter of luring each mob of customers through the dining area, where you get drinks and sides, to the wood-and-class-enclosed "holy of holies" in the back. It's here that you gather around a time-worn, smoke-encrusted counter, look up through the haze at the only menu and finally order your meat.

On the far side of the counter, things seldom slow down. Men in an odd collection of greasy aprons and hard hats move from pit to carving table to counter constantly, barely setting the butcher paper of meat in front of one customer before turning their eyes to the next. The line snaking through City Market's dining area is clear and orderly. In the pit room, however, it disintegrates into a mob, with only the pit guys to try taking people in some order.

On this particular day, the dining room seems the unchoreographed epitome of Texas barbecue. Some tables are filled with casually dressed Hispanic couples and families, happily chattering in Spanish as they pass around dripping papers of beef brisket, pork ribs and smoked sausage. Other tables, including four pushed together, are packed with African-American families dressed as though for a special occasion. It isn't a Sunday, but there's a definite "back from church" feel—perhaps for a wedding or a funeral. Either point in the life cycle requires great barbecue, it seems, and these folks clearly know where to come and get it. So does the lone cowboy sitting near the front window, gazing out between chews at the railroad tracks beyond the blinds. He seems removed, isolated by time and space, from the joyous din deeper in. His butcher paper is almost empty.

Meat at City Market is cooked over post oak. "Some people," offers Joe, "like mesquite, but I say it burns too hot. With post oak, you have more control over your heat." Sides are pretty much limited to potato salad and pinto beans. On this day, two employees pick through dried beans spread across a table along the wall, pitching the good ones into a pail for cooking.

There's a strong grocery store vibe to City Market, one that the Ellis family clearly goes considerable lengths to maintain. Service is friendly, especially when someone is filling your cup from the drink dispenser, but it doesn't concern itself much with your table. That's your space, it says, almost as though you were taking your food home but got too lazy within a few steps of the pits.

"My favorite part is watching people eat our barbecue," Joe says, glancing around at this home-away-from-home. "Every day at least one customer comes in and says this is their first time, and before they leave they tell us how good it was. That tells us we're still doing a good job."

LULING'S BAR-B-Q LULING

ADDRESS: 709 E. DAVIS STREET, LULING
PHONE: (830) 875-3848
ESTABLISHED: 1989
OWNER: LEE CHAMBERS
BEST BITES: PORK TENDERLOIN, JALAPEÑO SAUSAGE, POTATO SALAD, MACARONI AND CHEESE, SMOTHERED CABBAGE (WHEN AVAILABLE), HOMEMADE BREAD PUDDING
PAYMENT: CREDIT CARDS

"Course, I'm not the barbecue cook," says D'Ann Trimble, putting the required reverence into her voice.

That tells the tale, at several levels, about barbecue in Texas and about Luling's "other" barbecue place. With City Market just on the other side of the high-

way, the place called Luling's Bar-B-Q might as well insert the word "Other" into its official name. That's how people are going to think of it, even though it was founded nearly two decades ago. The original eatery built by A.W. Reid and his wife burned down in 2000 but was rebuilt as the small, café-like space it is now, owned by Lee Chambers.

The thing about Luling's Bar-B-Q: Like that rent-a-car company many years ago, it has to try harder. And trying harder is where D'Ann fits into the business plan. She's been a cook in places all around here for 23 years, and most of those places were cafés and restaurants that didn't have the word "barbecue" by any spelling in their name. They were places that rose or fell serving good food...and based on the things she's making now, it was good food with country simplicity and abundant flavor.

No one's complaining, especially not the "barbecue cook," currently taking a break from his smoke at one of the tables. Or the cadre of old-timers scattered around the small dining area, not seemingly together but happy to complete each other's sentences sharing facts, dates and anecdotes with any visitor who asks about the place. Across the highway at City Market, you're in Luling, Lockhart's barbecue kid brother. At Luling's, you're in Mayberry—and happy to be here.

"We make all our stuff here," says D'Ann, stepping out in front of the counter so she can point better at what's on the steam table. "Our broccoli and beans are our best sellers among the sides, day in and day out. So's our cabbage, whenever we have it, like today." She points to the bowl atop the counter, filled with the smothered leafage and a version of what country folk have always called "pot likker."

"The secret is adding a little water, but not too much," she explains. "We sauté the onions with the bacon in a little butter first, then we add the cabbage and that bit of water. I mean, you don't want to boil it. Just steam it a little, I guess."

While little earth-shattering is offered from Luling's barbecue pit, the things that make it onto the carving station are all excellent: warm, smoky and well-seasoned. Pork tenderloin is a surprise, since pork elsewhere tends to be ribs or the occasional thick chop. These thin slices of the "other white meat" certainly give diners an option. But then again, so do the beef brisket, all-beef sausage (original or jalapeño), chicken, pork ribs or turkey breast.

As D'Ann explains, any brisket that's left at the end of a day—or any that's "overcooked" crisp and caramelized along the outer edges—is detoured to a special bowl for use in Luling's chopped beef sandwiches. Like a child who outshines his or her parent, this sandwich might be the best brisket going.

As part of "trying harder," D'Ann has encouraged the owner to expand Luling's menu more and more. Not only does she get to create specials each day—announced on a sheet of paper taped to the counter—she gets to fix turkey and dressing on Sundays and even steaks and seafood to drum up business in the evening, when people might be tempted by something other than barbecue.

For dessert, Luling's sets out some desirable coconut cream pie, pecan pie and what D'Ann calls "Eye-talian cream cake," plus the fluffy bread pudding she makes from the end pieces of that omnipresent white bread.

"I'm just gonna put the specials on my sign, along with what's on the next day," says the cook who's not the barbecue cook. "I pretty much know what people like to eat."

SOUTHSIDE MARKET & BARBEQUE, ELGIN

....

ADDRESS: HIGHWAY 290 AT HIGHWAY 95 NORTH, ELGIN

PHONE: (512) 285-3407

ESTABLISHED: 1882, THIS LOCATION IN 1992

OWNERS: THE BRACEWELL FAMILY

BEST BITES: ELGIN HOT SAUSAGE, BEEF BRISKET, SMOKED TURKEY, POTATO SALAD, BROWNIES

PAYMENT: CREDIT CARDS

Bryan Bracewell doesn't look 125. But as the third-generation pit boss and, more formally, chief executive officer of Southside Market in the tirelessly touted Sausage Capital of Texas, that's about how old he feels some days.

As Bryan explains it, plenty of central-Texas barbecue joints can look back to when they were fresh meat markets that only sold smoked brisket and sausage on the side, a function of using up scraps and less desirable cuts that otherwise would have been wasted. Southside Market can do that, too. But as what he insists is the oldest barbecue joint in the state—the sprawling operation on Highway 290, 19 miles east of Austin—can turn back the clock farther, to a mythical, too-good-to-be-true time when barbecue made house calls.

"This business started in 1882," he says, "when a man named William J. Moon started selling fresh beef and pork from a wagon door-to-door." Bryan pauses to readjust his cap a bit, letting the picture of a meat salesman making his rounds settle in. "The barbecue was kinda born out of necessity. If he didn't sell it fresh, he cooked it over an open fire and sold it as barbecue. That's what they did back in those days, when there wasn't any refrigeration as we know it now: salt it, smoke it, cook it, eat it."

Over the past 125 years—in fact, within four years of getting started—Moon's meat operations found a permanent home to replace that old wandering wagon. Yet beneath the somewhat high-tech and definitely high-volume aspect of Southside Market today, you see that "salt it, smoke it, cook it, eat it" is still pretty much the business at hand.

The Bracewell family runs one of the larger barbecue restaurants and markets in the state, along with the connected processing plant that turns out all-beef Elgin Hot Sausage (or Elgin Hot Guts, as old-timers colorfully call it) for supermarkets and restaurants, along with the Elgin Hot Sausage Co., which sends out trucks to distribute same. Along the way, the mission has spawned so many branded retail sidelines, from Southside Market caps to T-shirts to gift boxes, the space all around the long, communal tables has come to resemble a carnivore's Cracker Barrel.

At times, the volume can be staggering: something like 2 million pounds of Elgin hot sausage made and sold fresh or smoked each year by a total of 85 employees. The average busy Saturday night at the restaurant might go through 2,000 pounds. And the busiest single day ever at Southside saw 8,000 pounds of sausage head out the door. Of course, that was the Friday before the Fourth of July weekend, when every Texan with so much as one piece of charcoal to his name was heading outside to fire up the grill.

"Any time people are getting together in the backyard is a good time for us," Bryan says. "In a lot of other areas, sausage is a kind of side note, whether they're making their own or using somebody else's. In Elgin, sausage has always been center of the plate."

Bryan waves a hand in the direction of the serving line, and several plates come out to prove it. There is sausage on each one of them, pretty much in the center and definitely delicious. But that doesn't prevent a host of other meats from hitching a ride...some very tender and smoky brisket (this is Texas, after all, Bryan notes), along with some wonderful smoked chicken, turkey and ribs.

Though the siren song of side dishes was resisted until the Bracewells moved into their current location in 1992, that battle was fought and lost a long time ago. There's potato salad, coleslaw and beans, all prepared fresh each day. Southside even pickles its own jalapeños, which is impressive for a place that also claims to have handed out more than $1 million worth of crackers over the years.

Desserts are simple, just a few brownies and little pies, but there's no sense of deprivation—thanks to an entire ice cream bar scooping Blue Bell made in nearby Brenham. "My dad's sister is head of research and development there," explains Bryan with a smile, "so in a

roundabout way, the Bracewells have a hand in that, too."

The Bracewell family hails from South Texas but moved to San Antonio so Bryan's grandfather Ernest could pursue a career in sales with Armour Meat Co. In making his rounds for Armour, he visited Southside Market, of course, which had passed from William J. Moon to Lee Wilson back in 1908, and from him to Jerry Stach and Van Zimmerhanzel in 1944.

Having bought his partner out, Jerry sold the business to Ernest and his wife, Adrienne, in 1968. Their son Billy started working at Southside Market at the age of 12, which apparently became a kind of family tradition. Bryan got started doing little jobs around the market when he was also 12. Many years of Southside jobs—and a degree from Texas A&M in food science in meat later—the third generation seems comfortably in charge.

"We're all about the food," Bryan says, summarizing his family history to way of what it serves. "The No. 1 thing we can't let get away from us is the quality and consistency of our product. At Southside Market, we can never have a bad day producing sausage."

MEYERS' ELGIN SAUSAGE ELGIN

ADDRESS: 188 HIGHWAY 290, ELGIN
PHONE: (512) 281-3331
ESTABLISHED: 1949
OWNERS: THE MEYER FAMILY
BEST BITES: SMOKED HOT LINKS, BEEF BRISKET, PORK GARLIC WRAP, COLESLAW, BANANA PUDDING, SMALL PIES
PAYMENT: CREDIT CARDS

Anywhere else in America, kids might wish they were an "Oscar Mayer wiener." But kids growing up in the Sausage Capital of Texas should probably be singing a cute, catchy jingle about R.G.

Meyer's sausage instead.

Meyers', one of two huge operations in Elgin that distribute tons of sausage throughout Texas and far beyond each year, bills its core product as "Real Texas, Real Good." And most assuredly, there's a factory that makes it that way. Yet the fact remains, even in this age of federal inspections and near-surgical cleanliness, people are more interested in devouring Elgin-style sausage than in ever watching

it be made. That fact finally dawned on the Meyer family, inspiring them to keep the wholesale side of things for major profit but to add a restaurant that would warmly welcome the public into the world Rudolf Karl George Meyer created officially in 1949. Unofficially, he'd been making his German sausage in small batches for friends as far back as 1915.

"Sausage is our biggest thing," says Becky Meyer, whose husband, Gary, is a fourth-generation Elgin sausage maker. "When people taste it, their eyebrows lift up and they say, 'Oh, wow!' It's delicious...what else can I say?"

Gary and his brother Gregg moved home from Austin, a good 20 miles away, when their father died in 1989. Their intention was to run the family sausage business. The only trouble was: People kept turning up at the Meyer plant on

Main Street and asking where the restaurant was. Well, the brothers had to say, there wasn't one. Still, these constant queries put the idea front and center in the brothers' minds. By the late 1990s, when the longtime Biggers Barbecue location on Highway 290 came up for sale, they bought it and jumped right in. Meyers' opened on Friday the 13th, Becky relates—Feb. 13, 1998—and the family's luck has been good ever since.

As at their chief competitor on the same highway a couple blocks away, sausage made with pork or beef is "center of the plate" at Meyers' restaurant incarnation, but the menu certainly doesn't stop there. From the huge smokers using oak wood come not only standard-issue Texas beef brisket, available sliced on plates or chopped with sauce for sandwiches, but nifty St. Louis-style pork ribs (cut uniform thickness for more even cooking), pork steak and some amazing pepper-lime smoked chicken.

Sandwiches take a few unusual twists, customer favorites being the pork garlic wrap and beef sausage wrap. "Wraps" are meant to sound relatively modern, but they're mostly just meat held in a slice of bread, something Texans have been doing since before the birth of the Republic.

For dessert, Meyers' fans have been known to eat their weight in banana pudding with its mandatory vanilla wafers, but those in favor of portion control head for the five-inch pies available daily in five or six different flavors.

As Becky tells it, the family success story is all about a recipe. It came from Germany in the late 1800s, presumably starting to attract attention on the day Henry Meyer settled in central Texas. He was the father who taught it to R.G., thus making him the favorite dad in all neighborhoods the Meyer son ever called home.

The spices were right, Becky explains, as was the grind of the lean pork trimmings (called "coarse" or "chunk") that went into the natural pork casings and eventually into the Meyer smoker. After going pro in 1949, R.G. passed the recipe and the business on to his son Buddy a decade later, with the next generational chance bringing in Gary and Gregg 30 years after that.

In the Age of the Internet, with Meyers' now shipping sausage to individual customers nationwide, Becky doesn't mind if her kids and their cousins show an interest in the family business. But she's smart enough to know that, in this day and age, running such an operation isn't for the faint of heart. With the restaurant business one of the few that's even more grueling than the sausage business, it especially isn't for anyone who merely drifts in because he or she has the right last name.

"You have to have a passion for it," she says, smiling and waving Gary off to drive their teenage daughter to a doctor's appointment. "If you don't have the passion, you're not going to do well, and the business isn't going to do well. You can't leave this business just because it's 5 o'clock. I tell my children: This is going to have to be in your heart."

RUDY MIKESKA'S TAYLOR

ADDRESS: 300 W. 2ND STREET, TAYLOR
PHONE: (512) 365-3722
ESTABLISHED: 1952
OWNER: RUDY "TIM" MIKESKA
BEST BITES: BEEF BRISKET, SMOKED SAUSAGE, PORK RIBS, POTATO SALAD, BANANA PUDDING
PAYMENT: CREDIT CARDS

More than a century after leaving their Bohemian Czech homeland, passing through Galveston and making their way to central Texas, the Mikeskas are the First Family of Barbecue.

There are other dynasties, of course, other generational sagas. Indeed, most are found living and working within a brisket's throw of Taylor, in towns like Lockhart and Elgin. But the Mikeskas

had the foresight to do the one thing destined to make them unique in the universe of Texas barbecue. They had nine children, and they made sure that boys and girls alike all knew their way around cutting, smoking and selling meat.

Today, Rudy Mikeska's in Taylor is the oldest and highly unofficial flagship of a great line, with 10 or more outposts at any given time stretching from Temple through Columbus as far south as El Campo. Despite name recognition verging on a single "brand," Mikeska's Barbecue is no single business. Each eatery belongs on its own or in a small cluster, now all owned by a tangle of Mikeska cousins as friendly with each other as they are independent.

"That's the only time we ever work together," says Rudy "Tim" Mikeska, pointing to a famous *Texas Monthly* photo of his father and three brothers gathered to cater barbecue for 18,000 people in the 1980s. "For a job. For something so big we need the help."

He thinks a moment, perhaps conjuring up the ghost of many a Christmas past. "We are completely separate. We share our family and our love for each other, but we don't share a whole lot else. We all use different seasonings, we all use different recipes, we all charge different prices. The only thing that's the same is when you write us a check. You write 'Mikeska' and it'll get cashed."

Tim's grandparents settled on a farm outside Taylor and embarked on the two careers most Czech men in Texas chose between: raising cattle and butchering cattle. Since Grandpa Mikeska was adept at both, this evolved during the Depression into what was called a "meat club." By this practice, with roots deep in the Old World, a butcher traveled from farm to farm throughout the region, slaughtering and portioning in return for some of the meat. "They were very poor," Tim says admiringly of his grandparents, "but they were never hungry."

Two main components of the Mikeska family tree were Catholic faith and love of their adopted country, the place that had allowed their labor to lift them slowly from want. Four Mikeska sons, including Tim's father, Rudy, fought in World War II, and four of their younger brothers fought in Korea. By 1952, as America enjoyed its postwar expansion, Rudy saw a chance to own his own business after cooking for his in-laws at Taylor Country Club. He opened a tiny barbecue stand, eventually building the business to three locations before letting it shrink to a more manageable level in one in 1972.

"I started working here when I was 7," Tim remembers. "Back then, I had to stack those old wooden Coca-Cola crates so I could reach the table to make sausage—you know, flipping them to make the links. My dad would say I had to make four to the pound, and I got really good at it. I had no choice. My dad would cut four off from what I'd done and go weigh them. I had to know just where to put my thumb, because that was money."

Today, Rudy Mikeska's is open as a restaurant only three days per week, at least partially the result of a recent brush with cancer that forced Tim to reorganize his life around his wife and children. He seems more than happy to concentrate on catering and the busy e-commerce Web site he designed and built himself, since those things are easier to manage than being open as a restaurant X number of hours per day X days per week. Besides,

he laughs, his online customers around the world are a tad easier to make happy than Mrs. So-and-So around the corner, who phones to complain the brisket she picked up and took home is cold.

With regular large-scale catering jobs—going back to the many barbecues his dad threw for his pal Lyndon Johnson and many other Texas politicos—Tim needs firepower. He relies on oak for heat and smoke in the four large Roto-Flex smokers that turn meat like a carousel in Mikeska's kitchen, as well as in the mobile Southern Pride rotisserie.

Brisket gets not only a coating of pepper-crunchy dry rub, but the chance to marinate in it for a remarkable seven days—even that reduced from the 21 days favored by the late Rudy himself. Briskets get smoked 12 to 18 hours, then are allowed to cool and go into the refrigerator, then end up back on the smoker to cook about 4 hours more. The result: tender meat whose "smoke ring" is also a bit of a "spice ring," showing where the Middle European curing with pepper, salt and other seasonings has worked its magic.

The second most popular meat at Rudy Mikeska's is the perfectly ground and deliciously seasoned sausage Tim has been stuffing and linking here since he was 7. This is made in a special room off the kitchen, and is still tied in links by the skillful handwork turn-and-twist that father taught son long ago.

"I remember when I was a teenager, this salesman came in with a machine he said could link better and faster than any person ever could," Tim recalls with a grin, replicating the Paul Bunyan legend for clearing Minnesota timber. "My dad tells this guy, 'Oh, my son can do that.' So we had a kind of race. And I could link more sausage than his machine could, so my dad didn't buy one. Suddenly, I'm standing there and I realize just how much work I could have saved myself. And I think: What the hell did I just *do*?"

TAYLOR CAFÉ
TAYLOR

ADDRESS: 101 N. MAIN STREET, TAYLOR
PHONE: (512) 352-2828
ESTABLISHED: 1948
OWNER: VENCIL MARES
BEST BITES: BEEF BRISKET, PORK RIBS, SAUSAGE,
POTATO SALAD
PAYMENT: CASH AND CHECKS

When Vencil Mares came ashore in Normandy in June of 1944, he wasn't thinking much about barbecue. The Cistern, Texas, teenager had his gaze fixed on the long road ahead—miles and miles of treacherous hedgerows, French towns connected only by mud, and a patch of forest that by snowy Christmas would be known as The Bulge. As a medic attached to the 102nd Evacuation Unit, inch by inch across Europe into Germany, Vencil would see less of the spoils of victory than of its exceedingly high cost.

"Whenever they expected a lot of casualties," he remembers in the barbecue joint he's run for more than 50 years, "we moved up as close as we could right behind them."

Since Vencil joined the Army at age 16 and ended up in England awaiting the invasion, he had thought relatively little about his postwar career—until, that is, he had to find one. Today, he assures anyone who asks that he had no plans to

spend his life in the food business. Still, when he spotted a job cooking barbecue at Southside Market in Elgin in 1946, he grabbed it. After two years there, he stumbled on the chance to buy his own place in Taylor, just 15 minutes up the road. As Vencil expresses the timelessly American sentiment: "If I could do it for the man, I could do it for me."

On this particular afternoon, with his café awash in waning light, Vencil sits at the back of his long bar beneath the sign proclaiming ABSOLUTELY NO ALCOHOL. The sign must refer to hard liquor, since every one of the eight or ten men positioned around the bar is sipping on a bottle of beer. Indeed, without the signage provided by the various beer companies, the place known officially as Taylor Café but universally called "Vencil's Place" would have little decoration at all.

The man's 84 years have taken their toll, as has a recent leg injury during a nasty fall. Yet Vencil still shows up at his place every morning at 5, only an hour after his pit man comes in to cook meat. More amazingly, he usually sticks around to close at or around 11 p.m….hours later than most Texas barbecue places have locked their doors.

Despite the stoop the years have put in his frame, Vencil is able to move as needed about the bar or walk back to his office (a tiny space littered with hunting trophies, caps celebrating various sports teams and farm equipment, and an entire shelf of cigar boxes holding all the place's financial records). "It's my computer," Vencil jokes, barely able to raise his head high enough to see all the cigar boxes. "It tells me what month and what year and what I need."

Like many of his generation, Vencil takes pride in his life and his work without ever seeming boastful. Pleased by the attention that has come his way in recent years—including an article in *USA Today* that called his brisket one of the 20 best dishes in America—Vencil merely shrugs and mumbles something about working on the same thing for half a century making you pretty good at it.

There are parts of his business he has given up—outside catering jobs, for instance. "I'm getting too old to fight that truck," he says simply. But the food served at Taylor Café to go with all those beers remains classic Texas barbecue, from the brisket cooked 8 to 10 hours over post oak to the ribs to the sausage.

By all accounts, including his own, Vencil has no particular plans to retire and no specific vision what will happen to Taylor Café when he stops reporting for duty every morning. Surely, he can teach others how to make his brisket or his special barbecue sauce or his potato salad, although he has no exact plans to do so. For the time being, Vencil insists his health is good and there's no reason he can't go on for years to come.

"I don't drink and I don't smoke," he proclaims, then winks at his late-afternoon visitor. "And I gave up chasing women."

LOUIE MUELLER BBQ, TAYLOR

ADDRESS: 206 W. 2ND STREET, TAYLOR
PHONE: (512) 352-6206
ESTABLISHED: 1949, THIS LOCATION IN 1959
OWNERS: BOBBY AND TRISH MUELLER
BEST BITES: BEEF BRISKET, BEEF RIBS, HOMEMADE HOT SAUSAGE, POTATO SALAD, COLESLAW
PAYMENT: CREDIT CARDS

If it weren't for the free Wi-Fi that's available to customers bearing laptops, you'd probably swear you were stepping into another time—or at least into another place. Bobby Mueller has invested considerable effort and money in the brick barbecue joint his father founded to make you think he hasn't invested at all. Since he has a "new" section made to look just as old as the original, you're pretty sure that isn't the case.

"It's just the character of the old part of the building," says Bobby, taking a seat at a wooden table between the counter and the screened door, resting his hands on the short pants beneath his apron. "We got one up on that, I guess. What sets everything up here is the building itself; that's what most of our customers tell us. We started off in a little shed somewhere else in 1949, but we've been right here since 1959. And we mostly live by word of mouth, since our product is always good."

Though Taylor often takes a backseat to Lockhart, a quick jaunt up the highway, Louie Mueller BBQ joins Taylor Café, Rudy Mikeska's and Davis Grocery to make the town a kind of "second capital of barbecue." And barbecue being the personal, subjective thing it is in Texas, there are surely those who would rather visit Taylor than its larger, more touristic counterpart to the north. Truth is, both towns serve terrific barbecue…but sitting in the sifting natural light of Louie Mueller's with a cool breeze coming in through the doorway, it's tempting to refill your iced tea from the urn against the wall and refuse to ever leave.

The place is huge, cavernous, as though you could play basketball inside, which is exactly what ladies teams once did in the 1920s. For most of the rest of its history, the building was the single most appropriate precursor for a barbe-

cue joint in central Texas: a grocery store that sold fresh meat.

When Louie Mueller took over the location four years after World War II, he started emphasizing barbecue over other products but did so within the limited range of his German heritage: smoked meat served on butcher paper, with little concern for side dishes, utensils or comfort. Bobby bought his father out in 1974, having worked in the family business off and on between stints of school and military service. As the new generation, he understood what was happening to his father's business; he almost immediately added potato salad and coleslaw, made from his mother-in-law's recipes. A few additional side dishes became part of the menu over the years, along with smoked chicken and turkey.

As though in reflection of the setting, there are far more things Bobby and general manager Lance Kirkpatrick refuse to change. All smoking of meats, including the beef brisket, the sausage Bobby makes from 100 percent beef and the ribs of either beef or pork, is still done over oak—with no other wood added unless there isn't enough oak available. To achieve the flavor Bobby is looking for, every bit of heat and smoke comes from wood, with no contribution from charcoal or gas.

As for the side dishes, often an element that barbecue joints feel justified in farming out, potatoes are boiled for chopping and cabbage is shredded for coleslaw every single day. No desserts are offered beyond ice cream.

Bobby Mueller is a man of few words, perhaps believing in that Texas adage that a man's actions speak louder. His actions are quiet, careful and repetitive, those of an old-fashioned Texas pit boss who understands that to lose focus is to risk a customer's meal. And to risk a customer's meal, in this worldview, is to risk everything.

He thinks of his father every day, of course, since his father's name is over the door. But he also knows that a good deal of the fame surrounding Louie Mueller

BBQ (including a 2006 James Beard award in the American Classics category, plus features on the Food Network and the Travel Channel) has come to the place since Louie Mueller's son became the boss.

The odd sections of wood and brick around the dining area seem to blend seamlessly beneath a layer of something darker than smoke and thicker than time. Whatever that something is, Bobby knows it's the single most important thing he has to sell. "The hardest part is concentration, putting out a good product," he says simply, shifting in his chair to gaze at the sunlight on the street beyond the screened door. "All the cooking here is human and wood. We do no artificial cooking."

DAVIS GROCERY AND BARBECUE, TAYLOR

ADDRESS: 400 S. ROBINSON STREET, TAYLOR
PHONE: (512) 352-8111
ESTABLISHED: 1994
OWNER: JAMES DAVIS
BEST BITES: MUTTON, BEEF BRISKET, BONELESS PORK, ELGIN SAUSAGE, COMEBACK JUICE, PECAN AND SWEET POTATO PIES (DURING THE HOLIDAYS)
PAYMENT: CASH AND CHECKS

If you ask James Davis why he's devoted so many years of his life to barbecue, he'll probably answer you in two parts. First, he has been a minister of the Christian gospel even longer than he's been a pit master. And second, he might inadvertently remind you of Flip Wilson's old line "The devil made me do it." Except, in James' case, it'll always be the opposite.

"We started out as just a small grocery store across the street," relates James, pastor of the Rising Star Baptist Church. "We had no idea we were going to sell barbecue. I never had cooked it, except for weekends with my son. But then one day, as I was passing this old worn-down building, the Spirit of God spoke to me

smoke curling around meat from a glowing wood fire.

"My dad and his friends used to give rodeos and cook meat right in the ground, the way just about nobody does anymore," James remembers. "They had this big patio dance parlor. They'd cook, and whatever was left over at the end of the day, they'd cover it up with these burlap sacks. You'd go down the next morning and uncover all that barbecue and that aroma––Oh, man!"

Today, Davis Grocery is one of the few barbecue joints in central Texas that looks like both parts of its name. While the aroma of meats smoked out back fills every breath you draw inside, your eye flits comfortably along shelves filled with breakfast cereals, rice and pasta mixes and canned foods, with soft drinks available from the shelves or from the cooler.

If barbecue is your choice, you can order at the counter and then watch James or Danny prepare your plate: your choice of meats along with the typical barbecue sides. The beans are made from their sister's recipe—their sister considered "almost a carbon copy" of the mother who taught both boys so much about cooking. Meats are usually smoked over mesquite, unless as on this day, only oak is available.

James is especially proud of his barbecue sauce. Squeeze-bottled onto a plate loaded with brisket, two types of sausage, two types of pork ribs and even mutton (tender breast meat with ribs), this sauce is a sweet revelation. Since he believes the sauce accounts for a lot of the grocery's return customers, James has a name for it as catchy as the flavor. He calls the stuff Comeback Juice.

"When you're not on the beaten path, you have to always do a little better job," he says. "Sometimes this business gets tough, you know, and people can be harsh and crude and cold. But there's an expression we like to use: The will of God won't take you where the grace of God can't protect you. I kinda have to look at it that way."

and said, 'This is where you need to be.' "

James put down a $200 deposit on that decrepit building in 1991 and managed to get it repaired enough to open by 1994. That place served for a little over a decade, becoming a gathering point for Taylor residents both black and white. Doors opened for James with the continued success, and by 2005, he was able to build a new place from the ground up.

"It's my pulpit right here," James says, joining his brother Danny behind the counter to slice up brisket, ribs and sausage for a first-time visitor. "If you had been in here an hour ago, you would have heard me explaining to a young woman about a time before her time. If you can't get them into the church, then how are you going to get them to learn that? Well, that's how I teach them, with barbecue. Whatever and whoever comes along, that's what we do."

For all of the surprise James expresses that God called him to make barbecue, in truth the calling began in his earliest years. His father worked as a cowboy around Taylor and even participated in one of the area's last cattle drives. Part and parcel to that work was cooking barbecue to feed not only others along for the trail rides but the hundreds or thousands who attended various livestock shows. If Moses first met the God of the Israelites in that burning bush, you might say young James met Him in the

COOPER'S OLD TIME PIT BAR-B-QUE LLANO

ADDRESS: 604 W. YOUNG STREET (WEST HIGHWAY 71), LLANO
PHONE: (325) 247-5713
ESTABLISHED: 1963
OWNERS: THE WOOTAN FAMILY
BEST BITES: THE BIG CHOP, BEEF BRISKET, PRIME RIB, SMOKED JALAPEÑO SAUSAGE, PORK LOIN, POTATO SALAD, BLACKBERRY COBBLER
PAYMENT: CREDIT CARDS

In the bigger-better-best boy's club of Texas barbecue, where anything and everything is a secret, it's hard to say how much innovation there actually is. Unless, of course, you are Cooper's—which for half a century has been preaching a gospel that's different and arguably heretical.

While every other corner of Texas was perfecting its methods for slow-smoking meat with indirect heat funneled in from fireboxes, Tommy Cooper's father was insisting that the higher heat achieved by having coals directly underneath produced more exciting results. The process gave birth to what might be called the "Llano style of barbecue," followed by all who cook meat nearby but by virtually no one anywhere else in Texas. Tommy Cooper perfected his father's recipe from Taylor when he opened Cooper's in Llano in 1963. And after Tommy's untimely death in an auto accident in 1979, his technique passed through an intermediary until it settled upon the Wootan family, who lived across the street.

"We call it cooking cowboy," explains Jason Wootan, whose father, Terry, bought the Llano location in 1986 and currently is working on plans to franchise. "It was all in place to an extent under Tommy. But the show's gotten a lot bigger now."

Bigger seems an understatement to a visitor walking around the old-fashioned pits outside Cooper's buffet line and its indoor picnic tables arranged beneath a dozen or more glass-eyed hunting trophies. As Jason leads the al fresco tour, it's unavoidable to realize that you are witnessing a process unlike any other...a process its practitioners believe will give them the best barbecue time after time.

Cooking begins when whole pallets of mesquite wood are forklifted into what look like iron furnaces and set ablaze until they're reduced to glowing embers. These embers, in turn, are transferred by reinforced 12-foot shovels to trays within seven metal cooking pits. Meat cooked in these pits drips incessantly, igniting conflagrations among the coals and sending up virtually the only smoke these briskets and other meats will ever see. Thus, barbecue at Cooper's is a good deal less smoky than most found elsewhere—a function of this limited smoke mixed with the shorter-than-usual cooking times over direct heat.

Since the beginning at Cooper's, and carried forth reverentially by the Wootans, a quirky cooking method has been delivered to customers by an even quirkier delivery system. The faithful line up outside at the brick "serving pit," the place all cooked meat ends up after spending time in the "holding pit." You stand beside the pit, asking questions and pointing to this or that piece. Each choice is lifted by long fork onto a plastic tray, preferably after going for a swim in

Cooper's vinegar-based sauce, and then carried inside by the customer for weighing. Pricing is not by the piece or the serving here, but by the pound.

Once your meat is wrapped in butcher paper, your tray makes its way along the buffet line, taking on side dishes, fruit cobbler and a cup for sweet tea in the process. Cooper's soupy-delicious pinto beans are there for the taking, on a counter by the drinks out in the dining room.

Any list of Cooper's greatest hits has to begin with The Big Chop, a moist and flavor-packing 2-inch pork chop cooked and served on the bone. Other success stories include the beef brisket, cooked over hot coals for less than 5 hours, and the smoked sausage made at Cooper's adjacent USDA-inspected plant. This sausage comes in a "regular" style blending pork and beef, as well as in an all-pork jalapeño variation. Such meats are joined on the cafeteria line by what Jason calls "deli meats," from beef jerky and smoked beef to summer sausage and snack sticks (like a Slim Jim, he explains, only better).

On any given day, especially on weekends in summer, the line leading to Cooper's serving pit can stretch around the block. It can also be a study in demographic diversity, ranging from doctors, lawyers and CPAs from Austin, San Antonio, Dallas and Houston to large gangs of bikers fresh from the dusty road—"You know," says Jason, "the kind that aren't yuppies in disguise." They all come here to Llano because it's clearly a cool thing to do, and also because the barbecue served by Cooper's and just about everyone else in town is different from the barbecue served anywhere else.

Slight exceptions to this rule have been made over the years for meats cooked by other members of the Cooper family, from that original location over in Taylor to later spin-offs in Round Rock and Junction. In one of life's fascinating circular motions, the Wootans recently brought in Tommy Cooper's son Terry (actually named after Terry *Wootan*) to

operate the first Cooper's franchise in New Braunfels. Someday soon, predicts Jason, there will be additional franchised Cooper's in Fredericksburg, Fort Worth and beyond.

It's a safe bet that all will continue to treat "smoking" as a four-letter word, keeping those mesquite coals glowing brightly and flaming wildly to cook heretical barbecue for a new generation of Texans.

INMAN'S KITCHEN LLANO

ADDRESS: 809 W. YOUNG STREET (WEST HIGHWAY 71), LLANO
PHONE: (325) 247-5257
ESTABLISHED: 1967, THIS LOCATION IN 1986
OWNERS: MYRTLE AND HORACE OESTREICH
BEST BITES: TURKEY SAUSAGE, JALAPEÑO AND CHEESE TURKEY SAUSAGE, BEEF BRISKET, PORK RIBS, SMOKED TURKEY BREAST, COLESLAW, HOMEMADE BREAD, APPLE PIE
PAYMENT: CREDIT CARDS

If you were going to create a new taste sensation in Texas, a place that treats even pulled pork as though it's a personal insult to beef, you probably wouldn't do it with turkey. Yet that is exactly what Lester Inman did back in 1960, perfecting a recipe for smoked turkey sausage and selling it mostly to deer hunters at a small gas station he owned. At first,

people stopped in for gas and merely sampled the sausage absentmindedly, as Texans do with beef jerky today. But before long, they were pulling in—or even driving a bit out of their way—to buy this marvelous thing Lester had invented, applying an old German recipe handed down to his wife to the Pilgrim's bird from Thanksgiving.

Lester started offering his sausage at a coffee shop he ran at a local hotel, and he finally convinced one of the waitresses there, a lady named Myrtle, to become his business partner in a new barbecue place called Inman's Kitchen.

That was in September 1967. In less than a decade, Inman's had outgrown a couple of locations in Llano, inspired Lester's brother Francis to open Inman's Ranch House in Marble Falls...and that waitress' husband had joined the business. When Lester passed away in 1988, the couple bought the founder's half of the Llano location and committed themselves to his legacy, turkey sausage and all.

"The uniqueness of the sausage definitely does bring people in here," says Horace Oestreich, who operates this Inman's and the connected 4,000-square-foot dance hall that functions as a catering venue with his wife, Myrtle. "We've been a tradition for so many years."

Of course, Horace won't give away the recipe for Lester's turkey sausage, but he will talk about it a little. For one thing, he explains, since it's sausage and not Thanksgiving dinner, the emphasis is on dark meat. White breast would be too dry to hold together. And mostly for flavor, there is a bit of beef blended in—no pork, he insists.

The regular sausage Lester created for his gas station remains the biggest seller, but Horace and Myrtle have come up with a popular modern variation that's studded with jalapeño and Swiss cheese. In its link form—and especially in the larger lobes, a shape most associated by Americans with bologna—it resembles nothing so much as a coarse and delicious French country pâté. That's proba-

bly not an allusion that would be good for sales, but it helps give things a global perspective.

"Our sausage is real lean, with no additives or fillers," says Horace. "Most times you go to buy sausage somewhere, you read the label and put it right back down. Not here. We use only the good stuff."

Like most couples running a restaurant, Horace and Myrtle don't worry much about division of labor. If a thing needs doing by the owners, one of them will simply do it. Still, within the Texas tradition, Horace is the de facto pit master at today's Inman's Kitchen, working his way around the five open pits— no electricity and no gas—that keep the meat coming for the restaurant, for weddings and other events in the former Rambling Rose Dance Hall, and for off-site catering jobs large and small.

For Inman's beef brisket, which they sell a lot of despite the fame of turkey sausage, there's only the simplest of dry rubs followed by 6 to 7 hours in mesquite smoke. Other, lighter meats go in a separate pit, with their smoke coming from post oak. In an increasingly competitive barbecue universe (and with the iconic Cooper's just a couple blocks away), the couple added pork ribs, chicken and turkey breast after they moved to their large current location in the waning days of 1989.

Sides are straightforward at Inman's, and all are made from scratch: coleslaw (a nifty sweet-sour balance with unexpected poppy seeds) and potato salad dished up with your order, plus pinto beans and barbecue sauce kept warm in what seems an antique stove or furnace at one side of the dining room.

Your best bet for dessert is probably the apple pie, though peach, pecan and cherry are nearly always available as well. One thing you won't see here are the bags of commercial white bread so much a part of many Texas barbecue joints. In one of Inman's biggest surprises, they actually bake their own. Thicker cut than commercial, even their white bread has flavor, though far less than the dark they sell as Bavarian.

To Myrtle, who spends most of her time with customers and staff while Horace concentrates on his solitary pits in the back, none of this is exactly rocket science. What she clearly treasures is the memory of Lester Inman, who started doing one little thing well in a gas station long ago and nurtured it into a legacy of kindness worth preserving. "We try to greet everybody," she explains, as though not sure what other option there might be. "And we try to call the people by name, if we know 'em."

PEETE MESQUITE MARBLE FALLS

....

ADDRESS: 2407 HIGHWAY 281, MARBLE FALLS
PHONE: (830) 693-6531
ESTABLISHED: 1992
OWNERS: WAYNE AND LANELL ANDERSON
BEST BITES: PORK SPARERIBS, PORK STEAK, BEEF BRISKET, COLESLAW, MACARONI SALAD, PEACH OR BLACKBERRY COBBLER
PAYMENT: CREDIT CARDS

San Antonio native Wayne Anderson studied at the Culinary Institute of America and worked as a chef for 30 years in 10 states before deciding Texas barbecue

would be his culinary final resting place. As for most who choose barbecue, however, he hasn't gotten much rest since.

"I'm in here at 3 or 3:30 every morning, getting the fire going," he reports, his eyes smiling through his glasses and his cap sprouting a gray ponytail he probably wouldn't have gotten away with at Omni or Marriott. "After all those years as a chef, I have to have quality. With barbecue, if you don't know what you're doing or trim the fat too early"—he laughs—"or stick the whole thing in the microwave, then what you end up with is your own fault."

Wayne and his wife, Lanell, first came to this area, often called the Lake Country, in the mid-1990s. Back then, Wayne was still doing what he'd always done, serving as executive chef for the posh resort at Horseshoe Bay. The area made him happy, even if the job seldom did. So when he and Lanell stumbled on Peete Mesquite, run by an older gentleman as something of a hobby since moving here from Johnson City in 1992, they realized they had a mission.

"He didn't even have a sign out front," says Wayne. "It took us almost two years to talk him into it. And, well, the first thing we did was put up a sign."

Not surprisingly, with his culinary credentials, the visible change outside was nothing compared with the tireless if less visible changes in the kitchen and the pit area out back. For all his cooking of everything else over three decades, Wayne had never cooked barbecue...so he set out to eat in 50 or 60 places across Texas and decide just what he liked. Talking with pit masters and reading cookbooks, he connected the dots between what he liked and what you did to make it that way. And through it all, in ways few barbecue guys have the background to understand, he applied the principles of flavor—and any kind of flavor—he'd learned as a trained chef.

"What makes us unique is having a rotisserie run off of nothing but mesquite," he says, taking on an almost

scholarly air, undercut by the bemused look he gets thinking about all the barbecue he's seen. "A lot of places are mostly about gas or electricity. But me being an executive chef, I just couldn't go that way."

Wayne finally adopted an unusual combination of direct and indirect heat. The indirect method, usually just called smoking, he borrowed from the broadest traditions of Texas barbecue and the German-Czech butchers who perfected it in the Hill Country. For this, he burns mesquite wood in a firebox off to the side, letting its heat and smoke waft its way in with the meat and cook it "low and slow."

To achieve his goals for meat as a chef—including the wonderful caramelized color that smoking seldom produces—Wayne also shovels hot coals from his firebox right under his briskets and pork ribs, thus applying direct heat when his training tells him the time is right.

From his two smokers holding 700 and 400 pounds of meat, Wayne takes what's usually his No. 1 seller—beef brisket, given a nice covering of dry rub (17 spices, blended by the chef) at the start. If he gets what he ordered, he prefers smaller briskets of less than 9 pounds, these needing to cook only 6 to

8 hours. But when his purveyors deliver only 14-pounders by "mistake," the cooking time goes up to 9 to 14 hours.

Gifted with the same rub and smoked for 3 hours, Wayne's pork spareribs are to him the most exciting thing on the menu. And if not the ribs, then it has to be his unique "pork steak," cut from the shoulder, covered with a mixture of dry rub and brown sugar and smoked until it's all spicy candy outside and pinky flaky on the inside.

"I can eat that pork steak every day, and I just about have for 10 years," Wayne says with a smile. "It's a tough job, but somebody's gotta do it."

Lanell, who worked as a CPA for 25 years before joining Wayne in the barbecue business, is a godsend. She works behind the counter from opening to closing, a constant customer presence as Wayne races back and forth to the pit, and then handles all the books and the taxes. Paying her husband one of the highest compliments in the business, she puts on her CPA hat and says simply, "He's real good about watching his food cost."

As an executive chef, Wayne knows well the job is every bit as much about purchasing as about cooking: buying the best when it matters, handling it well, and fitting those expenditures into the overall fabric so the numbers work—or, in his case, so his wife doesn't yell at him.

Most of the meat at Peete Mesquite represents a bump up from the barbecue norm, as does the chef's obsessive insistence on making nearly everything from scratch. From the coleslaw to the macaroni salad to the peach or blackberry cobbler, here is food made by someone who learned from the ground up, who understands exactly what makes something taste wonderful, and who takes no shortcuts while also taking no prisoners.

"I wanted to finish my life in a small town," Wayne says thoughtfully. "Sure, I figured I'd do fine dining here—I *wanted* to do fine dining. But back then, 10 years ago, they'd have ran me out of town. I just knew Marble Falls was a nice place to be."

GEORGETOWN BAR-B-QUE
GEORGETOWN

ADDRESS: 723 W. UNIVERSITY AVENUE, GEORGETOWN
PHONE: (512) 864-7389
ESTABLISHED: 1977
OWNERS: DONN AND MYRA SUBOCZ
BEST BITES: BEEF BRISKET, SMOKED SAUSAGE, PORK RIBS, PORK LOIN, CHOPPED BARBECUE, POTATO SALAD, BANANA PUDDING
PAYMENT: CREDIT CARDS

Growing up Lithuanian in western Massachusetts, Donn Subocz knew somewhere between little and nothing about Texas barbecue. Still, by the time he was ready to take on the Lone Star State's fabled food after 20 years in the military, the fact that he'd spent his childhood working in his family's meat market didn't hurt one bit.

Though he loved smoked brisket from the moment he sampled it, his was not the admiration of one who knew nothing, but of one whose experience told him what he was tasting was impossible.

"I was fascinated," Donn admits of that first encounter, which took place near the end of his career running restaurants, clubs and bars for the U.S. Army, including two stints in Vietnam. "I'm very familiar with beef brisket from the East Coast, but that's always served as corned beef. I just couldn't understand how they got the meat so tender by smoking it, instead of simmering it in liquid the way you do with corned beef."

Donn's fascination obviously rang as something of a challenge, for he embarked on an obsessive quest—accompanied before long by his wife, Myra, whom he met when he was working in Texas at Fort Hood—to perfect methods for every minute aspect of barbecue.

Donn's first place, which he opened shortly after his retirement from the military in 1977, was a mere 1,200 square feet, with all the important business being conducted in two 55-gallon oil drums that had been welded together. Over the next three decades, despite these humble beginnings, Donn would profitably launch, sell and lease no fewer than seven barbecue joints between Austin and Georgetown, several of which still do nice business under their original name, Donn's.

"The first day I think we took in $65, but eventually we broke the $300 mark," Donn recalls. "At the time, Myra was working as a benefits administrator. The first time our daily sales reached $300, I called her and told her she'd better give her two weeks notice. I needed some help."

Clearly not the sort of guy to retire and play golf, Donn operated most of his early places with only his wife. That, he says, is why he's managed to own only one place at a time, instead of building a chain. He certainly has the know-how, after running foodservice in Army officers clubs that fed thousands. It wasn't about not knowing how to cook barbecue, he confesses, but not knowing how to let go.

"I thought I was the only person who could do it right," he explains. "But each time I did it that way, I burned out. This is the first place I've let go some, with five employees besides me and Myra. But I'm still here at 5 every morning to check the briskets. I do all the carving for cus-

tomers all day, and I usually don't leave 'til 9 at night. It's the brisket that's the most difficult to be consistent, day after day after day."

At Georgetown Bar-B-Que, which Donn and Myra opened near the end of 2003, those oh-so-pampered briskets get covered with a dry rub made to his recipe. And since Donn has come a long way from those jerry-rigged oil barrels, they go into a Southern Pride rotisserie overnight over a fire of green mesquite. This pit master can go on at some length about why green wood is so much better than dry or seasoned wood, since its moisture keeps it from ever catching fire during the night. Such a flame-up, he says militarily, would be "putting yourself in a negative air situation." And that would be a bad thing.

In addition to Donn's tender brisket, he and Myra fill orders all day for the smoked sausage (plain from Elgin, jalapeño from Hallettsville) and for the pork ribs. Sandwiches can be made from "chopped barbecue," an appealing combination of beef and pork, or from chopped chicken. This chicken is actually more pulled than chopped, but when Donn tried billing it as "pulled chicken," it never got ordered.

Georgetown Bar-B-Que keeps side dishes simple: homemade potato salad with very little mustard, a super-creamy coleslaw and some cumin-tinged pinto beans. Desserts are handled with similar minimalism: pleasant banana pudding and a shifting array of cobblers best served with ice cream.

At some point, as with the six barbecue places that went before, someone will probably walk into Georgetown Bar-B-Que and make Donn an offer he can't refuse. The guy who never even tried to cook barbecue before he'd retired the first time says he just might do it this second time. Then again, he says, "I'm the type of person that can't just sit around."

FUSCHAK'S PIT BAR-B-Q, SAN MARCOS

ADDRESS: 1701 S. INTERSTATE 35, SAN MARCOS
PHONE: (512) 353-2712
ESTABLISHED: 1966
OWNER: MORGAN FUSCHAK
BEST BITES: BEEF BRISKET, FAJITAS (ESPECIALLY IN A TACO, DIPPED IN BARBECUE SAUCE), BARBECUED CHICKEN, PORK RIBS, JALAPEÑO CORN, BANANA PUDDING, CHOCOLATE PUDDING WITH FUDGE BROWNIE
PAYMENT: CREDIT CARDS

When the 21st century was still young, a developer approached the Fuschak family with an offer to buy the barbecue place their mother had started four decades earlier, intending to tear it down and put up a pharmacy. The offer was unexpected, even unwanted—and, after a bit of back and forth, way too good to turn down. Still, since there wasn't enough money for family members and key employees to retire comfortably, oldest brother Morgan Fuschak did the next best thing. He and his siblings hauled their rotisserie smokers up onto flatbed trailers and carted them to a sparkling new location on the interstate between Austin and San Antonio.

"My big brother did this for us," says Danny Fuschak, obviously touched but also smiling through his walrus mustache beneath eyeglasses and a baseball cap. "When our counteroffer was accepted, we didn't know if we'd rebuild or not. But our family and a lot of other employees depended on this place for our living. Everything Morgan has done, he's done for this family."

Fuschak's Pit Bar-B-Q today is a bit of a time warp, a bit of a contradiction in terms. Founded by one woman who worked as a waitress in a franchised joint and got the opportunity to buy it in 1966, this new/old Fuschak's blends extremely traditional Texas recipes with some of the comforts of a modern restaurant. Enough of the old décor made the trip, right

along with those smokers, that old-timers say the family must have moved the building. Yet issues of stability, cleanliness and efficiency were addressed by this being brand-new construction.

Morgan had a promising career of his own when his mother called in 1975. She was seriously ill, she told him, and needed him to stop what he was doing and keep Fuschak's going. Within six months, Danny joined his brother in the business, and he has worked nowhere else in the three decades since. "There's not a soul in this family—and I mean kids, nieces, nephews—who hasn't worked down here one time or another," Danny says.

Back at the old place, most of the serious cooking was done on a brick pit, but even there the family used one or two Ole Hickory rotisseries to help them through big catering jobs. Today, the brick pit is but a memory, and three Ole Hickorys wait just beyond the kitchen for the Fuschaks and their pit guys to cook meat over a mixture of post oak and hickory. They tried mesquite early on but didn't much like the taste. "Besides," Danny says, "mesquite made my eyeballs burn."

Brisket is the most popular meat at Fuschak's, dusted with the family's dry rub and smoked 18 to 24 hours. All other meats—from smoked sausage and fajitas to chicken, turkey and pork ribs—go on in the morning when Danny comes in around 6. By then, the kitchen is humming, with cooks using two 10-burner Vulcan stoves to turn out beans, barbecue sauce and one of the place's most striking side dishes, jalapeño corn.

"It's like creamed corn except it's not," laughs Danny. "Morgan's wife used to serve it at Thanksgiving and Christmas, and I know I looked forward to it all year long. That was only two days a year. Now it's a hit seven days a week."

Several of the other sides are made in-house, including a nifty version of coleslaw. Desserts seem a bit of an afterthought, as they do in most meat-centric barbecue joints. But even so, a handful of sweet-tooth home runs has emerged over the decades. The banana pudding goes in for the layered look—vanilla wafers, then sliced bananas, then banana pudding, then more vanilla wafers—while the dark chocolate pudding all mixed up with chunks of fudge brownie is a total blast from the past.

In catering mode, with all three smokers and all 20 burners going strong, Fuschak's can serve barbecue to 3,000 or more people at a time, and does so on a regular basis. UT in Austin is a major client, Danny confirms, buying upwards of 10,000 meals in the course of a year.

"And there are, like, how many barbecue places in Austin? Like 500? And they come to us!" He ponders for a moment, not for the first or last time, thinking of Hill Country barbecue joints that get more press, the ones that are always featured in *Texas Monthly* or on the Food Network. "My mama put her heart and soul into this business. I don't need riches, but there's no reason we shouldn't get some respect."

GRANZIN BAR-B-Q NEW BRAUNFELS

....

ADDRESS: 660 W. SAN ANTONIO STREET, NEW
BRAUNFELS
PHONE: (830) 629-6615
ESTABLISHED: 1984, THIS LOCATION IN 2007
OWNER: MILES GRANZIN
BEST BITES: BEEF BRISKET, MARINATED TURKEY
BREAST, "COUNTRY-STYLE RIBS," GRANZIN'S TACO WITH
CARNE ASADA, POTATO SALAD, COLESLAW, PECAN PIE
PAYMENT: CREDIT CARDS

Miles Granzin thought he'd learned one thing moving his 23-year-old barbecue business from a 400-square-foot takeout joint to a new 6,300-square-foot restaurant that seats up to 180. But he learned the opposite thing instead.

"It's easier," he says, nodding an aw-shucks acknowledgement of the irony. "I couldn't believe it myself. And when I tell people, they figure I'm lying. But it is. In the old place, we were always climbing all over each other. And we had to cook things in small batches that now we just make all at once. Plus, of course, the building started falling down around us."

Miles grew up with German roots in a Texas town long famed for trotting out an oompah band at the drop of a schnitzel. Yet his world of brisket, sausage and ribs seems to exist apart from all that old-world charm, a theme park opened daily for the 3 million-plus tourists who come here, most in summer to tube the Comal and Guadalupe rivers. Miles' customers are mostly locals, meaning they don't stop showing up in the winter. And many of them, like some of his best employees

now enjoying the additional room, have been faithful since the beginning.

Miles started working in barbecue when he was 16, helping in the commissary for the San Antonio-born chain Bill Miller's. Eventually, his father came to live in New Braunfels at the edge of the Hill Country, and Miles was cajoled into following. He spent four years in a different kind of food business, working at the oldest bakery in Texas, a German place called Naegelin's by the courthouse. When a tiny barbecue takeout joint went out of business in 1984, Miles saw it as his chance to get back into a line of cooking he knew and loved.

"It was all to-go at that little place, with picnic tables in the back," he remembers. "It was so easy, and I was satisfied where I was at. I was learning the business and we were making good money, so when I thought about opening a bigger place, I always thought, Why do it? But then the old place started falling apart." Miles ponders his motivations. "Plus, my kids were getting old enough that I figured they should have something nice when I retire."

The new restaurant, opened in 2007, features much of the faux-rustic wood and rusty-looking metal that Miles had neither the money nor the space to install in the original. The counter area and front dining space, in fact, are made to resemble an Old West town, with a wooden façade that announces a saloon and a jail. And if it all sounds theme-park fanciful, nothing about the kids' high chairs should change your mind. Youngsters sit atop a studded black leather saddle. "We only had one of those when we opened," Miles reports, "but the kids kept fighting to get it. Now we have four."

Today, service is breakfast, lunch and dinner at Granzin's, with a lot still being taken out, but more comfortable dining available for 80 people inside, 80 more in a nice back party room, and 20 more on the veranda outside when the weather cooperates. Miles brought one of the pits he built at the old place to the new, and

ribs come cut in three shorter segments, supposedly so you can eat them with one hand while floating the river in a tube, your other hand free to hold your beer.

Side dishes are all produced in-house, including a potato salad on the sweet side, with limited tang from mustard, and a coleslaw much the same. In fact, a mixture of the two sides (not recommended officially) produced potato salad with the world's crunchiest texture—well worth a try.

One of the secrets to Granzin's longevity is using the same, high-quality raw ingredients, many of them made right in New Braunfels by relatives. Three styles of sausage come from a cousin— smoked, jalapeño and garlic—while all the breads and rolls are sent over fresh by brothers who own Naegelin's. In an unexpected multi-ethnic touch, the old German bakery even takes time away from its strudel to produce Granzin's 1,000 or so daily flour tortillas.

"I didn't have room to make them at the old place," Miles says with a grin. "So I bought them the machine."

then built two more that look just like it. Mesquite is his wood of choice.

Happily for his longtime customers, Miles' retention of many employees as the business moved down the street meant that nearly all their favorite flavors remained unchanged. They line up early each day for Granzin's breakfast tacos— especially the ones crafted around his smoked turkey breast, which (Miles explains) is first marinated in a blend of Italian dressing and mayo, which forms a crusty outside that keeps the meat super-moist within. As the morning fades, lunch orders start to favor beef brisket, which gets a dry rub before going on the smoke for 6 to 8 hours.

"It's as tender as it can be," says Miles. "You can't let it get too tender cuz then it wouldn't work on the slicer. We like kinda thin slices here, compared to some places I've been. I like to roll my brisket up and dip it in our barbecue sauce."

Many know to order the "country-style ribs," which come boneless and aren't actually ribs at all. What they are is smoked strips of tender pork shank, lightly dusted with mellow kosher salt. Actual

TEXAS PRIDE BARBECUE ADKINS

....

ADDRESS: 2980 EAST LOOP 1604, ADKINS
PHONE: (210) 649-3730
ESTABLISHED: 1996
OWNER: TONY TALANCO
BEST BITES: SLICED BEEF BRISKET, CHOPPED BEEF SANDWICH, BABY BACK RIBS, SMOKED SAUSAGE, "GERMAN POTATO SALAD," COLESLAW, PEACH OR PECAN COBBLER
PAYMENT: CREDIT CARDS

Long before Tony Talanco moved to this piece of windswept highway where the Hill Country flattens out toward South Texas, he learned how to barbecue from his grandparents and parents.

That founding generation—a man from the Italian seaside town of Pescara and an Irish-American woman from

Texas—knew relatively little about the food business when they started in the 1920s. What they understood, like most people in that time and place, was hard work.

By the time Tony's father was growing up, his parents were running a combination filling station, restaurant and tourist court (that precursor to the great American motel) on the banks of Leon Creek in San Antonio. According to Tony, their eatery was more than a place to get fed. It was a place to get elected.

"Back in the '30s and '40s, there was no TV, so candidates couldn't reach voters the way they do now," says Tony. "The way they got people to elect them, here in Texas anyway, was by throwing a free barbecue with beer.

"My grandfather used to drive down to John Nance Garner's ranch in Uvalde, when he was a congressman or later when he was FDR's vice president, pick up halves of beef and ice it down in the back of a Model T pickup. The roads were nothing but gravel then, so this drive was an all-day affair. They'd barbecue the meat all night long, and the next day they'd have a big political rally."

Tony's grandfather lived until 1947. By then, his grandmother had been joined in the business by Tony's father and uncle, both of whom had known the operation intimately since way too early in their lives. And since father wouldn't have it any other way for son, Tony's upbringing was the same.

"I grew up icing down the beer when I was 6 or 7 years old, cleaning tables and sweeping floors," Tony recalls. "It was an exciting time for me to be a kid. I loved it. We had an old motorcycle dirt track, with races on Sundays and crashes and everything, and I used to go around picking up the empty bottles. Every day seemed to be like going to the fair."

Over the years, Tony tried a few things on his own. He had a successful go at country cooking—chicken-fried steak and the like—and then, in a different setting, at Mexican food. At some point,

though, he remembers having an unforgettable dream of finding an old filling station like the one his grandparents used to run. It was a delicious memory... so delicious that when he couldn't track down such a place, he decided to spend more than three years building one from the ground up.

"I bought this property as raw land, and then I collected all this old gas station and farm equipment," Tony says. "This place looks so authentic that, well, I've had people tell me they remember stopping here when they were kids." He smiles. "I don't say anything to that, really."

Texas Pride has grown into an impressive complex. Outside the antique-filled barbecue restaurant is a huge area with a stage for live music, picnic tables, room for dancing and a playground for the kids. Though the first incarnation of this area was built around fish fries on Friday nights, Tony now manages to weave his barbecue through the very different audiences that attend Biker Night or Classic Car Day. As Tony sees it, people come here once from Austin, San Antonio or Houston for some special event. They'll come back again and again for the barbecue.

After years of struggling with a 30-foot brick pit, Tony went over to a Southern Pride smoker. He uses mesquite wood and smokes his dry-rubbed briskets 10 to 13 hours. "I like hickory best in terms of flavor, but there just isn't a lot of hickory around here," he points out. Other popular meats include the pork sausage Texas Pride makes in-house and the baby back pork ribs they cook until the meat almost falls off the bone.

Popular side dishes include a strange spin on "German potato salad" (combining bacon and onion with mayonnaise, served cold instead of warm) and the creamy-sweet coleslaw with celery seed and cider vinegar. Peach cobbler is Texas Pride's best-selling dessert, though pecan cobbler (like pecan pie except looser) is starting to give that barbecue-joint classic a run for its money.

GOODE'S
ARMADILLO PALACE

Dominoes,
Pool and
Shuffleboard

Cold
Goo

GOODE CO. TEXAS BAR-B-Q, HOUSTON

....

ADDRESS: 5109 KIRBY DRIVE, HOUSTON
PHONE: (713) 522-2530
ESTABLISHED: 1977
OWNER: JIM GOODE
BEST BITES: BEEF BRISKET, SAUSAGE, POTATO SALAD, JAMBALAYA, HOMEMADE BREADS, PECAN PIE, CHOCOLATE CREAM PIE
PAYMENT: CREDIT CARDS

Jim Goode was an artist above all else. It just took him a few years to discover he was meant to paint his greatest works with smoke.

By the mid-1970s, Jim had trained as a commercial artist and taken up residence in a Houston studio with a handful of others similarly inclined. Together, they high-octaned their way through the need-it-yesterday world of designing logos, laying out magazine ads and spinning out illustrations, all things that required a lot of hand labor in those days before computer graphics. Though the future looked bright enough for the artist, with any thoughts of Texas barbecue relegated to weekends with family and friends, a strange notion began to take hold as the thrill of being a commercial artist began to grow thin.

"My dad was one of those real go-to guys, and he was always a perfectionist," says Levi Goode, using the "P word" about his father for the first of about a dozen times. "He was the kinda guy that you could take him something at 5 in the afternoon and get it back in time for your meeting at 9 the next morning. He just got pretty tired of all that, so he decided he would open either a bait camp or a barbecue place."

To the disappointment of bait-camp fans everywhere, opportunity came knocking from the other direction. Jim was in the habit of stopping for barbecue at a little mom-and-pop place that had served Houston since the 1950s. One day

when he stopped, mom was struggling visibly, with pop nowhere in sight. Jim asked the woman if her husband was around, only to learn he had passed away. Clearly, running a barbecue place alone was not high on this mom's personal wish list, though she hadn't yet given much thought to what she might do about it. As he generally did in his art studio, Jim had some pretty good ideas.

"My dad only had about $6,000—and $3,000 of that was receivables, you know, the check's-in-the-mail type thing," Levi remembers. "He gave her what little cash he had, and she pretty much handed the keys to him. That lady was out of there the next day."

Ownership of the place changed just before Labor Day 1977. Over that long holiday weekend, Jim and various family members worked around the clock to get the restaurant in order: deep cleaning in the kitchen, general sprucing and maintenance in the dining room, plus a new look in all public areas achieved more with style than substance. Old license plates, weathered concert posters and various hunting trophies became the décor of Goode Co., and they remain so to this day. An uncle who had cooked in the Army during World War II came in to assist for a while, making foods and also helping Jim refine his recipes.

Opening on a shoestring, and a short one at that, Jim had virtually no money for mainstream advertising. His focus for the first two or three years in business, according to his son, was on being his own best perfectionist—experimenting with wood 'til he settled on green mesquite (higher moisture content, less harsh flavor), trying different spice blends for a dry rub until he had one worth setting in stone, auditioning purveyors until he gave up and decided to make almost everything himself from scratch.

This included not only turning out Goode Co.'s four kinds of barbecue sauce, but grinding and stuffing his own sausage and even baking his own bread. Wonder of wonders, Goode Co. not only bakes its own specialty breads—like the immensely popular onion buns and jalapeño cheese loaf—but the most traditional, arguably least interesting bread of all time, plain Texas white.

The payback, on the good days anyway, was near-complete control over quality. Over time, the even bigger payback came to be word-of-mouth, soon spilling the cafeteria line all around the dining room and out the front door.

The moral of Goode Co.'s story is that once you hear opportunity knock, you probably need to keep listening. By the time the barbecue place was going strong, Jim had already grabbed up an old Del Taco location across the street and turned it into his own peculiar blend of taqueria and hamburger joint, complete with mesquite cooking, and constructed a commissary to help with high-volume, big-labor items like barbecue sauce, spice blends, sausage and all those loaves of bread.

In 1986, Jim drew on his childhood along the Texas Gulf Coast (in Freeport and Clute, with plenty of fishing trips to Surfside Beach) by opening the first of two Goode Co. Seafoods, followed by a second barbecue place in 1989 and a Hall of Flame retail store across from the original restaurant in 1993. With the advent of mail-order sales via the Internet, the family morphed that store in 2004 into Goode's Armadillo Palace, a music venue that hosts shows five or six nights a week to the tune of Texas comfort food.

While not "officially retired"—indeed, a huge banner outside the mother ship proclaims Jim Goode is "still at the reins"—Jim has turned day-to-day operation of the empire over to Levi and settled in to work on "projects." After all, any new restaurants the family launches will need menus and kitchen designs, not to mention a certain amount of stuff on the walls. Most of all, what each new eatery will need is exactly what the old ones needed when it was their turn: an artist who's also a perfectionist.

PAPPAS BAR-B-Q HOUSTON

ADDRESS: 1217 PIERCE AT SAN JACINTO, HOUSTON
PHONE: (713)659-1245
ESTABLISHED: 1967
OWNERS: CHRIS AND HARRIS PAPPAS
BEST BITES: CHOPPED BRISKET, BEEF RIBS, PORK SPARERIBS, STUFFED BAKED POTATO, CUCUMBER SALAD, MACARONI AND CHEESE, POTATO SALAD, PECAN PIE, CARROT CAKE
PAYMENT: CREDIT CARDS

Mary Pappas isn't your typical Texas pit boss. In fact, she grew up in a well-to-do Greek-American family with a wide assortment of profitable restaurants in their collective blood. And she went off and earned an MBA from Harvard Business School to seal the deal.

Today, Mary is grappling with the same delicate balances of wood type, smoking apparatus, and time and temperature that equally haunt and fascinate anyone making barbecue in any corner of the Lone Star State. Starting in 2003, with the family's absorption of the struggling Luther's chain, Pappas Bar-B-Q went from six locations to 20. And Mary went from generally working in her family's business to focusing exclusively on barbecue.

"It's the original," she says of the Texas cooking style and her family's work within it, starting with one place called The Brisket House in downtown Houston in 1967. "Every day I get to work with some of the founding team members who've been there for the journey we've been on. It's sort of the heart of what we do."

Like many Greek-American families, the Pappas clan has a definite patriarch—H.D. Pappas, who came to America from the mountains of central Greece at the start of the 20th century and started running small cafés. After adventures in several states, H.D. found success in Dallas—enough success, in fact, that he could extract from his children a now-legendary promise to *never ever* be in the restaurant business. They did the thing right next door, though, selling and distributing restaurant supplies, which brought them south to Houston.

It was a member of that first American-born generation who fudged on his promise just enough to learn all he could about Texas barbecue and open The Brisket House. Part of the complex and interwoven tapestry of Houston's Greek restaurant families, Tom Pappas gave the city one of several barbecue joints owned and operated by Greeks. It's unlikely he foresaw that, with the next generation led by Chris and Harris Pappas, that small family business would take its place within a substantially larger concern.

"My father and uncle never had their sights limited to one restaurant," Mary says, explaining the difference a generation or two in America can make. "They always had a much bigger goal." She lets go with a girlish giggle. "And I have to brag on them a little; they really love what they do."

These days, "what they do" involves upwards of 75 restaurants belonging to seven or eight concept categories and spread over Texas, Arizona, New Mexico, Colorado, Georgia, Ohio and Illinois. The eateries range from the ultra high-end Pappas Bros. Steakhouse in Houston, to casual burger and seafood places, plus airport food kiosks and colorful tributes to Tex-Mex (Pappasito's) and Cajunized Gulf Coast seafood (Pappadeaux). In recent years, the family has even added a fun Greek eatery named in honor of Mary's grandmother, Yia-Yia Mary's.

Still, for Mary herself and fellow group leader Scott Harvey (who came up through the ranks), barbecue is literally the air they breathe. The Pappas method, perfected years ago by "Uncle Tom" Pappas and a general manager named Selvos Escobar, involves slow-smoking with hickory in a rotisserie pit with a firebox, thus creating indirect heat. The brisket that is their biggest seller (sliced or chopped, or served in tacos at break-

fast or stuffed into a baked potato for lunch or dinner) is dusted with a dry rub and set to smoke for a minimum of 14 to 15 hours. A similar fate awaits Pappas Bar-B-Q's three types of ribs—spareribs, baby backs and mastodon-like beef ribs— except the rub is different.

Side dishes are made fresh daily at each location and include the Big Three. A couple of Mary's favorites from the 12 or so that rotate through include a sweet-and-sour cucumber salad and a lushly traditional macaroni and cheese.

For dessert, the family is probably proudest of its pecan pie, though fan clubs have also grown up around their vanilla cheesecake with bright red strawberry sauce and their peach cobbler. A recent addition is super-moist carrot cake, with more than a little cream cheese icing.

"Greeks always want to work for themselves," Mary says, asked to explain not only her family's success but that of Greek immigrants serving every type of food in America throughout the 20th century. "For us, it's all about being independent and being your own boss. Plus, it's that whole Mediterranean thing." She smiles. "I can't imagine getting together with my family and there not being too much food."

DEMERIS BAR-B-Q HOUSTON

ADDRESS: 2911 S. SHEPHERD, HOUSTON
PHONE: (713) 529-7326
ESTABLISHED: 1964
OWNERS: YONNY, FRANK N., FRANK G. AND GEORGE N. DEMERIS, BILLY VLAHAKOS
BEST BITES: BEEF BRISKET, SMOKED SAUSAGE, HAMBURGERS, GREEK SALAD (ESPECIALLY WITH FAJITA MEAT ON TOP), JALAPEÑO CORN, APPLE COBBLER
PAYMENT: CREDIT CARDS

At one time or another, the Greek-American Demeris family has cooked and served everything from soup to nuts—doughnuts, that is. Yet it was only when a younger generation discovered its "inner Texan" and started dishing up barbecue that fame and relative fortune began to accrue. Today, the family not only operates one mother-ship restaurant and two satellite locations but a catering division that keeps five trucks on the street. Demeris has sliced and diced brisket for upwards of 8,000 people at a time.

As most diners know, Greeks who came to America have long been drawn to the restaurant business. In the Deep South in particular, from Savannah to Montgomery to Jackson, it seems the majority of chicken-fried steak, meat loaf and other café favorites is prepared by some guy with a Greek accent, a blue-and-white Greek flag beside the cash register and a poster of the Acropolis somewhere on the wall.

In a sense, Houston is no different, with its annual Greek Festival making clear just how huge and successful the local Greek population has become. Still, it took quite a few steps for the Demeris family to settle on barbecue once they made it into this country through Ellis Island, traveling to Texas by way of a stint in Joplin, Missouri.

"I think it's because of our independent spirit," says Billy Vlahakos, who now owns Demeris Bar-B-Q with four cousins whose last name is on the sign: Yonny, Frank N., Frank G. and George N. "It's because they can do this for themselves. In a restaurant, you can take and do and apply what you learn. With a limited amount of book knowledge and a lot of hard work, Greeks could always just go ahead and do this."

"Doing this" in Texas is what the Demeris family and its extensions have been all about. Before there was a wildly successful barbecue restaurant and certainly before there was a catering division doing not only barbecue but some of the fanciest party food in town, there was something called the G and N Café in downtown Houston (much like those Greek-owned cafés in almost every Southern city) and also a Shipley's Grill (named because it agreed to serve Shipley's doughnuts, along with other menu items). Plus, restaurants in two downtown hotels and something called Carol's Kitchen—"where the Starbucks is now," Billy and Yonny point out.

The family had plenty of experience dealing with food and people, and also with the ups and downs of a family business with brothers, sisters and cousins, not to mention in-laws. At some point, a few family members split off from the cafés to work in a Greek-owned barbecue place called Steve's. Years later, when they heard about the opportunity to buy a barbecue place of their own—one of several at the same location since the 1930s—they jumped in and made it their own.

From 1964 on, Demeris Bar-B-Q has operated from an ever-expanding compound, growing the physical plant as business changed and expanded. Of those evolutions, the rise of catering was cer-

tainly the most significant, particularly when the family decided to move beyond barbecue to things like spaghetti and fajitas, eventually anything a particular client wanted.

In the restaurant today, beef brisket is the best-selling meat, followed at a distance by smoked sausage and chicken. Jalapeño corn, creamy and spicy at the same time, joins more typical items like potato salad, coleslaw and two kinds of beans among the lengthy list of sides.

For dessert, a rotating selection of pies is offered—cherry and lemon meringue among the most popular—plus apple and peach cobbler, cookies and brownies topped with ice cream.

With five family members in the driv-er's seat, there's seldom any lack of a Demeris to keep the operation running smoothly, even when a 1,000-person lunch order comes in without any warning. "By this point, barbecue is easy," says Yonny. "Running the restaurant is easy. It's catering lunch for those 1,000 people that's the biggest challenge. It's because we're a family business and we don't like to ever tell anybody no."

BEAVER'S, HOUSTON

ADDRESS: 2310 DECATUR STREET, HOUSTON
PHONE: (713) 864-BEAV (2328)
ESTABLISHED: 2007
OWNERS: MONICA POPE, ANDREA LAZAR, JON DEAL, JEFF KAPLAN, ADAM BRACKMAN
BEST BITES: SPICY LAMB WRAP, BEAVER WINGS, STUFFED PEPPERONCINI ANGELS, BEEF BRISKET, BISON AND BEEF MEAT LOAF, BRAISED GREENS, KILLER COLESLAW, PHILLY MAC AND CHEESE, BANANA PUDDING, HOMEMADE BREAD
PAYMENT: CREDIT CARDS

It's hard to imagine a more awarded or admired Houston chef than Monica Pope, whose obsessional mantra of "fresh, seasonal, local" made the menu at her former Boulevard Bistro and now at her t'afia sound a lot like the farmers market she

hosts there every Saturday. Chef Dax McAnear is no slouch when it comes to fancy either, after stints at popular foodie meccas like 17 and benjy's.

When these two get together, you'd expect a festival of thoroughly chefed-up, big-ticket engineering based on foie gras, caviar and truffles, right? Wrong!

Taking over a longtime Houston icehouse—yes, a place that initially sold ice but came to concentrate on the "next generation," aka ice-cold beer—Monica and Dax have thrown considerable caution to the winds, and considerable smoke as well. The place they've opened together has all the trappings of a *glorified* icehouse, including the ice-cold beer; yet instead of mere bar snacks, there's topflight barbecue developed with a serious eye to scientific method. And there's more sauces, appetizers, side dishes and desserts than you'd find at any *six* barbecue joints anywhere else.

"A lot of the cheffies in town don't really legitimize barbecue," Monica says, "so in some ways it's a big risk for us to do this. We actually want to keep that old, humble Texas barbecue, but we do want to input our ideas and our passion into it. We're not trying to be 'foo-foo' and fancy, put everything on a plate and compose it. But we can't really excise our culinary minds either."

"I grew up in a trailer park," adds Dax, perhaps with a wink, "so this is my kind of food. Happily, Monica is letting me trashify everything."

Monica doesn't like the notion of "fancy barbecue," any more than she enjoys off-putting phrases like "fine dining." "It's not fancy," she insists. "It's just food." Yet by any measuring stick available (other than Beaver's delightfully casual feel and absolute lack of dress code), some measure of "fancy" applies.

All the food is made from the best ingredients possible, including many things from artisanal ranches and farms that get named virtually in prayer on the menu. Many things normally bought by barbecue joints are made from scratch here. Many recipes with three or four ingredients, from dry rub to coleslaw dressing to banana pudding, here have seven or eight. And most tellingly, many dishes associated with a single cooking method (such as traditional smoking) are subjected here to two or three, most ending up in the deep fryer. As a general rule for life: The more cooking processes used and the more pots dirtied, the more trained chefs are in the kitchen.

As far back as the 1930s, the icehouse called Doody's was a beer-with-barbecue gathering place for its inner-city neighborhood. Over the decades, as often happens, regulars took to calling the place "Beaver's" after its owner, and after Beaver's death, his widow made the name official. By the coming of the new millennium, Beaver's was edging toward a memory. Perhaps its best chance at new life would have made it a music club for New Orleans musicians displaced by Hurricane Katrina, headed by trumpet great Kermit Ruffins. But that dream died along with its lead developer, a local real estate guy named Robert Brackman. It was Robert's son Adam who one day looked at the building with Monica and

decided on a plan in his father's memory. Keep the name, keep the beer, keep the barbecue...*add* the chefs.

The renovation took nearly a year, all done in an upgraded icehouse style, whatever Monica and Co. figured that would look like. Most strikingly, the yellow walls were covered with murals themed around the beaver—yes, that industrious little animal—branching out to one eye-catching evocation of a huge orange-and-green chain saw. Monica's partner Andrea Lazar refers to all items gathered around this theme as "beaverobilia," but the place and its list of wines, cocktails and more than 65 beers have a bit of class nonetheless.

Since the old Beaver's had a pit—a simple box with five shelves that Dax dismisses as a "smoke closet"—the chef set about not only learning how to use it but developing an entire technique for forcing it to produce its best. Wood, for instance, became the subject of an extended science experiment, with all kinds of woods sampled at different times and temperatures, each result carefully rated and recorded. The result: Beaver's smokes its meats over a combination of oak and maple.

Meats tend to get covered with a dry rub and left alone for half a day or more, then smoked at 200 degrees according to their dimensions—Beaver's "Harris Ranch" briskets upwards of 17 hours, and some special-cut thick and fatty pork ribs an outlandish 12 hours before being finished in the fryer. "It's only a special, maybe one Wednesday a month," Dax stresses of these particular ribs. "It'll be almost by invitation, with everybody getting only one or two."

Beyond the smoked meats, Monica and Dax have come up with truly extraordinary appetizers (cream cheese-and-smoked-pork stuffed pepperoncini— "Bread it. Fry it. End scene," instructs the menu), side dishes (Philly mac and cheese topped with sweet-stewed tomatoes) and desserts (homemade banana pudding with "Lilla" wafers, named after Monica and Andrea's young daughter).

In a sure departure from Beaver's ice-house days, there's a nifty kids' menu available, plus at least one lonesome-looking high chair in the dining room.

"We look at everything more like chefs do," says Dax, who likes to assure his uppity peers that barbecue is the original Slow Food. "We're not saying the guy using only salt and pepper sucks. We're only adding what we as chefs want to taste. We're asking what we can do from our arsenal."

PIZZITOLA'S BAR-B-CUE HOUSTON

ADDRESS: 1703 SHEPHERD DRIVE, HOUSTON
PHONE: (713) BAR-B-CUE (227-2283)
ESTABLISHED: 1934
OWNER: JERRY PIZZITOLA
BEST BITES: PORK RIBS, BEEF BRISKET (ASK FOR THE CRUSTY OUTSIDE PIECES), DEBONED BARBECUED CHICKEN, POTATO SALAD, COCONUT CAKE
PAYMENT: CREDIT CARDS

Before there was a Pizzitola's Bar-B-Cue, there was a Shepherd Bar-B-Q Stand, the creation of John Davis and his wife, Lela. The original location is no more, a function of sitting squarely in the path of Interstate 10. But for nearly three decades before that superhighway carved its concrete signature across Houston, Shepherd Bar-B-Q was one of five or six places that carried the "black barbecue"

style to a larger, wider and whiter audience. Many of the great business names of mid-20th-century Houston—the same names that now grace the city's concert halls, office buildings and libraries—came in to let John Davis cook barbecue for them.

"Sure," remembers Jerry Pizzitola, "when I went traveling with my dad to other parts of Texas—the central part especially—we ate in places like Hinze's and Mikeska's, all part of that Czech and German tradition. My dad loved barbecue, *anybody's* barbecue. But back here in Houston, barbecue pretty much *was* African-American barbecue. It's all we had, really, the East Texas style—and it's the style I really came to love."

As Jerry tells it, Shepherd Bar-B-Q was not only a great place to eat but a beloved social fixture. While from the 1930s on, its diners were segregated—Davis sent his white customers to the back door and kept his black customers out front—the joint attracted both races in nearly equal numbers. The dining experience was no-frills, with only brisket and a little sausage for meats. "Takeout" in those early years meant bringing your own cast-iron pot and letting John or Lela fill it up for you. As Christmas approached and families planned their get-togethers, the number of such pots covering every open space in the Davis kitchen was staggering.

"When I took over, John and Lela had no stove, just the two open brick pits," Jerry recalls, thinking of the "new location" the couple moved into ahead of the interstate in the '60s. "Just the two brick pits and one chopping block. Except for the meats, they cooked everything at their house about a block away and carried it over. There was no ice, just a little cooler along here that didn't cool anything much. And here was the cash register, right in the kitchen. No one cooked or cut or cashed out except John and Lela—never."

The workload on the Davises was considerable, opening nine hours a day, six days a week, 11 months a year. Yet even the month they closed became part of their legend: October, the entire month, so John could catch a train to wherever the World Series was being played. He was afraid to fly, but he wasn't afraid to give up a month's revenue to take in his favorite sport.

Things continued that way until 1981, when Jerry walked in to have lunch one day and found the place different, changed, depleted. Lela had died in 1979, but John had kept it going the best he could. With his death only weeks earlier, Shepherd Bar-B-Q was clearly more than the survivors could handle. Sadly, Jerry saw another Houston landmark threatened with extinction.

As luck would have it, Jerry was just leaving his family's wholesale sandwich business after a falling-out with his father, and going through a divorce as well. Something about Shepherd Bar-B-Q called out to him, an amateur pit guy who'd competed in a few cook-offs. It took him nearly two years to talk John and Lela's heirs into letting him lease the place— and to hire a series of key cooking staff (Christine Lewis, Carlton Gould and David Reynosa) who are with him to this day.

Despite John Davis' emphasis on beef brisket, Jerry slowly evolved the place to focus more on pork ribs and chicken. This seemed a natural function of cooking with open-pit direct heat, rather than the indirect heat associated with all those brisket-loving smokers.

For customers who insist on their brisket, Jerry recommends his favorite pieces—the crusty, caramelized slices and chunks from the outside. If there could be such a thing as "candy from the grill," this would be it.

As befits a place Jerry renamed Pizzitola's, many important recipes come from his extended Italian-American family, who started off in Houston running a fruit stand and a tiny neighborhood grocery. Side dish recipes come from Jerry's mother, as do those for the banana pudding, coconut cake and chocolate cake.

"This place," Jerry explains, "just had in it a lot of years and a lot of 'stand-for' stuff that usually gets skipped in this business when you multiply and try to do volume. We want to do volume here, don't get me wrong. But we want to keep that stand-for stuff that this place, that John and Lela, always had."

RUTHIE'S PIT BAR-B-Q NAVASOTA

ADDRESS: 905 W. WASHINGTON (HIGHWAY 105 WEST), NAVASOTA
PHONE: (936) 825-2700
ESTABLISHED: 1976
OWNERS: JAMES AND RUTHIE HENLEY
BEST BITES: BEEF BRISKET, PORK SHOULDER, ELGIN SAUSAGE, POTATO SALAD
PAYMENT: CASH AND CHECKS

Even Texas barbecue fanatics, a breed found in all 254 counties, would consider Louis Charles Henley pretty hardcore. Since the day the ramshackle joint bearing his mother's name opened for business 32 years ago, Louis hasn't just smoked all the meat himself with a blend of post oak, pecan and mesquite. He has chain-sawed and chopped all the wood to make the smoke.

Admittedly, Ruthie's volume is small compared to some of the big boys, and its attitude is essentially: Come and eat 'til it's gone, cuz we aren't fixing anymore. But the fact that for more than three decades Louis has responded to phone calls from local ranchers about this or that tree being available by jumping into his truck and going to get it, seems as tied to Ruthie's culinary philosophy as some French chef choosing the goose for his foie gras or some Italian chef digging around the tree roots for truffles.

And Louis' proudest achievement in all these years of cutting up wood seems to be getting injured only twice.

"That's right, that's all," he says, interrupting a late lunch of tender brisket and what might be the best pork shoulder anywhere to show off his scars. He points to his knee, which lost a fight with a chain saw some years ago, then swipes off his hunting cap to reveal a thin line along the top of his skull. "This one was just about three years ago. But that only makes two times. I'd say that's pretty good, wouldn't you?"

According to Louis, his parents, James and Ruthie—still listed on the menu as owners—were traveling around Texas nearly 40 years ago and stopped in some out-of-the-way county seat for a sandwich. Apparently, the sandwich was an epiphany. "My mama said, 'We got this house. We gotta open up a barbecue place.' "

"This house" had once been the country "playhouse" for prominent Houston attorney Roy Moore, but it had already been towed around the Navasota area a couple times. With the barbecue plan, the house was moved again, lasting in much the same form from 1976 until someone broke in, robbed the place and set it on fire in 2005. By this point, Louis *had* to rebuild, using parts of another old house that must not have looked very different. Louis had no choice: Ruthie's Pit Bar-B-Q was famous.

"We've been in _Texas Highways_ around at the clippings that they were buri I better start calling ing to get another copy. on us in Madrid, Spain. They thing in London, England."

Louis was pit boss at Ruthie's from Day 1, learning his craft for two years from his Uncle Clyde, who came in from Austin. With his uncle and others helping, Louis worked the old house into shape to serve as a restaurant and built a brick pit out back for smoking. And he embarked on forming a set of standards, a set of rules he can now recite with the unflinching authority of _Larousse Gastronomique_.

For wood, there's mostly post oak, with just a little bit of pecan and mesquite for flavor. For dry rub, there's something simple, little more than seasoned salt, black pepper and garlic powder. For meat, there's beef brisket that cooks 12 to 13 hours in the pit, plus the pork shoulder Louis calls by its grocery store name, Boston butt, smoked until it shreds and crumbles into tender piles of flavor. There's Elgin all-beef sausage, smoked a long time "until the grease all runs out, not like they do over there in Elgin." And there's "mutton," a different touch in Texas to be sure: ribs of older lambs, something older customers line up for and eat 'til it's all gone.

One thing there definitely *isn't* at Ruthie's Pit Bar-B-Q is marinade for the meat, especially not the kind a fellow working somewhere else might inject using one of those hypodermic needles. "No injections!" Louis exclaims, seeming to get worked up about this topic. "You know, any time you put somethin' in a sauce and let it sit, that's marinatin'. That may be cookin', but it ain't barbecuin'. In barbecuin', it's the smoke that tells the tale."

NEW ZION MISSIONARY BAPTIST CHURCH HUNTSVILLE

ADDRESS: 2601 MONTGOMERY ROAD, HUNTSVILLE
PHONE: (936) 295-3445
ESTABLISHED: 1979
OWNER: NEW ZION CHURCH, OPERATED BY HORACE
AND MAY ARCHIE
BEST BITES: PORK RIBS, BEEF BRISKET, HALF CHICKEN,
SMOKED SAUSAGE, POTATO SALAD, BUTTERMILK PIE
PAYMENT: CASH AND CREDIT CARDS

In Texas, it's hard to argue against barbecue being the Lord's favorite food. But at New Zion in Huntsville, it's even harder to argue that cooking the stuff isn't the Lord's work as well.

Since 1979, when Annie Mae Ward dragged a pit onto the property and started cooking lunch for workers building the church, the place has become an offbeat landmark in a town equally famous for its larger-than-life statue of Sam Houston (aka "Big Sam"), its university named after the same hero and the nation's most notorious Death Row. Somehow, when your platter of barbecue lands in front of you on a table plastered with furniture and lawyer ads, it's easy to forget any and every other reason your life might bring you to Huntsville.

"Mrs. Ward had a stroke about four years ago and couldn't do this anymore, with the long hours and all," church deacon and current pit master Horace Archie explains. "I'd helped them out for a summer or two, so they showed me the secrets and told me this place was mine to watch over."

As Horace's vocabulary implies, he sees the New Zion barbecue operation not exactly as a job and surely not as just another business, since profits directly support church activities. And when he isn't cooking meat on the barrel smoker outside or serving as deacon, or being lured back in small doses to his previous occupation as a painter and carpenter, Horace finds more than enough to do as New Zion's Sunday school superintendent. Still, he takes obvious delight that even here in the Deep South, a preacher like New Zion pastor Clinton Edison can replace traditional "fire and brimstone" with the gentle smoke wafting upward from oak, hickory, mesquite and pecan.

"Like Mrs. Ward always said, there is no secret in our barbecue," Horace recites, leading a visitor out to the pit he *does* use past the one he almost *never* uses. The bad one, he explains, has its wood right under the meat, making the cooking process, literally, one long ordeal of putting out fires. He much prefers the pit that's closer to the road, which features a firebox at one end so the meat gets only heat and smoke, with no flame.

"God is our secret. He do it all. I say a little prayer every morning and just come on in and get started. Sometimes it goes the way you want it to, and sometimes it don't. But God is always in charge."

Considering the number of entertainment, sports and political celebrities who make their way to New Zion each week during its four-day barbecue run, Horace is well aware he's performing on a bigger stage than he might ever have imagined. It was Annie Mae Ward who worked here well into her 80s and set a high standard, not only for food but for media visibility. The walls of New Zion's barbecue joint are peppered with articles from newspapers and magazines across the nation. And in the church's most amazing recognition, its barbecue and Mrs. Ward herself were featured on the CBS *Early Show*—recognition under the headline "Holy Smoke" among the 10 best places to eat *in America*.

"A lot of people saw that show and still remember it when they come see us," says Horace. "We get people from New York and California all the time, lining up at the counter just like everybody else. And all the sports teams know about us before they come to Sam Houston State. They come a day ahead of time, mostly, so they can eat all they want here and it don't interfere with their performance."

Though the barbecue served by New Zion is mainstream delicious, some of the techniques are definite departures from the mainstream. For one thing, Horace is one of the few pit masters in Texas who doesn't smoke his brisket overnight, preferring to come in each morning about 5:30 to get the wood going and cook his briskets in a single 6- to 8-hour stretch. Quite often, he serves it sliced or chopped the same day it starts out on the smoker. As a result, the fork-tender beef at New Zion is less smoky-tasting than most

other examples—a matter of personal preference—featuring instead the char-grilled flavor associated with steak.

Other items, like the half chickens and pork ribs, seem to carry more smoke than the brisket, while the spiced blend of pork and beef in the sausage would probably still taste good if it saw no smoke at all.

Side dishes are extremely spartan: a scoop of mustard-yellow potato salad and a pool of mild red beans, plus a deli pickle and a slice of onion. Desserts, however, seem heaven-sent to make up for any deprivation. All baked here, best-selling sweets include pies of sweet potato, buttermilk and pecan.

Just those few items, ordered at the counter and served to you at one of New Zion's 52 seats, are enough Wednesday to Saturday to attract a line that often stretches out the door, past the smoking pit and around into the parking lot behind the sanctuary.

"It all helps out the church," Horace emphasizes. "I love to see all the people eating and telling me how great it is and coming back again and again." He smiles broadly, tongue softly touching cheek. "It might even help me get to heaven."

LEON'S WORLD'S FINEST IN & OUT BBQ HOUSE GALVESTON

ADDRESS: 5427 BROADWAY STREET, GALVESTON

PHONE: (409) 744-0070

ESTABLISHED: 1987

OWNER: LEON O'NEAL

BEST BITES: PORK RIBS, BEEF BRISKET, LEON'S RICE STEPPED UP, POTATO SALAD, FRESH PIES

PAYMENT: CASH AND CREDIT CARDS

It isn't every day you meet somebody who got into barbecue by way of bail bonds. But that's what Leon O'Neal was doing when the barbecue bug bit him—in the least pleasant of places and the least pleasant of ways.

"You see now, when you bail a guy out of jail, he's happy to pay you back at first," Leon remembers from those days, more than two decades ago. "But after being out awhile, he kinda starts forgetting. So this partner and I were rocking along for a year and a half, and then it was like there was no money coming in. Everybody just stopped paying. So we put our heads together and wondered if bail bonds was a good business to be in for the long haul. We decided to make something to offset these losses."

If "long haul" was the new business plan, the thing they "made" represented anything but something new for Leon.

"I've always cooked," he says simply, and he doesn't mean it like some guys say "I've always watched football" or "I've always collected stamps." Besides starting in the kitchen as a kid and polishing his skills at Prairie View A&M, Leon spent 25 hard years as a cook in the military. Tours of culinary duty took in all the usual places stateside, plus Vietnam and Germany. Along the way, he developed a special talent for making generals happy with food, even General Westmoreland while he was commanding the U.S. forces in Southeast Asia.

"Everywhere I went," says Leon, "I cooked. And now we'll do the same right here. We'll cook anything for anybody, anywhere."

Sitting in one of his booths beneath a wall covered with newspaper clippings, Leon swipes a few strands of thick white hair back under his black Stetson. "We've catered a wedding in Washington, D.C., and two funerals in Los Angeles. We've shipped to Harvard University. I cooked the very first dinner party in Washington for Sandra Day O'Connor after she joined the Supreme Court. They could get anybody to cook them anything, but who they wanted was me."

Leon's barbecue joint blossomed on the ground floor of what had been the bail-bonds enterprise. The space had been used for storage and, to be honest, it still seems to be. Though the booths and tables are uncluttered and clean, most other horizontal spaces are covered with paperwork of undetermined origin. The high countertop you order food over is thick with correspondence, phone directories, advertising flyers and signs for local fund-raisers, while a side table lies buried beneath fresh-baked pies. Leon's sells these whole for takeout, or you can order a slice for dessert. Though workers race in and race out for a quick bite, more than a handful make room for a slice of pie.

As a prelude to pie, customers at Leon's—whether they're longtime locals, celebrities or tourists stepping off a cruise ship—go for the pork ribs and beef brisket. Side dishes are straightforward, except maybe Leon's version of dirty rice, without the slightest hint of liver or any other organ meat. "I call it Leon's Rice Stepped Up," he explains. "I took the dirty out and stepped it up with fresh jalapeño peppers. They eat it and be sweatin', but they keep on eatin'."

Thinking back over the past 20-plus years, Leon sees making good barbecue as pretty simple, really. As though ticking off a grocery list, he'll tell anyone what it takes: "You need a good pit," he says, describing his 25-footer made of steel with triple doors for meat and double fireboxes. "You need good wood (pure oak, because it 'cooks clean'), good meat and good seasoning (he blends his own, naturally).

"Oh," he remembers, "and you need a good sauce. Some folks like sauce and some don't, but you gotta have a good sauce. That's the key to having folks say 'I'll be back.' "

QUEEN'S BAR-B-Q
GALVESTON

....

ADDRESS: 3428 AVENUE S, GALVESTON
PHONE: (409) 762-3151
ESTABLISHED: 1976
OWNER: SANDY KERZEE
BEST BITES: SMOKED TURKEY CLIFFHANGER, BRISKET CHILI (IN SEASON), POTATO SALAD, GREEN BEANS WITH SMOKED HAM, PIÑA COLADA CAKE, FRUIT COBBLERS, HOUSE-CHURNED VANILLA ICE CREAM
PAYMENT: CREDIT CARDS

Sandy Kerzee doesn't like to think of her life in barbecue as a deathbed promise to her daddy. But today, as she watches her kids help run the business in an old grocery store near the seawall and teaches simple tasks to her grandchildren and great-grandson, that's pretty much how it's worked out.

"I grew up in Galveston but always wanted to live in the country," she says. "That's where I was happiest, not here with all the lights and the noise and the traffic. But two months before my daddy was going to retire from running this place, he had a massive heart attack. I kept it going, even though I didn't know a thing about all that cooking stuff. I'd ask him questions in his hospital bed, but mostly I'd just say, 'Daddy, now you don't worry about a thing.' I learned the hard way, that's for sure. But I kept this business going for him."

This business had been constantly changing throughout the family's history here, going back to the day Clifford Earl

Putnal bought it as a grocery store that older Galvestonians remembered making deliveries by horse and buggy. Clifford always saw the place as a grocery store, but as in so many other tales across Texas, he started smoking meats and selling them as a sideline. The barbecue sideline kept growing more popular as Queen's reputation spread—that had been the grocery's name, and when Clifford talked about changing it one time, the locals begged him not to. Somewhere around 1976, Queen's started billing itself more as a restaurant, even though it still sold some grocery items, too.

After her father's death, Sandy and her siblings worked out a deal to sell the place. Two guys said they wanted it, which was more than any of the siblings could say. But when that deal fell through at the last minute, Sandy felt pressure from the rest of her family to keep her father's legacy alive. And by then, try as she might to deny it, she'd gotten pretty skillful around the 15-foot pit full of brisket, ribs, chicken and turkey. She wanted to live in the country so bad she could taste it...but she decided that, all things considered, she'd better taste her father's style of barbecue instead.

Sandy's single indulgence involved the décor, or what had been the lack of same. Remembering the houses she loved in the Texas countryside, she brought in 100-year-old, rough-hewn wooden wagon wheels and barn doors from rural areas and attached them to every bit of table, wall or ceiling that could support extra weight. And all the while, she steered Queen's toward its new life as what she lovingly describes as a "hole in the wall."

She recalls, "Even when my daddy was here, people kept saying, 'You need to sell that barbecue and get rid of these groceries.' So each time he sold out a shelf of groceries, he'd put in a new table. Since he's been gone, it's been a lot of hard work, but it's been a blessing. With all this new stuff, I thought: If I can't be out in the country, I'll just bring the country right here."

Throughout the early years, there was a separate building behind Queen's that housed a run-down neighborhood bar. "My daddy," says Sandy, "was a Christian man and he didn't like that bar being there one bit." After Clifford's death, when the bar's lease ran out, Sandy took over the building and expanded Queen's to get more dining space. Her father's dream had come true, in more ways than one.

A lot of things are done the old-fashioned way here, by decision and of necessity at the same time. Meats are cooked just as Clifford cooked them, including the smoked turkey embellished with cheese and ranch dressing by Sandy's son to become the place's most popular sandwich, best served on a toasted jalapeño cheese bun. It's called the Cliffhanger, after her father, of course.

Other exquisitely homespun touches include the brisket chili in cool weather— "People start calling every day to see if we're making it yet"—the piña colada cake, the peach or blackberry cobblers, and the vanilla ice cream churned right in the Queen's kitchen.

Along the way, Sandy let burgers sneak onto the menu, cooking them in the smoker like any other Texas meat. But the best she'll do for french fries are bags of potato chips, just like her daddy used to sell at Queen's Grocery. "I don't fry anything," she says proudly. "I'm not a short-order cook here. And I never want to be."

JOE'S BARBEQUE COMPANY, ALVIN

ADDRESS: 1400 E. HIGHWAY 6, ALVIN
PHONE: (281) 331-9626
ESTABLISHED: 1975
OWNER: JOE SALADINO
BEST BITES: BEEF BRISKET, PORK RIBS, SLICED SMOKED TURKEY BREAST, POTATO SALAD, FAJITA BUFFET (THURSDAYS), FRUIT COBBLERS
PAYMENT: CREDIT CARDS

Texas is filled with tiny shacks serving barbecue, little old joints dishing up brisket, ribs and sausage beneath a hand-lettered sign you can barely read, with only a curl of smoke above the roof for advertising. And then there's Joe's Barbeque Company.

Joe Saladino proudly tells you his place is a "mom-and-pop," not anybody's idea of a chain restaurant. And he gleefully relates the mythology of Joe's beginnings three decades ago, with a cluster of only four tables. But if a seat in this huge, often bustling dining room doesn't convince you you're not in mom-and-pop "Kansas" anymore, a stroll out back certainly will.

There, in addition to huge, rustic black pits that seem to hail from the Republic of Texas, is a long row of bright stainless steel smokers, each turning out enough smoked meat to feed the gathering multitudes. On the day of our visit, not only are 2,000-plus expected to come in for lunch or dinner—many drawn by the all-you-can-eat buffet, built today around fajitas—but the place is catering barbecue for the President of the United States and 1,500 friends at a nearby nuclear power plant. What's important for all to know about Joe's, south of Houston in what Texas baseball fans think of as "Nolan Ryan Country," is that this *isn't* an unusual day at all.

"I guess we kinda stretch the picture of mom-and-pop a little, don't you think?" Joe smiles, leading a visitor on an impromptu tour. He makes an introduction to his son, who has the benefit of culinary school in ways his father, grandfather and great-grandfather never imagined. By definition, young Joey holds the future of Joe's in his chef-trained hands.

"He's the fourth generation of our family doing barbecue," relates Joe, once Joey has raced back to cooking for the President. "He has to learn the things that change, the things you have to keep up with. Mom-and-pops really are a dying breed—and when they're gone, they're gone. To lose that, I think, would be sad. If he continues to stay in a mom-and-pop, he'll have to stay ahead of everybody else. He'll have to do a better job than they do."

The story of Joe's Barbeque Company is extraordinary, especially outside the realm of corporate ownership, multiunit operations and all-American franchising. Joe Saladino's Italian ancestors came to America with the immigrant crush in the late 1800s and ended up working small farms near Bryan, Texas. Though it seems a bit late in the timeline, family legend has them traveling by "covered wagon" south to the Alvin area.

Before long, Joe's grandfather and then his father were operating a barbecue place in Houston, setting the stage for the next generation in then-tiny Alvin. Nearby in Clear Lake was NASA's mission control, with its hungry workers and big-budget government entertainings, and it wasn't all that far to M.D. Anderson and the rest of Houston's famed Medical Center.

"We do the big boys," Joe says today,

and as you struggle to understand how a mere four tables could become 325, you begin to see the outline.

As business volume grew through the roof over the decades, adjustments had to be made. All the meats are still smoked at Joe's—using post oak for brisket and other slow-cook items, mesquite for quicker fajitas and cut-on-premise steaks. Other things had to be ordered in. Joe's sausage, for instance, is custom-made near Sealy, while the potato salad may be Joe's mother's recipe but requires a supplier to turn out the 5,000 pounds devoured each week.

Other customer preferences include the chicken-fried steak, the thick slices of jalapeño bread and the four fruit cobblers with self-scooped Blue Bell ice cream.

"Oh sure," Joe says, shaking a hand here and there among regulars arriving for a business lunch upstairs, watching the day's buffet crush begin to pour in through the door. "I get fed up sometimes and want to retire. But what am I going to do? To keep from driving my wife crazy, I'll probably just go out in the backyard and barbecue something."

DICKINSON BBQ CO. DICKINSON

ADDRESS: 2111 FM 517, DICKINSON
PHONE: (281) 534-2500
ESTABLISHED: 2005
OWNERS: TOM AND LINDA KEYWORTH
BEST BITES: BEEF BRISKET, SAUSAGE, STUFFED BAKED POTATO, CANDIED YAMS, BREAD PUDDING
PAYMENT: CREDIT CARDS

Tom Keyworth and go-to guy Tim Brewer had been in the lumber and hardware business for years. In fact, even though barbecue had played a regular part in Tim's life going back to his youth in West Texas, things like two-by-fours, nails, washers and faucets had been a far *more* regular part since coming to this water-

stripped coastal area between Houston and Galveston. Barbecue was what *other* people did, or maybe what you did to relax on weekends—until dramatic changes occurred in what Tim now calls "the original plan."

"The original plan was to open a third hardware store," he says. "But then, Tom and I both decided we were burned out on lumber and hardware, and it turns out Tom had been wanting a barbecue joint for a long time. I'd cooked for him and his wife a few times, and one night at dinner he just asked me if I could do this with him." Tim smiles at the memory. "I asked if I could have some time to think about it. And Tom said sure, I could have as much time as it took me to finish my beer. I looked down, and it was half gone already."

As anybody walking beneath the American flag painted on corrugated iron into Dickinson BBQ Co. can surmise, Tim and Tom made a deal over beer that night. And as it turned out, the décor of the restaurant they would build benefited mightily from their previous careers.

As a hands-on guy around lumber and hardware, Tim was able to push and pull the general contractor as inspiration

demanded—not to mention doing tons of the work himself. Whether he's pointing to the "hairless" barbed-wire fence that runs along the drive-thru lane or brushing his hand across a shiny wooden tabletop, Tim makes typical "pride of ownership" seem lame by comparison. For him, Dickinson BBQ Co. brings "pride of buildership" as well.

As barbecue joints go, Tim considers this one a "cut above everyone else." There are plenty of extras in any direction you glance—shadow boxes on the walls holding pictures, maps or other graphics (handmade by Tom's mother), corrugated iron and aromatic cedar, and doors copied from those found in horse stalls. "No," Tim laughs, "these haven't really been in anybody's old stable."

Tim is especially proud to show a visitor the mural that covers much of the drive-thru side, looking for all the world like the creation of some Cowboy Monet. With Impressionistic explosions of color and light, the mural on corrugated iron dissolves through scenes from different regions of the state—from the gator-filled swamps of Southeast Texas through the bluebonnets of the Hill Country to the vast, brown cattle lands of West Texas.

For Tim, getting the joint built was only the beginning. He had given Tom the idea, after all, by cooking for him. And while Tim's wife is often working at Dickinson BBQ, from the office to the cafeteria line, he's in charge of anything that comes from the kitchen. The usual suspects (beef brisket, pork ribs, sausage, chicken and turkey) come from lounging beneath his homemade dry rub, then spending quality time (up to 20 hours for the brisket) in the pit out back. Tim prefers a mixture of pecan and hickory wood, insisting there be no oak or mesquite anywhere in sight.

When it comes to side dishes, he pushes past typical items to offer green beans, macaroni and cheese, black-eyed peas, corn, carrots and candied yams, plus 1-pound baked potatoes stuffed with another 6 to 8 ounces of meat.

For dessert, there's traditional banana pudding and a decent selection of pies, but Tim has created a craving for one sweet that's a bit different—old-fashioned bread pudding.

"I unleashed the beast, I guess," he says. "I can't keep the bread pudding in here. I suppose, if you wanted dessert, you could go to the Dairy Queen next door. But I'd rather have something good for you here than make you have to walk someplace else."

BILLY'S OLD FASHION BBQ, JASPER

ADDRESS: 1601 N. MAIN STREET, JASPER
PHONE: (409) 384-8384
ESTABLISHED: 1988
OWNER: BILLY MAHATHAY
BEST BITES: BEEF BRISKET, PORK RIBS WITH BILLY'S DRY RUB, BARBECUE SAUCE, POTATO SALAD, PEACH COBBLER, SOUL FOOD (WEDNESDAY NIGHTS)
PAYMENT: CASH AND CHECKS

Billy Mahathay was a long-distance trucker—"I hauled everything there *was* to haul," he says proudly—before he was shown his life's true calling by the Ghost of Barbecue Past.

"My uncle had a barbecue place right next to here, back in the 1930s, I think," says Billy, settling his lanky but almost regal frame into one of his dining room's three booths. "That old building was still there, all the time I was coming up. When I decided to do something on my own, I opened that old place to do barbecue again, and I ran it for six or seven years.

"My uncle's old pits were still sitting back there, just the open fire with all your meat on top. But then the place burned down. Some neighbors got together—black and white—got me some money and put me back in business."

Billy's Old Fashion BBQ is something of a landmark in a town whose only other landmark is nearby—Lake Sam Rayburn.

Most people who pass through here without living here for generations are heading to a vacation house on the lake. But these days, thanks to word-of-mouth from the locals, an increasing number of visitors find their way in for some barbecue. Though the place is little more than a quickly erected shack, it does boast a wheelchair ramp—surely a function of the Americans with Disabilities Act. Con-sidering the number of older locals who stop in primarily to pass the time with Billy, that ramp may come in handy over the years.

As he promises in the place's name, Billy keeps everything as "old fashion" as he can. He smokes his meats—the briskets up to 24 hours—over hickory with something extra thrown in for flavor. He is partial to sassafras, when he can get it.

The moment he knows they're ready, he sweeps the meats away from the fire and rushes them into the refrigerator for a "rest" before slicing them. This way, he insists, they're not so quick to crumble. Billy is a man who likes his meat to be meat, not mush. He slices and keeps the brisket ready to serve, but not in any sauce. "Some of my customers don't want sauce," he reports. "They just like the taste of smoked meat."

In addition to their work at Billy's, he and his wife cook regularly for church

functions around Jasper. "The white churches and the black ones," he stresses, "we cook for them all. Even the Mexican churches."

In addition to such feeding of the multitudes, Billy does something every Wednesday that clearly gets his culinary juices flowing. Wednesday night is Soul Food Night, letting him work his way through classics like smothered chicken, rice and gravy, turnip greens and black-eyed peas, almost always with peach cobbler for dessert. These are foods, you understand as Billy shares more of his story, that he came by honestly.

"When I was a boy coming up," he remembers, "my mother took sick, and I had a grandmother who lived with us who couldn't see, and I had a brother and sister, too. I had to come out of school to work. I threw papers, and I worked at the drugstore. But most of all, I had to do the cooking. They depended on me, so they would tell me what to do and how to do it. I kept it all in my mind, and I've been cooking ever since."

Like a lot of small-time barbecue guys, indeed like mom-and-pop owners whatever food they serve, Billy is unsure how his place will make it into the next generation. He shows off the pictures of his son around the dining room, along with news clippings of the lad's scholastic success, but after his hard life, he wants something less hard for his son. As the man who's still there to put on the brisket every day and there to take it off, Billy knows there's no way to make this food that's *not* a hard life. You need to be present, every moment—and there's only one guy Billy feels comfortable committing to such a tireless ordeal. That would be Billy.

"I won't ever retire," he says, leaning back to take in photos of his son atop the soft-drink cooler, as well as of his parents and grandparents peppering the patchy wallpapered walls. "I'll always cook. I got some customers who can't, so they really depend on me. I may shut it down a couple days a week, but I won't ever retire."

WEST TEXAS STYLE BAR-B-QUE, SILSBEE

ADDRESS: 3078 HIGHWAY 96 NORTH, SILSBEE
PHONE: (409) 385-0957
ESTABLISHED: 1985
OWNERS: RICHARD AND NITA NOLEN
BEST BITES: BEEF BRISKET, PORK RIBS, CAJUN RICE, POTATO SALAD, HOMEMADE YEAST ROLLS, FRESH-BAKED PIES
PAYMENT: CREDIT CARDS

In the modern world's restaurant culture, much is made of The Promise. The Promise is something you're supposed to keep, obviously, a kind of expression in your marketing and, hopefully, in your personal greeting that tells a customer what good things to expect. At "Chockie" and Nita Nolen's barbecue joint, they understood about The Promise before The Promise was cool.

"Good Food...Mean Women" promises a sign right beside the front door.

These days, that promise is being kept better than ever. West Texas Style Bar-B-Que is one of the few such places in which the entire experience is delivered by women. Chockie sits with a buddy at a table, the two discussing the weather and such beneath their cowboy hats while the friend devours a chopped beef sandwich. On this day, they invest a good deal of energy discussing a new photo of

Chockie—the man holding up an ugly garfish he'd caught nearby that weighed close to 100 pounds.

Behind the counter, Chockie's wife, Nita, their two daughters and several other women of no particular relation double-time through orders to knock down the line at the register. "And," says one of the women as she flashes by, perhaps with a wink, "we're even meaner when we have a headache."

Richard Nolen, known to all as "Chockie," started this place with his wife more than two decades ago. He called it "West Texas" not because he forgot this was East Texas but because he wanted to smoke with mesquite, a technique few cooks in the area would support. Still, that doesn't hold back the line that forms here every lunch and dinner—and it doesn't keep Chockie or, increasingly now, his daughter Alma and her husband, from driving all the way to West Texas to fill a trailer with the deep red wood.

Asked to explain the place's success, Chockie spins a few yarns about his years in the Army or with Halliburton (it's hard to tell them apart in his stories), but then asks a visitor to wait for Alma. When Alma finally does break free of the rush and grabs an iced tea from the table off to the side, her mother joins in.

"The important thing," says Alma Byars, "is still having fun doing it. We don't hire nobody to cook. We do that— me and her (a nod to Nita) and my sister." Alma's smile turns conspiratorial. She looks quickly at her mom, then at the visitor. "Let me tell you what she got for her sixth birthday: a hoe to hoe out in the garden."

"We had 52 acres," Nita adds. "That was our only food."

"My mother's worked hard all her life," says Alma.

Apparently all things are relative, since Nita would strike most folks as working hard right now. She passes through the dining room constantly, asking customers if their food is all right or offering to refill their coffee. Behind the

counter, she's a whirlwind as well, helping this young woman figure out something on the register before showing that one how she wants the ribs cut.

For a trip through the kitchen and out to the smoker, Alma takes over, making sure to point out each thing that's being made from scratch along the way. There, as though to verify their story, sits the trailer that she and her husband just drove in from West Texas, some of the mesquite still waiting to be stacked. And there, on crusty racks inside the long black smoker, brisket after brisket breathes in the heat and smoke of a Texas far from Silsbee.

Every morning in the kitchen—actually a row of white stoves in the smoking shed, to keep the heat out of the dining room—"Chockie's Girls" indulge in their single greatest culinary extravagance. In a restaurant climate that increasingly buys all desserts from vendors, West Texas Style Bar-B-Que bakes its own pies. The result is close to irresistible, sitting atop the counter for all the world to think it's 1947. There's perfect pecan, coconut cream, lemon and chocolate under golden-browned peaks of meringue, pumpkin during any cool weather and leading up to the holidays.

"Let me tell you how we started with our pies." Alma smiles outside between the stacked mesquite and the smoker, Nita out of earshot. "When my mother was pregnant, she'd bake two pies at home every day. She'd eat one, and the other one was for us. One day we put some of ours that was left up over there for the customers, and it just created a monster. We've had to bake pies here every morning ever since."

CAROLINE'S QUALITY B-B-Q, KOUNTZE

ADDRESS: 320 3RD STREET, KOUNTZE
PHONE: (409) 246-8050
ESTABLISHED: 2000
OWNER: CAROLINE WILSON
BEST BITES: CHOPPED BEEF SANDWICH, BAKED POTATO WITH BEEF, POTATO SALAD, CAJUN RICE, MINI SWEET POTATO PIES
PAYMENT: CASH

The plain brown building—like the "plain brown wrapper" it resembles—has no sign out front. It did at one time, but not anymore. Once you step in through the unmarked wooden door, you can read the laminated menus on the three tables referencing "Caroline Wilson/Owner" and "Arthur L. Yarbough/Helper." These words say more than any sign ever could about two people who finish each other's sentences.

Caroline's Quality B-B-Q has no right to be as famous as it is. Open only three days a week, with no sign and no advertising, and a nondescript location on a nondescript street a block off a nondescript drag through a nondescript East Texas town. But there the place is. And

nothing makes the delicious contradiction clearer than a request to shoot a few quick photos.

"Oh, we had a guy in here shootin' just last week," says Arthur. "Who was he with?"

"I don't remember," says Caroline, "but he sure had a lot of equipment."

"Yeah, he had all these different cameras and lights and this thing that measured how bright it was. He was climbing around here for hours..."

"With his son..."

"*Texas Monthly* maybe. Or somebody."

"I got his card somewhere."

Caroline and Arthur are not a vaudeville act. They're two people who do intense and exhausting work hour after hour in an extremely tight space. And they stay busy, mostly because everybody in the neighborhood knows who, what and where they are.

An inquiry from a visitor driving up and down each street gets him pointed back to a building he'd already passed, notable now for an orange cone that seems to relate to parking in the yard. On closer inspection, there actually is a sign off to the side, one of those meant for letters like "BBQ" or "Half-Price" or "Come On In." The sign is blank, and has been for some time.

"Somebody tore my sign up," Caroline explains, seeming surprised that anyone would ask. "They took a stick to it and knocked all the lightbulbs out. We don't really need a sign, though. We work too hard in here to need a sign." Arthur completes the intriguing thought: "There's a lot of famous people out there with great big flashy signs. And their food is *nothing*."

Somewhere in that bizarre notion is the truth about Caroline's. Within these walls, whether at the counter picking up takeout or waiting for your meal at a table, you become convinced that only a place this uninterested in success could possibly turn out food this good. No part of this notion may be true, of course—and different parts may be true at different places. But under the spell of Caroline and Arthur, you come to believe you'll only eat in plain brown buildings without any sign from this point on.

The menu is Texas with a side order of soul. As you'd expect, Arthur is the barbecue cook, smoking his pork ribs, beef brisket, homemade links and chicken over oak in a pit out back with its own 16- by 16-foot building. He lets on that he'd like to mix in mesquite sometimes for extra flavor but, "We're down here and mesquite ain't. Besides, it's really not the wood that do it." He smiles, playfully catching Caroline's eye. "It's the cook!"

The kitchen area is visible and as simple as simple can be. There's a counter only feet from where Caroline takes your order—and standing at it, Arthur cuts any and all your meat. Anything that needs to be kept warm, from the barbecue sauce to the baked beans, gets to sit in its own Crock-Pot. There's a stack of baked potatoes, hinting at what has become one of the place's biggest hits: a huge spud, broken open and mounded with chopped beef and sauce. At the tail end of one day's lunch, these potatoes are virtually all that walks out the door, in orders of four and six, bound for construction sites all over Kountze.

Popular side dishes include excellent potato salad and peppery Cajun rice made with smoked sausage, while desserts are limited to mini sweet potato or pecan pies baked for the restaurant by a local lady.

"Everything here is good," summarizes Caroline, "and everybody knows it."

"You got copycats," adds Arthur, "people who come in here and—how you say— dissect everything we do. But they still can't do it. It's like the great basketball players. However long you study 'em, you can't do what they do."

CHUCK'S BAR-BQ AND BURGERS, EVADALE

ADDRESS: CORNER OF HIGHWAY 96 AND HIGHWAY 105, EVADALE
PHONE: (409) 276-1100
ESTABLISHED: 2006
OWNER: CHUCK HOWARD
BEST BITES: CHOPPED BEEF SANDWICH, POTATO SALAD, STUFFED BAKED POTATO, REDNECK NACHOS, TATER TWISTERS
PAYMENT: CREDIT CARDS

You arrive at Chuck's Bar-BQ and Burgers just as a lunch crush piles in from a highway construction job, so there's no time for the man to sit down and chat about the meaning of life. Instead, he promises he'll tell you what he can between orders and invites you into his kitchen. He positions you over by the door heading out to his smoker with the time-honored restaurant kitchen warning: "Everything in here is hot, sharp or slick."

Chuck Howard backed into the barbecue business, automotively speaking. In fact, what he sold before barbecue was cars, whether unloading them on his own or managing and motivating the salesmen who did. But the pressure got to be too much, he says, and (nodding to the hungry workers mobbing his window) not the *good* kind. It was time for a change, Chuck says—in how he made a living, and in how he lived.

"When I quit drinkin', I started cookin'," he puts it simply, before shouting to the women filling Styrofoam boxes to tell him what they're waiting on. "I'd barbecued for years, for friends and family. You know, anytime somebody needed food for some event. They always said it was real good, but I wondered if they were just being nice. So I was curious more than anything else. That's why I started out in an old toolshed I just drug over here."

Chuck smiles, then washes his hands—as he does again and again, barbecue's answer to Lady Macbeth. "I was in that toolshed for 10 years."

The only part of the operation that's still outside by that shed is the black smoker. Using pecan or hickory, depending on what he's cooking, Chuck does all his meats over a traditional slow fire, then carts it into his brand-new, sparkling kitchen. The feeling here is barbecue-meets-short-order, both of those being jobs Chuck handles in a flourish of chopping, slicing, frying and portioning. The boxes come to him loaded with sides—with his mother-in-law's potato salad, for instance, or in the case of burgers, with waiting toasted buns. It's up to Chuck to fill all the open spaces with goodies from his smoker or from his short-order flat-top grill.

Chuck winks, as though he's about to share the secret of a long and happy life. "Look at that," he says, lifting a burger off the sizzling surface. "Look at those marks. From the grill! I do all the burgers outside first, smokin' 'em right along with all the other meats. Then when somebody orders 'em, I sear 'em right on this old flat top. In between, I keep 'em in

what I call my swamp water. Look at this." He lifts some of the liquid with his spatula, letting it run back in little rivers into the bright silver tray. "Believe me, that ain't no Worcestershire sauce!"

Most of Chuck's menu is time-honored Texas: beef brisket sliced or chopped, plus some nifty smoked pork. As good as the sandwiches are on those toasted buns, it's worth ordering a plate just to get your choice of two sides. The potato salad is as good as promised ("I was married to her daughter for 12 years before she'd give me the recipe!"), as is a colorful array of other specialties ranging from "redneck nachos" to "pork on a stick."

When Chuck and his family replaced the toolshed recently with a former real estate office, they opted out of french fries for something they've dubbed Tater Twisters. Instead of the freezer required to keep commercial fries, Twisters need only a special device to spiral-cut potatoes, skin and all, into something resembling an ongoing potato chip. These cook up crisp by the basketful in the only fryer in Chuck's kitchen.

During the briefest of lulls, his dining area for once noisier than his ordering window, Chuck remembers the choice he and his wife made all those years ago—and the day they tried to launch their new lives in that smoky old toolshed.

"We opened in the pouring-down rain without telling anybody," he says. "I told my wife, 'This way we won't get too busy.' I'll never forget. We opened at 11, and by 2:30, I finally had about two minutes to go put my OPEN sign up."

Confirming with the ladies that there's nobody waiting on anything, Chuck shrugs contentedly and goes over to the sink to wash his hands again. "We work our hiney bones off here. But it's worth it. It's all about pride. We try to make a living, but there ain't no big money in this stuff. We mostly just like doin' it."

BELLI DELI BAR-B-Q KIRBYVILLE

ADDRESS: HIGHWAY 96, $2^1/2$ MILES SOUTH OF
KIRBYVILLE
PHONE: (409) 330-5537
ESTABLISHED: 2002
OWNERS: JON AND PAT SORENSEN
BEST BITES: BEEF BRISKET, PORK RIBS, POTATO
SALAD, CHILI, GUMBO
PAYMENT: CASH AND CHECKS

"Yesterday I only sold one chopped beef sandwich," says Jon Sorensen, nearly four decades after escaping South Dakota for Texas by way of Vietnam, Africa and Malaysia. "But some days I sell 20."

Jon glances around the tiny kitchen of the trailer he uses as a roadside stand, making his seated listener feel less like a brief drop-in than a lifelong neighbor invited for coffee. "This isn't a four-star restaurant," Jon observes with a grin. "It's a minus-star restaurant. But it depends on what you want. Do you want good food, or do you want to go someplace just to brag about it?"

Jon's question is common among Texas barbecue joints, but seldom as much as at Belli Deli Bar-B-Q, a tumbledown outpost on the highway just south of Kirbyville whose various propped-up hand-lettered signs seem to take up more ground than the place itself. There's only one table, under the shade beside the front door, but it's not at all clear whether even that is intended for dining.

According to Jon, this 34-foot trailer represents an ongoing memory of a larger restaurant he and his wife, Pat, used to operate next door. But it's also the public face of an odd collection of home-based businesses they run behind the scenes, from making jams with the fruits they grow in their orchard to raising freshwater fish. "It would be nice to make some money one of these days," Jon sighs in a gravelly voice reminiscent of radio's Wolfman Jack. It's clear, though, that if

money were all he were interested in, he would have led a very different life.

After serving in Vietnam, Jon found himself in the oil industry—today he's certain he worked in "39 different factions"—until cancer reduced his abilities to do most jobs. Before long, after handling different tasks around the world, all he could do was cook on the rigs in the Gulf of Mexico, whether their nearest land qualified as Texas, Louisiana or Mexico. It was this experience, and the praise he received for his handiwork, that convinced Jon to take the mission onshore. He built his own 10-foot smoker, naming the contraption "Igor." It's what he's cooked on as long as he and Pat have been at this location, whether serving at tables in their restaurant or through the window of their barbecue stand.

Jon's operation seems passionate and nonchalant at the same time. He doesn't seem desperate to wave cars in from the highway, an act that might help, based on the way most simply speed by. Yet he also makes it plain there's nothing he won't cook and no one he won't cook it for.

"If you come in and don't mind waiting for a baked potato, I'll bake a potato for you," he assures. "And if you tell me you want some fresh vegetables, I'll go to the store and get maybe some cauliflower, and I'll cook that for you." Jon stops, then takes the notion deeper. "Nobody, especially nobody with kids, is going to go hungry around me. Even if you don't have a dime, if you're hungry, you're going to get a sandwich here."

The passionate belief in feeding people spills directly into Jon's fascination with what they're fed. In the smoker named Igor, Jon cooks beef brisket, pork ribs and sausage over a mix of oak and pecan, with wood from his fruit trees for accent. Pear and apple impart a pleasurable sweetness to any meat, he says, or maybe they just take the bitterness out. He admits he's not sure which.

In addition, on the small gas stovetop inside the trailer, Jon can whip up hamburgers, hand-battered catfish and french fries, along with a selection of soups, chili and gumbo the moment the weather turns cool.

"Everybody asks what I'm doing here," Jon concedes, stepping out onto his front step to light a cigarette. "But I live right here. We do everything right here. I tell people: I'm here because of love and lust and age. I'm politically motivated, and I'm poetically involved." The big Dane from South Dakota grins broadly in the bright morning sun. "Food has its own kind of poetry."

GATOR JUNCTION
WALLISVILLE

ADDRESS: 24620 S. INTERSTATE 10, WALLISVILLE
PHONE: (409) 389-2401
ESTABLISHED: 1999
OWNERS: LINTON AND VANESSA GIVENS
BEST BITES: BEEF BRISKET, PORK RIBS, POTATO SALAD, BOUDIN, JAMBALAYA
PAYMENT: CREDIT CARDS

Some Texas barbecue businesses credit newspaper, radio or television advertising for their success, while others go in for couponing and other forms of direct mail. Still others, with a more futuristic turn,

have created Web sites, blogs and e-mail blasts. Linton and Vanessa Givens aren't the least bit shy about telling you what's made their Gator Junction barbecue successful—the thousands of "food critics" pretending to be truckers covering Interstate 10 between Jacksonville and San Diego. Those guys and gals, say Linton and Vanessa, are the best advertising money can't buy.

Sometimes, though, the spreading of the Gator Junction gospel catches even Linton a little by surprise.

"There was this fella—no, I don't recall his name," says Linton, taking a short break from weed-whacking his property along the I-10 feeder road, "from right over there in Hankamer. He was an oil field kinda guy, and he went off to work in Scotland for a while. And he and this Scottish guy, you know, end up going out for a few drinks. After a while, this Scottish guy starts talking about barbecue, saying as how the best barbecue he's ever tasted was at this little place on the interstate between Houston and Beaumont. Well, this guy from Hankamer finally says, 'That's Gator Junction, and that's right by where I'm from!'"

It being such a small world doesn't diminish the dreams of Linton and

Vanessa, who bought Gator Junction going on nine years ago and set about an upgrade of its culinary offerings while expanding the physical plant. Previously, Linton had owned a cafeteria, learning the dos and don'ts of barbecue from an elderly African-American cook there.

Today, he is unapologetic to food snobs that his place also functions as a gas station and convenience store—after all, no one makes anybody pull off the interstate to eat. He just knows the daily from-scratch production of beef brisket and pork ribs, plus smoked turkey, chicken and sausage, plus some excellent sides like potato salad, coleslaw and baked beans, makes his a Texas barbecue joint that needs to take a backseat to nobody. And being just over an hour from Louisiana, he feels entirely justified making and serving the Cajun sausage called boudin, as well as the sausage-and-rice concoction known as jambalaya.

"We sell gas, and we sell beer and cigarettes," Linton says. "But barbecue is our big deal here."

A while back, business had increased to such a degree that more kitchen space was required...even with all the smoking of meats being done in an old-school black pit behind the building, with a huge covered stack of red oak logs behind that. Linton and Vanessa decided to expand the kitchen and add some tables while they were at it. This split the dining area into two sections flanking the cash register, each section trying to be more rustic and essentially more corny than the other. Whimsical alligators have several roles to play in the otherwise Tall Texas décor, while small gator figurines share space on each table with that signature bottle of Louisiana hot pepper sauce.

"The expansion hasn't really started paying for itself, you know, in terms of bringing in more business," says Linton. "But at least it's given the girls more room to cook in the back."

WILLY RAY'S BEAUMONT

ADDRESS: 145 INTERSTATE 10 NORTH, BEAUMONT
PHONE: (409) 832-7770
ESTABLISHED: 1994
OWNERS: MIKE AND MILLY DOUGAY
BEST BITES: ST. LOUIS RIBS, SMOKED SAUSAGE, POTATO SALAD, BAKED BEANS, PEACH COBBLER
PAYMENT: CREDIT CARDS

You might consider calling Willy Ray's the Barbecue House That Tamales Built.

Though a long way from Hispanic South Texas or even the heartbeat of Hispanic Texas in San Antonio, Mike and Milly Dougay parlayed an excellent recipe for tamales into a restaurant that grew from 12 seats to 120, taking on a "bar and grill" identity along the way. The Dougays sold The Tamale Co. after seven years of success, deciding to concentrate on making and selling their now-famous tamales wholesale. But like many who get out of the restaurant business, they obviously missed the aggravation. They turned the profits from selling lots of tamales into creating Willy Ray's.

Unlike some barbecue joints that come from humbler origins (and are, by any business definition, seriously "undercapitalized"), the Dougays by this point had the wherewithal to make the new place exactly what they wanted. They started with the menu. Aware that most restaurant success stories these days are built around offering something for everybody,

they decided to do that with the Texas barbecue tradition. In fact, there's nary a flavor or a food type found within that tradition that doesn't turn up somewhere on Willy Ray's extensive menu.

"The day before we opened," Milly remembers, obviously pleased to have some challenges behind her, "my husband just multiplied the sauce recipe he'd been using at home, and it wouldn't come out right. He made sauce and made sauce and took it around to all our neighbors to taste. He stayed up all that night working on that barbecue sauce, saying he would perfect it. And he did."

Mike actually had some "training" in the making of Texas barbecue. While he grew up in Lake Charles, Louisiana, that was close enough to the Texas state line for his father to know that true mythological barbecuing wasn't the same as anybody-can-do-it grilling. Milly says her father-in-law would slow-cook meats in the backyard for 8 hours, 11 hours, whatever they required to be tender and infused with delicious wood smoke. Mike carried that same philosophy, with an assist from chefs Fidel Maldonado and Sergio Esparza, into his born-again experience of the restaurant business.

Each batch of Willy Ray's beef brisket or pork roast, for instance, is cooked over red oak all night, 14 hours, before it's ready to pass muster. TV foodie David Rosengarten once described the pork roast here as "pornographic," and he definitely said it like it was a good thing. The ribs, cut St. Louis style for uniform cooking, are done in $1^1/_4$ hours, tender and tumbling off the bone.

Though the list of smoked meats at Willy Ray's is long and varied, the list of side dishes is even more intriguing. These include not only homemade versions of the standards (the sweet-mustardy potato salad comes from Milly's mother), but quirky rethinkings of turnip greens (which, in turn, get made into a cheesy turnip green casserole on Thursdays), dirty rice gone smoky with chopped brisket, a surprising carrot soufflé that even carrot-haters love, and exemplary baked beans...that last a friend's recipe with plenty of brown sugar, bell pepper and onion.

Having come into the barbecue business with the broader experience of owning a popular Mexican restaurant, Mike and Milly understand the importance of dessert to both pleasure and profit. They do offer their version of barbecue-joint banana pudding, but their changing list of desserts can also include cheesecake, Key lime pie, French silk chocolate pie, homemade bread pudding with rum sauce, and a super fruit cobbler—peach, naturally, being our favorite.

As Milly tells it, you can ask her to fix just about anything at Willy Ray's and you'll probably get it. But you'd better not try the same thing at her home. "My husband is the chef in this family," she insists. "I did my thing about cooking when my children were growing up. Today, if I can eat out somewhere every night of the week, that's just fine with me."

BROUSSARD'S LINKS + RIBS BEAUMONT

ADDRESS: 2930 SOUTH 11TH STREET, BEAUMONT
PHONE: (409) 842-1221
ESTABLISHED: 1993
OWNERS: LEONARD AND CAROLYN BROUSSARD
BEST BITES: HOMEMADE LINKS, PORK RIBS, BEEF BRISKET, RICE DRESSING
PAYMENT: CREDIT CARDS

Leonard Broussard has all the admirable earmarks of an African-American from southwest Louisiana: a French family name, a legacy of Catholic faith and a passionate belief in the transforming power of education. But when you're sitting with him in his screened green-and-yellow veranda eating the links and pork ribs he smoked this morning, don't you dare try to tell him he's not a Texan.

"Oh, but I am," he says with mock impatience. "I've lived here all my life. All I know about Louisiana is what I learned in high school geography."

Someone tasting his spicy rice dressing might beg to differ, but Leonard has a point. The Sabine River has proven such a porous barrier between Texas and Louisiana for so many generations that little things like family names, religious traditions and rice dressing have made the crossing regularly. And anyone interested in things Texan, anyone proud of the Lone Star State for its achievements, should be glad Leonard, his retired educator wife, Carolyn, and their two teaching daughters ended up on our side.

"I think me being here, with this business in this location, is some kind of divine intervention," Leonard muses. "When I was deciding to get into barbecue on my own, I had my eye on that red and yellow building across the street. But it seemed like a hand tapped me on the shoulder and said to check this out." He smiles. "There used to be a strip club here, you know. But it had been torn down for a long time before I got it."

Truth is, Leonard didn't foresee getting into barbecue whole hog, so to speak, even as he scouted locations in the early 1990s. He had worked at his uncle's barbecue place for five years in the '70s and decided he wanted to make "links" for a living—those peppery, yes, arguably "Cajun" homemade sausages so beloved in Beaumont-Port Arthur and little known anyplace else on Earth. So looking to McDonald's for inspiration—the original burger-only concept, not the current "something for everyone"—Leonard figured he could live by links alone.

"Links are all about TLC," he observes from decades of experience. "My uncle's was a good recipe, and I liked to make it. I made it very well, in fact. But a recipe can only carry you so far. It's like my wife's aunt. She could give you the recipe for her wonderful biscuits, but you could never make them."

As Leonard got serious about construction at his chosen location, he also got serious about the business of barbecue. In college, he'd studied sociology and history, and somehow these disciplines helped him learn everything he needed to know. He quickly figured out, for instance, that he needed to sell more than links. That would be, essentially, letting people walk away with too little, when barbecue could offer them so much. The pork ribs important in all African-American barbecue came next, followed by smoky-moist barbecued chicken.

Like most barbecue guys, Leonard became an expert on wood—choosing to use oak (preferably red oak) over mesquite or even the broadly popular hickory. And though he got started using an old black smoker behind his building, he eventually discovered and could afford the joys of a high-tech, wood-burning rotisserie inside.

The physical plant at Broussard's has expanded over the years, but the concept has never pointed the family toward having inside tables. Located on a busy commercial corner, the restaurant sees the bulk of its food going straight from the ordering window to people's cars. Still, as a kind of concession to customers not looking for takeout, Leonard has added the comfortable, spotless and attractive veranda. Or perhaps, it's more like an Old South screened-in porch, and nothing like the tumbledown, rotten-wood lean-tos so common in the barbecue world. "Dining in" at Broussard's combines the food quality of a restaurant with the simple pleasures of a picnic.

Educated to follow their mother into teaching, Leonard's two daughters have both worked at Broussard's and then returned to their chosen field. Maybe they'll return someday, Leonard shrugs affectionately, perhaps to start up a shipping division online. There's always room for the young, he believes, especially when you need innovation and technology. Even if his daughters stay teachers forever, you sense that Leonard both is and will be proud of them.

"Everybody has a niche," he says, relying on a word as French as his family name. "This is mine. This is what I like to do."

FAT MAC'S SMOKEHOUSE BEAUMONT

ADDRESS: 5555 CALDER AVENUE, BEAUMONT
PHONE: (409) 892-8600
ESTABLISHED: 2004
OWNER: BOB NORDBERG
BEST BITES: HOMEMADE LINKS, BOUDIN, BEEF BRISKET, SMOKED RIB EYE, CORN PUDDING, BOURBON PECAN PIE
PAYMENT: CREDIT CARDS

The way he tells the tale now, California-born Bob Nordberg was riding his motorcycle across Texas three or four years ago looking for the "best barbecue in the free world." Being Bob, when he decided he'd found it, he just had to buy the place.

As real estate goes, Fat Mac's Smokehouse didn't look like much. Or rather, it looked like a lot that was old and run-down. Still, as one of those guys who makes their money buying businesses, taking them to the next level and selling them at a hefty profit, Bob was hardly fooled. What he was looking at, at the time, was barely a year or two old. It was a casual theme restaurant built on the casual theme of Texas barbecue. And Bob saw (and, of course, tasted) plenty to like.

"My wife and I buy small businesses," explains Bob, who has traded his old life in San Diego "two seconds from the beach" for his new life based in San Antonio—keeping his San-ity, as it were. "She's more of a bean counter, and I'm more emotional. I'll get all hot and bothered about something. Then my wife gets hold of it and breaks down all the numbers. I was on a mission, but honestly, I wasn't interested in buying any restaurant. I thought I'd better buy this one before somebody else did."

Fat Mac's is a little hard to describe. If you take some real-deal Texas barbecue—the air around the open kitchen fills with smoke each time a pit man reaches for some meat—and then dress it up and out with corny, small-town Americana, you end up with a kind of Cowboy Cracker Barrel. Puns and other wordplays cover the walls, as do bits of faux rotting wood, old appliances, and nostalgic signs for gas companies and soft drinks of yore.

Happily for those who venture into Fat Mac's, neither the original owner nor Bob the California Transplant settled for merely the "look and feel" of Texas barbecue. They understood in their gut that everything was ultimately about the food, especially when you're dealing with food as iconic as barbecue. Both the pit inside and the large smokers out back are the charred, black numbers Texans over the generations have come to trust. Once all meats are marinated in a dry rub for 24 hours, they go in over red oak for as long as it takes. There's brisket, homemade links, chicken and turkey—even pork ribs, as in Kansas City, and pulled pork, as in Memphis.

Sides are a big deal within these oh-so-witty walls: dirty rice, green beans for those under orders to eat their vegetables, potato salad for those under orders to eat their mayonnaise and mustard, and a very flavorful yellow mush known as corn pudding. Desserts follow the same tongue-in-cheek, tasty party line, ranging from crisp-crusty apple or peach cobbler to the humble but delicious Rice Krispies Treats, with a mandatory stop along the way for bourbon pecan pie.

On Friday nights during crawfish season, in a town not only close to Cajun Country but surrounded by the young Texas crawfish industry, apparently all thoughts of ridin' and ropin' get pressed aside by a phenomenon Bob truly seems to enjoy. He loves his weekly crawfish boils so much, in fact, that a visitor can't resist asking if he ever feels like a traitor—you know, to Stephen F. Austin, Sam Houston, the Alamo and all that.

"Heck no," says Bob. "There's enough Louisiana influence around here. I mean, we couldn't do this in San Antonio. On Friday nights during the season, it's all about cold beer and crawfish, and believe me, the whole place gets stupid."

COMEAUX'S PORT ARTHUR

....

ADDRESS: 1848 BLUEBONNET AVENUE, PORT ARTHUR
PHONE: (409) 982-3262
ESTABLISHED: 1987
OWNER: EMMETT COMEAUX
BEST BITES: HOMEMADE LINKS, PORK BONES, BEEF BRISKET
PAYMENT: CASH

Emmett Comeaux's father came to Texas from Opelousas, Louisiana, an area rich in the Afro-Acadian-Native American intermingling that gave the world zydeco music. His mother came from Abbeville, a small town just south of Lafayette. By the time Emmett was born, the couple had settled near the Gulf of Mexico, amid the oil refineries and shipyards, in what Texans call the Golden Triangle. And Emmett was soon a child with a mission.

"When I was coming up, my dad used to always cook and my mom used to always cook," says Emmett, his deeply lined reddish-brown face gazing out through his ordering window beneath the hand-lettered NO CHECKS sign. He smiles, "And I was always in the kitchen, watching 'em."

What Emmett watched through those years at home surely included the greatest hits of southwest-Louisiana cooking—spicy soul foods like gumbo ya-ya, jambalaya, maque choux, sauce piquante. But they were also dishes born of necessity in a new place and time, using whatever was at hand, to feed the most people for the least amount of money. Among these items were the rough-ground sausages hand-tied with string known around Port Arthur as "homemade links" and the smoked pork neck pieces sold universally as "bones."

The boy who learned those dishes by watching his father and mother make them is now a grandparent himself...but they remain the biggest sellers at the red-paint-peeling barbecue shack that bears his family name.

"Barbecue around Port Arthur is like a history," he says. "These foods are part of our history. Everybody around here's got their own recipe, their own thing they do. My father made links all the time, and I was kinda watching him, you know. But he died before I could really get his recipe, so I had to work on my own 'til I got it right. It was a little slow at first, this business, back when I opened over on the west side. But then I came here and it kinda caught on. Today, I get folks hearing about these foods and coming in here to take some back to New York and California."

Despite this unexpected if undeniably limited kind of fame, Emmett seems to harbor few dreams of major success. He's not looking to build a bigger or better place—in fact, his current location has only one table. As he explains, "I don't specialize in no sittin' and eatin'." And he would surely be uncomfortable if anyone from New York or California talked to him about going "multiunit," selling franchises or making his face part of some logo high above an interstate exit.

Emmett seems content cooking homemade links and bones each day. His smoker is at home, so it's a safe bet his car smells mighty good. He also does some other standard items, like beef brisket or barbecued chicken, plus a handful of homemade sides. He seems content, too, with showing a visitor the best way to eat

his legendary links, covering a deep-red, string-dangling sausage piece with barbecue sauce, hot pepper sauce and yellow mustard, then rolling it up in a slice of white bread.

Most of all, Emmett seems content with a slow, steady trickle of customers throughout the day, all of whom tend to know that he shuts down in the morning to take his grandkids to school and in the afternoon to pick them up. He even has a handwritten sign—"Be Back at 4:00 p.m."—the sheet as weathered as the cook himself from being taped to the door, day after day after day.

JAWS BAR-B-QUE PORT ARTHUR

....

ADDRESS: 1448 7TH STREET, PORT ARTHUR
PHONE: (409) 985-6601
ESTABLISHED: 1984
OWNER: PUNARBASSI SANDY
BEST BITES: BEEF BRISKET, HOT LINKS, PORK NECK BONES, POTATO SALAD
PAYMENT: CASH

If there could ever be such a thing as a typical Texas barbecue cook, it's a safe bet Punarbassi Sandy would not be it. Born in Guyana, the English-speaking British colony at the top of South America, Miss Sandy (as she's known) went in and out of one marriage and started raising seven kids by herself before she met her husband—and, by a tangled path, found her future in Texas barbecue.

Arthur Washington Jefferson Sandy—besides having a name that sounded red, white and blue—was a diplomat for his native land, the Caribbean island of Trinidad. Perhaps due to the strong influence of India on his native cuisine, Sandy was no stranger to the immigrant culture from which his future wife would come. At the time of their meeting, Punarbassi ran a produce shop. As fate would have it, the diplomat went shopping for fresh fruits and vegetables.

"We met because of my produce," Miss Sandy remembers of "Mr. Arthur," who passed away in 2001. "And because he was a diplomat, he could travel all around my country. Before very long, we were going around together."

This ability to travel came in especially handy—in fact, it may have saved the couple's lives—in the late 1970s when Guyana grew violent with racial unrest. In the beginning of the troubles, it just seemed merely a matter of keeping ahead of the riots, but eventually it seemed best to leave completely. They came to the Port Arthur area in 1980, took one look at the local shipbuilding and oil industries and figured there was a need for good, inexpensive food for the thousands of laborers.

"At first we cooked the food we liked to eat in Guyana and Trinidad," Miss Sandy recalls with a knowing smile, looking much younger than her 60-plus years. "We made rice and peas just like back home, with plenty of sweet coconut milk...curry goat—now I can totally make that—and roti like they do in Trinidad. We fixed some wonderful foods, but unfortunately they didn't become very popular around here."

"Then somebody suggested we try American food, and we figured that in Port Arthur, Texas, American food had to mean barbecue. We cooked it and took it around to supermarket parking lots and to the refineries and the shipbuilding places at lunch. Before long, we were extremely popular. One day, we sold 700 barbecue sandwiches in Jasper. I don't never see people eat so much barbecue."

Eventually, after a falling-out with an early business partner, the Sandys settled on a small location in Port Arthur and named the place JAWS for a rearrangement of Mr. Arthur's initials. The emphasis was on barbecue's version of soul food, especially on their spicy rendition of beef homemade links and the pork neck pieces known in these parts as "bones."

All meats are seasoned and smoked on premises by Miss Sandy, who sends Styrofoam boxes to her cluster of tables inside, her picnic tables outside or to any of the cars waiting for takeout in the gravel parking lot.

Hurricane Rita, which devastated the entire region in 2005, did serious damage to JAWS Bar-B-Que—forcing Miss Sandy, her seven kids, 31 grandkids and four great-grandkids to evacuate to Houston. Now, she says, with her husband gone, all her family calls Houston home. "They all say they want me to move, to be closer, but what business do I have moving to Houston?" asks Miss Sandy. "You reach my age, there shouldn't be no talk about moving."

BUTCHER'S KORNER NEDERLAND

....

ADDRESS: 1155 BOSTON AVENUE, NEDERLAND
PHONE: (409) 722-4831
ESTABLISHED: 1995
OWNERS: C.J. AND JENNIE BREAUX
BEST BITES: SMOKED BRISKET, CHICKEN AND SAUSAGE GUMBO, BEEF TIPS OVER RICE, DIRTY RICE
PAYMENT: CREDIT CARDS

Scott Nutt is a masterpiece of multiculturalism. His Boston Red Sox cap balances the burnt-orange patriotism of his UT T-shirt. Happily for customers at the butcher shop and barbecue joint he operates for owners C.J. and Jennie Breaux on Nederland's main drag, he cooks more with what's under his shirt than what's under his cap.

Scott, who describes his job as "butchering, cooking, ordering, pretty much everything," says the building has been a gathering place in this typical on-again, off-again downtown for 100 years or more, operating mostly as a grocery store but always specializing in meat. Garner's Grocery, it was called for decades, and Scott pulls out old handwritten invoices and points around the dining room to cash registers and meat scales from the '20s and '30s to prove it.

"Really, it was just pretty much a meat market," he says. And a quick glance over to the current fresh meat counter shows that things have hardly changed entirely. "We brought in the barbecue and the catering in 1995. It's been good ever since."

Meat rules at Butcher's Korner, especially the steaks Scott cuts an inch thick every day. The important thing, he says, is that if Customer A wants hers cut an inch and a half thick, or if Customer B wants his cut two inches thick, he's happy to do that, too. Scott and the place's owners are well aware such service and the people who know how to give it are part of a dying breed, among the chain supermarkets filtering slowly down from Beaumont toward Port Arthur, with Nederland in the middle. That's just fine, they say. In fact, that's perfect for business.

While the meat market keeps a steady drumbeat of sales all day, lunch is prime time for the barbecue—or anything else Scott and his co-workers feel like cooking as a special. Everything, he says, is fresh, nothing frozen, and it's all made from scratch using the store's own recipes— many from the owner's roots in Breaux Bridge, Louisiana, on the edge of the wild, crawfish-rich Atchafalaya Basin. In fact, Louisiana gumbo dark with roux is the lunch special on Tuesdays and Thursdays in winter. "That pretty much goes quick," says Scott.

Anytime you have lunch at Butcher's Korner, joining the 150 or so locals who do, the drill is that Deep South classic: your choice of two meats and two sides. The meats might be brisket and spicy sausage or perhaps smoked chicken, while the sides range from standard potato salad and coleslaw to the Korner's signature dirty rice. Scott and friends turn out about 30 pounds of that each day, giving the rice sublime flavor by way of pork and pork liver.

All meats are smoked in the back with a combination of oak and pecan, including not only the meats the store intends to sell, and not only the turkeys it smokes each year for Thanksgiving and Christmas, but any deer, rabbit, duck, dove or anything else the area's many hunters drag in during the various seasons. Butcher's Korner can smoke the game whole or in pieces, or turn it into sausage according to its recipes or those of individual hunters. Sometimes, even things done against the butcher's will yield unexpected results.

"Take our jalapeño cheese sausage," says Scott, suddenly making us wish we could. "We really didn't want to do that. But somebody brought in a deer, and then he went out and got a bunch of jalapeños, and then he went out and got some cheese. We made it for him, sampled it and liked it, even gave some out to our customers. Before long everybody who came through that door was asking for it."

COWBOY RED'S NEDERLAND

ADDRESS: 1920 NEDERLAND AVENUE, NEDERLAND
PHONE: (409) 721-5774
ESTABLISHED: 2001
OWNERS: NICK AND BERTHA MORRISON
BEST BITES: FRIED BOUDAIN (CAJUN-STYLE BOUDIN), BEEF BRISKET, PORK RIBS, HAMBURGERS (ESPECIALLY THE OUTLAW, WITH THREE PATTIES), POTATO SALAD, BANANA SPLIT PIE
PAYMENT: CREDIT CARDS

In her six years managing Cowboy Red's, Candie Eaves has seen a lot of good things come and go, rising and falling with the fortunes of the community and of the individuals within it. The one thing she's come to recognize most profoundly is that, whether lives are heading upward or downward, in Texas people will need their barbecue.

"There's a lot of businesses on this side of town," she observes, "and not a whole lot of places to come in and sit down. But there's also our catering, to all the plants around here, which keeps us more tied up than anything. As many as we have cooks to make food and drivers to go there and deliver, that's how many lunches we can do. This morning we had six catering jobs come in, each for 20 to 25 people. And over at one plant, they had a big fire recently and lots of people are working overtime to get it up and running again. They call us all the time, maybe for 20 lunches and maybe for 50. The hard part is not knowing how many each morning until it starts coming in over the fax machine."

The restaurant owned by Nick and Bertha Morrison has an efficient, happy, almost fast-food atmosphere about it, one that's "gone to Texas" with a boost from some of Nick's trophies. No, not the blue ribbons or glistening medallions from local cook-offs on proud display, but the kind that have eyes staring blankly from the walls. Dark wood and deep-grained

leather saddles are most of what passes for décor within these walls, along with various words from the barbecue lexicon branded into the wood. There's a counter up front to place orders and smiling people to get things going in the kitchen. Cowboy Red's is like fast food's "better half," with the genre's fabled speed and lack of pretense balanced with some good and authentic Texas flavors.

Neither the dining-room atmosphere nor serving style came about by accident. Cowboy Red's started out, though no one here uses the term, as "barbecue fast food," with a tightly focused menu of pork ribs and burgers. That's right, Cowboy Red's was not shy about its fast-food inclinations, daring to specialize in the category's single most famous food item. Indeed, if you stand on tiptoe enough to read the fine print on all those awards, most of them came in for the ribs and the burgers. Over the years, however, success led Cowboy Red's away from its origins. So many plants phoned in orders every day and so many locals came into eat every day, that adding some variety to their diet was essential.

The menu expanded through and finally beyond barbecue, taking in all the

favorites of pop food culture. Buffalo wings were among the first things added, followed by a host of things from chicken-fried steak to fried catfish. Side dishes and desserts offer an intriguing contrast, perhaps even a delicious contradiction. With the unpredictable nature of its business—especially the workplace catering—Cowboy Red's logically starts a lot of its side dishes with commercial products, dressing things up with enough touches to call each side its own.

For desserts, though—an item even fancier restaurants often buy from vendors—Cowboy Red's actually has a local woman bring in homemade versions of banana cream pie, pecan pie and her crazy-popular all-time specialty: soda-fountain-nostalgic "banana split pie," complete with banana slices, pineapple, chocolate syrup and nuts.

"And then, we do breakfast," says Candie, relating yet another mundane detail of another typical day at the office. "You know, the usual stuff: eggs, grits, bacon. We open at 5:30 and we have a good crowd, especially our older men coming in for coffee. Sometimes they're waiting at the door when we get here to open up."

BILLY JOE'S BAR-BQ PORT NECHES

ADDRESS: 2029 MAGNOLIA AVENUE, PORT NECHES
PHONE: (409) 727-1482
ESTABLISHED: 1973
OWNERS: GARRY AND BRENDA RICHARDS
BEST BITES: BARBECUED CHICKEN, CHOPPED BEEF SANDWICH, COLESLAW, DIRTY RICE, GUMBO MADE FROM BARBECUED CHICKEN
PAYMENT: CREDIT CARDS

From Garry and Brenda Richards' perspective, barbecue is all about those Friday Night Lights.

Walk out their door and, yes, you're in Port Neches. But drive a minute or

two and you're in Nederland. This might not be such a difficult thing—many businesses, after all, are located in one town and close to another—except that Port Neches and Nederland have been bitter football rivals as long as anybody can remember. Some say 80 years, some say more. Yet for the barbecue place Garry and Brenda bought from Billy Joe (B.J.) Butler back in 2000 to enjoy their definition of success, they need to draw from both sets of football fans. They may not get around to mentioning it, but it's a little bit like selling barbecue to the Montagues and the Capulets.

Garry understands the ins and outs of this particular location better than most. He started working at Billy Joe's Bar-BQ when he was 14 and served as the place's night manager by the time he went off to college in Huntsville. That's a lot of high-school football Fridays, a lot of homecomings and, of course, a lot of Port Neches-Nederland battles royal. Garry watched these next-door neighbors interact through good times and bad on the football field, as well in the petrochemical industry that supports most families in the area, as well as through the hurricanes that sweep in from the Gulf of Mexico with barely a tall tree to stand in their way.

There were so many things about the place, quite frankly, that by the time

Garry finished college and married Brenda, he wasn't so sure he wanted to live up to his most-dramatic adolescent boast.

"When I went away to college, I told B.J., 'The next time I come home, I'll be comin' to buy you out.' But you see, by that time, I was running two restaurants in Huntsville. So one day, B.J. calls me and says, 'Remember what you said about buying me out?' I said I did remember, but I had a lot going on. He said, 'You should come on now.' So I did and we talked, and before long Brenda and I owned this place. We're here every day, pretty much breakfast, lunch and dinner, and it's been real good for us."

As it turned out, one of the most important parts of the Richardses' success at Billy Joe's stayed on after the purchase with the building and the name. Head chef Cleo Baltimore had been cooking for Billy Joe Butler almost since the beginning, and in the old days, when he wasn't barbecuing chicken on the rotisserie or chopping up beef brisket for sandwiches, Cleo was standing out on the street waving people in.

So many people noticed the white-haired African-American gentleman there on the street that some were concerned about him, calling the local newspaper or TV station and eventually inspiring a series of articles and reports. Cleo Baltimore became Port Neches' own version of a celebrity chef, before there exactly were celebrity chefs. And everybody in town, or in any town nearby, had to come try barbecue at Billy Joe's—you know, the place with that guy waving at you as you drove by.

"Cleo got his celebrity by being himself," relates Garry. "If he needed to get in here at 7 a.m. to get all his work done, he'd get here at 5 to make sure he had time to go out there. The longer he stands out there, the more a big deal he is. The thing is, if he misses more than two or three days, people come in ask if he's sick or if he's retired. They want to know just where he's at."

J.B.'S BARBECUE ORANGE

ADDRESS: 5750 OLD HIGHWAY 90, ORANGE
PHONE: (409) 886-9823
ESTABLISHED: 1972
OWNERS: J.B. AND MARY ARRINGTON
BEST BITES: BEEF BRISKET, PORK RIBS, SMOKED SAUSAGE, POTATO SALAD, PECAN PIE, BLACKBERRY COBBLER
PAYMENT: CREDIT CARDS

Billboards in Orange invite one and all to a "last taste of Texas," especially as Interstate 10 rises to cross the Sabine River and enter Louisiana. There could be many such final flavors, of course, but you won't find any more appropriate than meeting J.B. Arrington or sitting down with him to eat barbecue.

Like a lot of people in Texas, J.B. is a multifaceted kind of guy, and he has used his many facets to earn bits and pieces of a living here and there, from time to time. He calls himself a "teacher," for instance, yet reading, writing and arithmetic have never been his subjects. For years, the Orange native taught butchering in central Texas, before moving home to teach "vocational agriculture." There were always other jobs, however, things that never let him get far from the cattle business or the area's omnipresent oil industry. In fact, at various moments throughout his 82 years, J.B.'s motto might well have been: If you can't beat 'em, barbecue for 'em.

Not professionally, he stresses. For decades, making barbecue was something he did for love, and maybe for a bit of extra pocket change. But just over 25 years ago, something happened to J.B. that forced him to reconsider the path he, wife Mary and their children were traveling.

"I wanted to come home to Orange, you see," recalls J.B, making it sound like the most natural thing in the world. "I loved teaching, but me and Mary were just ready to come home. Then I broke my leg in a horse wreck, with three children and a pregnant wife. And while I was looking at recovering from this for a while, this old boss I had told me I'd better be in on Monday or he'd start docking my pay. Well, you know…it was right about then that Mary and I sat down and talked. About how maybe there was a better way to do this."

Not surprisingly, the serious talk led them home to Orange. And it led them into a business adventure nothing in their previous years together could have prepared them for.

The mechanics of barbecue were in place: the basic concepts of buying ingredients, cooking them over smoke and selling them for enough to pay for the groceries. Sometimes it wasn't exactly "selling" barbecue, J.B. explains—it was more like giving it away and setting out his hat for donations. But when they found a falling-apart abandoned house more or less hidden by the interstate highway, they decided it was time to get serious about feeding people.

The price for the house was fair, J.B. figured, but the place wasn't much. It required lots of work from J.B., Mary and anybody they could snag to help, hauling off dozens of truckloads of trash from the building and its overgrown lot. "I even found an old car back there," he says, as though that explains everything.

Still, after three years of selling barbecue from that old house, they jumped at the chance to start fresh. "Some guy over in Vidor said he wanted to buy the house and take it off," J.B. remembers. "I said. 'You give me $150 for the house and it's yours.' And then I said, 'You clean up the lot real good and I'll give you that $150 right back.' "

The new place that rose from the dust of the old has become a landmark in Southeast Texas, whether travelers are getting their "last taste" or their first. Considerable rustic décor has gone into the three dining rooms that wander off from the cafeteria-style counter, where J.B.'s grown kids and their spouses are likely as not to be the ones taking and filling your order.

Meats come in from one of three huge smokers in a separate building behind the restaurant, creating a cinder-block compound that resembles a small motel more than a restaurant. Hickory is the wood of choice here, whether in the big smokers or in the portable model J.B. drags off for charity events or competitions.

There are few signs of slowing down around J.B., who came in from "working maintenance" at his family cattle ranch to show a visitor around his family barbecue place. He is still in the restaurant from 4 to 7 most mornings, supervising prep for the day. The rest of the daylight hours, look for him at the ranch.

"Mary's been the backbone of everything," J.B. says, turning thoughtful. "She's done everything that anybody can do. She's sacrificed. And as tight as I am, she's still sacrificing." The man opens into an impish grin. "And she shall continue."

THE SMOKEHOUSE SAN ANTONIO

....

ADDRESS: 3306 ROLAND AT RIGSBY, SAN ANTONIO
PHONE: (210) 333-9548
ESTABLISHED: 2003
OWNER: LOUIS LIMON
BEST BITES: BEEF BRISKET, PORK RIBS, LAMB RIBS, SMOKED SAUSAGE, POTATO SALAD, RANCH BEANS, SWEET POTATO PIE
PAYMENT: CREDIT CARDS

Nestled at a four-way stop between shops devoted to tamales and mufflers, with plenty of police cruisers in the lot, The Smokehouse offers every promise of great inner-city barbecue. And five years into her family's adventure here, Tanya Limon Ollerbridez wants to keep it that way.

Tanya's father, who owns a local meat-packing firm, watched the demise of the place known for going on 40 years as Bob's Smokehouse from Ruben's Tamales across the street. It was his contact there, in fact, who filled him in on the difficulties the barbecue place was having since the death of its namesake and the assumption of duties by his kids. If barbecue can sometimes be an inspiring generational saga, sometimes it's definitely not. So the meat packager who sold meat purchased the barbecue joint that cooked it and sold it, then placed his wife and daughter in charge.

Happily, the new owner did the smartest thing any new owner can do: entrust the magic to those who knew how to make it.

"All the pit masters were here for years and years with Bob's," Tanya giggles respectfully. "Don't even try to put me on there, because it's not going to come out right. Every time our customers come in, they expect more than food—they expect a show. The guys are right there in the window in front of you when they're cutting your meat, making jokes and asking you which piece you want. One of my guys, when we're busy, keeps shouting out, 'Next in line, next in line!' I tell him he sounds just like a carny man."

According to Tanya, the customer base has gotten more diverse since her family took over in the summer of 2003. By the time Bob's had started to falter badly, financially as well as culinarily, even the flamboyant pit guys couldn't draw much of anybody from outside this ramshackle East Side neighborhood. Such people were still in evidence on this particular day, grabbing a bite between fixing mufflers, making deliveries and the like. But in addition to the number of cops settled in for lunch—always a warm reassurance—many tables were filled with businessmen in coats and ties. Outside, the parking lot serves as verification, with mud-splattered old pickup trucks alongside the shiny best of Mercedes, BMW and Lexus. Barbecue, at its best, can be one of Texas society's great equalizers.

Leading a visitor through some office space, past the toy-filled room where her baby and her sister's spend their days, Tanya delights in showing off The Smokehouse's ancient brick pits. No glinting rotisserie for this place, or for these pit guys either. They move swiftly through a ballet with each other, lifting this or that lid to grab a piece of this or that smoked meat, slamming it down on a counter to slice or chop, keeping up a spirited patter with the customers without seeming to stop for air.

All the meats served here get a generous attack of dry rub before they go into the mesquite smoke, then get mopped with a wet marinade at intervals during the cooking time. That number is about 18 hours for the brisket, naturally a great deal less for the ribs, the sausage made by Tanya's father or the chicken. Obviously,

this is a neighborhood that appreciates ribs, since The Smokehouse offers pork, two kinds of beef (short and even shorter "finger") and the rarely seen lamb.

While meat is the time-honored province of the pit crew, side dishes come mostly from Tanya and her mother. These include some all-American potato salad, crunchy-sweet coleslaw and ranch-style pinto beans. "A lot of people ask for baked beans," Tanya reports, "but I don't even know what those are." Desserts are peach cobbler, plus sweet potato pie featuring a rich cooked custard.

"My dad still has his meatpacking plant, distributing to a few companies," says Tanya. "He and his brother used to do barbecue and catering and stuff, so that's why he felt we could do this. He always said he'd never buy anything he himself didn't know how to do. He oversees things around here, and he comes in and cracks the whip whenever he thinks it's needed." She smiles. "Me and my mom, my two sisters, well...we're here all the time."

THE BARBECUE STATION
SAN ANTONIO

ADDRESS: 1610 N.E. LOOP 410, SAN ANTONIO
PHONE: (210) 824-9191
ESTABLISHED: 1992
OWNER: BOBBY PEACOCK
BEST BITES: BEEF BRISKET, PORK RIBS, SAUSAGE, PORK LOIN, SMOKED TURKEY, POTATO SALAD, PINTO BEANS WITH "FREE REFILLS," MINI PECAN PIES
PAYMENT: CREDIT CARDS

Bobby Peacock traveled all over Texas in the oil business, and the fuel that kept him going was barbecue. He tucked into the best in all the expected places, from Lockhart to Luling to Taylor, and also in a lot of tiny towns that barely made it onto the map, much less onto the Food Network. And all the time he was eating those slices of tender, smoky brisket, he

was asking himself: Why the heck can't I get good barbecue back home in San Antonio?

As happens occasionally in life, that question was reborn as a business plan.

"It's kind of a blur to me now," says Bobby, sitting at a table beside his son Stewart, who recently came into the business with one of those college degrees in finance and technology. "I just remember there was a slowdown in the oil business, so I spent six months doing the research. I mean, I ate barbecue everywhere. I got to thinking, if I go enough places, if I visit enough of these little towns with great barbecue, I might find me a guy who can cook it back in San Antonio. Then I'd go out and find me a place to put him. As it turned out, the guy I found has been here in San Antonio all along."

That proved to be one of those business relationships not destined to last, but at least it gave Bobby the faith to locate an abandoned Exxon station, renovate it into a barbecue restaurant and train a staff in the eccentricities of a very eccentric business. He found a good guy here, another over there, and still another brought in his younger brother. The team grew at The Barbecue Station, and so did its reputation for something not found often in San Antonio, birthplace of multiunit Bill Miller BBQ, Tom's Ribs and others: barbecue that wasn't cooked and served by a chain.

"You see so many great barbecue places in those small towns," says Bobby, "so I said: Let's do small-town barbecue in the big city, and it's been working well so far." He laughs. "This was just one of those conversations you have where you talk so much you can't turn back. It's commonsense stuff in so many ways. You just look at what's successful out there, whether you're pumping gas or selling barbecue or the CEO of a major corporation."

Having learned what's important in a Lockhart-Luling setting, Bobby has succeeded in delivering a no-frills, food-centric barbecue experience to San Antonio—going so far as to serve meat on butcher paper just the way those former butcher shops in the Hill Country do. He built brick pits into his version, mimicking the time-honored ways, but he also included a modern rotisserie to give him flexibility and speed. In terms of smoke, Bobby and his pit guys settled quickly on a blend of mesquite and live oak, perfecting the proportions as they went along.

As a result, they serve a delicious hybrid: the mesquite delivering that pleasantly acrid twang reminiscent of the South and West Texas styles, rounded and softened by the oak preferred in the central portion of the state. Bobby's brisket, which he's proud to report is Certified Angus, gets trimmed of considerable fat even before it goes into the smoker for 11 to 13 hours, during which time even more of the fat cooks out.

This is a big deal, he says, since many of his regulars hail from the affluent north side of San Antonio and tend to be health-conscious when not sipping carrot smoothies or busy with Pilates and yoga. All meats served here are a step up from the norm, and all are trimmed and cooked to be as lean as possible without drying out and giving up flavor—a delicate balance, to be sure. Lean meats sell unusually well within these walls, from the pork loin to the turkey breast. And even a traditional fat fest like sausage gets to shake off its past, thanks to the leaner recipe

Bobby dictates to the producers in fat-adoring Elgin.

Bobby and Stewart are currently looking to expand their catering business, which to date has focused on lunches at nearby hospitals. There's a lot of potential in catering, they realize, whether it's off-site or at the restaurant, which might inspire them to add a banquet room. One try at a second Barbecue Station after Stewart signed on proved a headache beyond its impact on the bottom line, but the younger generation with that finance degree is definitely keeping his options open.

"One store is enough for us right now," says Stewart. "With the catering, we can do it all from right here, without always having to run back and forth. You've got to keep on top of it. And the employees never run it just the way you want it run."

HINZE'S BAR-B-QUE WHARTON

ADDRESS: 8229 U.S. HIGHWAY 59, WHARTON
PHONE: (979) 532-2710
ESTABLISHED: 1970
OWNER: MICHAEL HINZE
BEST BITES: BEEF BRISKET, PORK SPARERIBS, SMOKED SAUSAGE, CHICKEN, FRIED CATFISH, CHICKEN-FRIED STEAK, CHICKEN TENDERS, BACON-ONION POTATOES, MERINGUE PIES
PAYMENT: CREDIT CARDS

Both sets of Michael Hinze's grand-parents farmed the cotton fields around Wharton. Yet by the time his parents, W.C. and Rosemary, had followed their lead into agriculture, one minor problem had presented itself.

"They just couldn't make no money at it," says Mike, who came into the Hinze household right about the time a momentous decision was being reached.

At first, the decision was embraced only by half, with W.C. continuing to farm while his wife took over a Dairy Freeze hamburger joint. Success with food was significant enough to convince the couple their future lay in that direction, with merely a change of meat on the plate. Somewhat to his chagrin, but also to his betterment, Mike found himself working in both the burger joint in town and then the barbecue shack on the highway that the family came to call its own.

"I think I was still in diapers when I started working, though of course I don't remember much about that," he laughs. "I know that by the time I was 6 or 7, my parents had me picking up the trash in the parking lot before I went to school every day. We all worked in this business—my mother and father, me and my brother, and my four sisters. My mother made sure we learned how to work hard, and I guess I should thank her for that now."

Customers were few and far between the first two or three years. For one thing, there was a fuel shortage going on, meaning people weren't just driving by day after day on leisure trips. For another thing, no one knew the Hinze's name (reflecting the German origins of

Michael's father's family, matched against his mother's Bohemian maiden name, Orsak) or associated it with terrific barbecue. Rosemary Hinze remembers using some of the family farmland as collateral to calm down their bankers, and fearing, with good reason, that two livelihoods might be lost at the same time.

"My parents almost lost everything those first couple of years, even though we always had really good product," he relates. "What really helped us was the truck drivers and—what did they call those things?—CB radios. That was a really big deal for us. The truck drivers took to stopping in for barbecue, and they let everybody know about us."

Business at Hinze's grew quickly, even if it was long overdue, creating by accident the restaurant's most striking physical characteristic. W.C. always loved pecan trees, including the two growing just outside his tiny barbecue restaurant. When the time came for the first of five or six expansions, he refused to let anyone cut down those trees. Thanks to a bit of casual engineering that might not even pass muster these days, a new and improved dining room grew up around the trees. As Mike reports, "All we have to do is water them every now and then."

By the time W.C. passed away in 1998, all six of his kids had committed to the business they'd known since childhood. Son Carl opened a Hinze's in Sealy, with plans to open another in Hempstead, and daughter Arlene opened a Hinze's in Bay City. Meanwhile, Michael came of age and purchased the Wharton original from his mother...and quickly convinced his three remaining sisters (Marlies, Donna and Lydia) to come work for him.

"I'm real lucky to have them here," says Mike. "Way back in the beginning, my parents and six kids lived in a 500-square-foot, two-bedroom house, so we're used to tight quarters. It was crowded, but we all got along pretty good. And we get along real good here. If somebody does something you don't agree with, you just talk about it and get on. I'm the big boss here, but I'm not the sort of person who acts like a boss. We all get dirty doing all the jobs, and we're not too good to do anything."

Democracy may reign in the Hinze's dining room, but not in the large open-sided pit area that stretches way out back. There, Mike is the undisputed pit boss, with all memories of side dishes and meringue pies fading inside the tumultuous swirls of smoke.

Mike uses two rotisseries fired with pecan wood, a Southern Pride for his brisket and an Ole Hickory for his pork spareribs, chicken and just about everything else. Cooking is done in these overnight, with finished meats moving into a couple of 20-foot homemade barrel smokers blessed with the least expected of features—double drawers that allow Mike and his guys to reach meat without sticking their faces deep into the smoke. Tales of necessity being a mother come to mind, especially when Mike demonstrates the single door that still swings up the old-fashioned way.

"My dad said we should keep that, so we'd never forget how hard this used to be," he says.

Mike's 16-hour brisket is king on Hinze's menu, dry-rubbed at the start and basted with a mop sauce near the end. Ribs and sausage come in next, followed by chicken, pork roast, ham and turkey. Not content with standard-issue potato salad, coleslaw and beans, Hinze's offers no fewer than 20 sides. The trinity is among them, of course, but so are bacon-onion potatoes and pinto beans, plus fried okra, several other fried favorites and something called "okra gumbo"—more like Creole okra and tomatoes, really.

For dessert, Mike and his sisters have become such masters of meringue that they're the only workers allowed to go near Hinze's coconut, lemon or chocolate pies. The fillings are amazingly light and flavorful, especially the coconut, and the meringues are lighter still. They're as close to weightless as you'll find this side of NASA.

"I remember they were running out of pies one day," says Mama Rosemary, who still comes into Hinze's every day. "So I asked if I could make some meringue, and the kids let me try, but it just never came out right. The next time they needed some pies and I offered to help"—Rosemary smiles—"they all just said, 'Oh no, Mom, we'll be okay.' "

AUNT JO'S BBQ VICTORIA

ADDRESS: 5303 U.S. HIGHWAY 77 SOUTH, VICTORIA
PHONE: (361) 578-5900
ESTABLISHED: 2007
OWNERS: THE JOSHUA FAMILY
BEST BITES: BEEF BRISKET, PORK SPARERIBS, POTATO SALAD, PUMPKIN BREAD, MINI PECAN PIES
PAYMENT: CREDIT CARDS

Monroe Joshua and Vic Salinas have shared most things for most of their lives—most things except a bloodline.

They've shared a strong, courageous mother who raised every child she met who needed raising, forming an extended African-American-Mexican family with a variety of last names, most of whom call her "Aunt Josephine." And they've shared the memory of a remarkable great-grandfather who amassed and developed 5,500 acres of South Texas land despite his worse-than-humble beginnings, as a slave.

"My great-grandfather came to own all these acres when black men shouldn't have been owning anything," asserts Monroe, a tall, distinguished-looking man with light coffee-colored skin. He points to the formal portrait on the wall, showing the stiff, dressed-up pose of another era but also a searing, fearless gaze that must have served Tom Joshua well. "He did anything he could for money after he got his freedom. He was a very hard worker. With some Mexicans from around here, he even cut down trees on what land he had and sold the lumber to the

local power plant. With all the money he made, he always bought more land."

Much has changed, of course, since the Joshua family began piecing together its ranch in Victoria County in the mid-1800s. The simple old farm road has become U.S. 59, a significant artery between Houston and the seemingly wild border country to the deep south. Some of the family's old buildings have fallen into disuse, including the old mill and the school Tom Joshua built for educating black children. But one roadside building has taken on new life recently after serving as the family's grocery store beginning in the 1920s.

Monroe, Vic and other family members bought the property from Josephine in 2000 and by 2007, they'd lovingly restored it into a barbecue joint notable for its cleanliness inside, its wooden picnic tables under the graceful trees, and the large effigy of a pig that is the business' main sign. "Look for the Pig!" is the Joshua family's mantra and message to anyone traveling along their stretch of highway.

"We have always barbecued for our cowboys here on the ranch, whenever we'd do roundups and stuff," explains Monroe. "We just decided to see how the public would like it. We draw a lot of our customers from the traffic going to or from Mexico, or just to or from Corpus." He smiles. "They seem to like it so far."

Behind the scenes, Vic spends most of his days working a glistening silver pit,

relying on mesquite for its signature smoke flavor. "Oak is our backup wood," explains Monroe, "whenever we can't get any mesquite." He notices that his listener doesn't quite understand. "Oh, we don't *buy* any wood—not with all these trees on our property. Anytime we need wood to barbecue, we just crank up the chain saw."

Aunt Jo's mesquite smoke tastes especially good on the thick slices of fall-apart brisket that's cooked 12 to 14 hours, but it also delivers a knockout punch to the place's tender pork spareribs. There are separate dry rubs for seasoning the beef, pork or poultry before it goes into the smoker, plus a wonderful, distinctive sauce for the eating afterward. It's sweet and tangy when you first taste it, but it leaves a warm trail of black pepper on your tongue that's equally pleasurable with beef and pork.

Side dishes travel no farther than traditional potato salad, coleslaw and beans, even though the onions provide a happy jolt. Instead of simply and typically raw, they are lightly pickled. Dessert choices include mini pecan pies baked by Monroe's sister and pumpkin bread baked by his mother. "We're keeping it very simple," he says.

Asked to define the lessons handed down to all family members by Aunt Josephine and by those memories of Tom Joshua, both Monroe and Vic answer separately with the same two words: "hard work." Considering the value placed on that quality on these 5,500 acres gathered for the future by a freed slave, it's not surprising this is something the younger generation is hearing about more than it sometimes wishes.

"My great-grandfather was the first black man around here to own property," Vic says, carrying a tray of reddish-brown, char-flecked briskets inside from the smoker. "We're in oil and gas and cattle, so we really don't have to do this. This is for our kids to have something to fall back on. I started doing hard work on this ranch when I was just a kid. Now our kids are going to, cuz I'm not going to just give it to 'em. It's a family thing. It's the way we are."

THE BAR-B-Q MAN
CORPUS CHRISTI

ADDRESS: 4931 INTERSTATE 37 SOUTH, CORPUS CHRISTI
PHONE: (361) 888-4248
ESTABLISHED: 1977
OWNER: MALCOLM DESHIELDS
BEST BITES: BEEF BRISKET, PORK SPARERIBS, SMOKED TURKEY, POTATO SALAD, WAFFLE CONES WITH ICE CREAM AND PRALINE SAUCE
PAYMENT: CREDIT CARDS

For decades, M.O. DeShields did just about everything there was to do in the food business except sell barbecue—which might, of course, have been the ultimate apprenticeship.

He drove a bread truck, ran a grocery store and doughnut shop, operated a fried chicken shack and then a short-order café, both of which quickly fell on their faces. Then one day, the owners of an old tavern down the street asked if he'd be willing to provide foodservice, thus saving them the trouble. M.O. thought about the proposition a little bit, then settled into a 200-square-foot corner of that saloon and started dishing up Texas barbecue.

"My father left Alabama at age 16 to cook in the merchant marine, so the food business has always been in our blood," says M.O.'s son Malcolm, sitting at the owner's table in the front of the barbecue restaurant he helped his dad open in 1977. "On the ship, he was cooking three meals a day for 300 people, so he figured he could handle just about anything."

With the addition of a kitchen to that saloon corner, The Bar-B-Q Man got pretty serious, as did the people who came from all over Corpus Christi to eat his barbecue. The tail may not have exactly wagged the dog, but eventually the tail tried to *buy* the dog. When the tavern owners refused to sell, M.O. took his show on the road, acquiring a plot of land with three run-down houses on it. M.O. and Malcolm knocked down two of those but used the survivor as the center of their restaurant. With growth in the business, another building was added in 1981, followed by a patio and cantina bar in 1987.

The bar was important to M.O., who'd

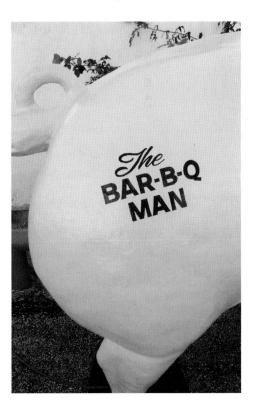

started his barbecue business inside one, after all. Not so to his son.

"My father enjoyed women, alcohol and having a good time," remembers Malcolm. "So the bar fit really well with him. I decided a long time ago I wanted to stay married to only one woman, and the bar didn't fit well with *that* at all. I've closed the bar down since we lost my father. The good thing is that everything within this six-foot Hurricane fence belongs to my family, and it's all paid for."

With so many customers loyal to The Bar-B-Q Man going back to M.O.'s time, it has been clear to Malcolm from the start that his job is to adjust whenever necessary but change nothing the customers will see, smell or taste. Recipes here are sacrosanct, nearly all going back to M.O. himself and prepared zealously by cooks who've worked here 25 or even 35 years. Malcolm sees this continuity as essential. While he's training new people under the old as time passes, he considers it well worth the investment to pay good people enough to keep them around.

"To have an employee in the same restaurant for 30 years is kinda weird these days," he agrees. "But when our customers come in and see the same faces behind the serving line and joke around with the same server in the dining room, that's really important to them. The first week of August, we close for an entire week. We've worked hard all summer, we're tired and kids need to get ready to go back to school. Everybody gets two paychecks on that Friday and then nine days off. We do the same thing again on December 24, except with three paychecks."

M.O. DeShields passed away in 1998, but you wouldn't know he was gone to look at the menu or the way items are prepared. Fact is, Malcolm had taken over the barbecue operation years before buying the restaurant from his father. The place seats up to 800 at a time and often does, though Malcolm stresses he likes things better with a little more breathing room. Meats are smoked in Southern

Pride rotisseries, what Malcolm refers to as "wood-burning convection ovens," essentially basting themselves as they turn in a sealed chamber.

Most popular meats here are the brisket and sausage, though the cafeteria line at The Bar-B-Q Man also entices with smoked chicken on the bone and smoked turkey breast off of it, along with tender and savory pork spareribs.

Following his father's lead, Malcolm offers only four side dishes: the trinity of M.O.'s recipes for potato salad, coleslaw and pinto beans, plus green beans. Favorite desserts include a waffle cone bearing vanilla ice cream and a topping of gooey-good praline sauce made up the road in Sinton.

"I hear people talk about my father a lot when they're eating here," Malcolm says. "The best compliment I can get is that I'm maintaining this business in my father's fashion. I'm really proud of that."

KNUCKLEHEADS CORPUS CHRISTI

ADDRESS: 819 N. UPPER BROADWAY STREET, CORPUS CHRISTI
PHONE: (361) 882-9997
ESTABLISHED: 2002
OWNER: LARRY WILLIAMS
BEST BITES: BEEF BRISKET, PORK RIBS, SMOKED CHICKEN, POTATO SALAD, SAUSAGE TORTILLA WRAP, SMOKED CHICKEN SALAD
PAYMENT: CREDIT CARDS

In outlaw-addicted Texas, the line between barbecue joint and biker bar can seem mighty thin sometimes. Knuckle-heads is one of those very few places, though, that strive to erase the line completely.

"What do you expect," asks grizzled, silver-ponytailed pit boss Earl Etter, "when you drive up and see five parking spaces for cars and 30 for bikes? We're a biker bar—oh, excuse me, a 'motorcycle-

friendly' bar. We serve everybody from bankers to bikers here, especially since these days most of the bikers *are* bankers."

The socioeconomic irony of this fact is hardly lost on Earl, who himself was a stockbroker for 10 years, presumably without the beard or the ponytail. In fact, over the years, Earl has been a lot of different things, even operating a crane for a year because he liked to play with substantially smaller toy versions when he was a kid. Riding a motorbike seems a given, but Earl insists it says more about his life that he now lives on a sailboat—a Morgan 386.

"I got my first sailboat when I was 12," he reports, "and I've had one ever since." Earl pauses to rub the gray stubble around his chin. "The whole point is not to have a plan. If you have a plan, then you're on a schedule. And if you're on a schedule, then you might as well work."

Knuckleheads combines, with no particular logic, the finer elements of a rough-tough bar on a lonesome stretch of highway with those of a faux 1950s diner—perfect, apparently, for that hard-to-buy-for biker-banker on your holiday gift list. The centerpiece of the main room is a long bar, behind which a waitress makes drinks and opens up bottles of cold beer. You can order food at the bar and consume it either at one of those high cocktail tables nearby or at rustic picnic tables in a smaller space behind. Both spaces wrap and warp around the kitchen, where Earl smokes meats in what he calls "nothing fancy," an old-fashioned box smoker powered entirely by hickory.

Biker memorabilia is everywhere inside the place, from the large motorcycle precariously suspended above your head as you sip a beer to the leather jackets pinned to walls like butterflies to the posters for past, present and future rallies. Again, the irony is in the fine print. Most of these events are sanctioned to raise money for un-bikerish good causes like breast cancer research. Something about black leather and all those little pink ribbons...

In addition to bikers and bankers, Earl says the joint is well supported by workers from local refineries, a fact helped along by its quirky location on the fringe of Corpus Christi's typically reborn downtown. At Knuckleheads, you're a long way spiritually from Joe's Crab Shack, the hometown-huge Whataburger or the posh Omni Hotel on the waterfront—or, for that matter, from the memorial to slain Tejano idol Selena, a source of lasting local pride. Within these walls, it's all about what you rode in on.

Lunch is the busiest meal for Earl, when all his entangled ethnicities and incomes cram in to stuff themselves with brisket smoked for 14 hours, as well as on the popular sausage wrapped in a flour tortilla—"the best ever," boasts the humble pit boss.

Most of the items and combinations are named thematically, as though the entire Hells Angels repertoire had suddenly become a subsidiary of Disney. You can order an "Easy Rider" (any two meats) or perhaps a "Big Biker" (your choice of three meats). Other specialties include the "Bone Shaker" (a tortilla filled with pulled smoked chicken) and the lovingly named "Softail" (a terrific smoked chicken salad).

"This was going to be a bar with a little barbecue," Earl observes, knowing better than most what happens to the best-laid plans of mice and men. "Instead, it turned out to be a barbecue joint with a little beer. No, it wasn't a surprise. We had to do things better than everybody else because of our location. Really, you go past here on your way to nowhere."

BAD BRAD'S BAR-B-Q JOINT, PORTLAND

ADDRESS: 1807 U.S. HIGHWAY 181, PORTLAND
PHONE: (361) 643-5000
ESTABLISHED: 2004
OWNERS: MIKE MORGAN, RUSTY KELLY, JOEL HOSKINSON
BEST BITES: BEEF BRISKET, PORK RIBS, SMOKED TURKEY, HOME FRIES, ONION RINGS, FRIED OKRA, FRUIT COBBLERS
PAYMENT: CREDIT CARDS

The five childhood friends behind Bad Brad's wouldn't want you to think they're bringing Oklahoma barbecue to Texas, which would be as unacceptable in barbecue as it would be in football. No, the five guys in question grew up around Portland and graduated from Portland High School and Texas A&M before lighting out for the territories—lock, stock and smoker.

After considerable success with Bad Brad's in places like Stillwater and Yukon, two of the guys and a friend decided to try their hand cooking Texas barbecue in the actual state of Texas. So far, what worked for Bad Brad's in Oklahoma is working in their hometown, with one notable exception.

"That damn smoked bologna must be an Oklahoma thing," says partner Mike

Morgan, poking a long fork at the offending knob sharing the tray with real meat like brisket, ribs and sausage. "They sell a ton of it up there. Down here, it's like one bologna can last you just about forever."

Disappointing bologna sales notwithstanding, Bad Brad's has encountered few major problems on the road to its first Texas success. Some customers hobble in from the 44,000 cars that pass on the highway each day. Others come from the town of Portland as well as from nearby Corpus Christi, attracted by solid, consistent food...a fun, casual atmosphere...and the chance to order hard liquor in addition to beer and the omnipresent iced tea. While Mike says the place looks a lot like the outlets in Oklahoma, he and his buddies had the good sense to cover the walls with Texas football memorabilia.

"I knew I wanted to come back here," says Mike. "This is home, and that was always the plan. We found this little piece of land right off the highway, and it was pretty cheap back then. It seemed like a pretty good location."

Actually, there was a modicum of desperation mixed in with major opportunity, as Mike had just been laid off from his job. It was then that one of his friends who'd gone to Oklahoma showed up unexpectedly. Surely over a few beers, the two started talking life, love and barbecue, and before the conversation was over, Mike had agreed to head for Stillwater to learn the barbecue business. This was easy enough there, since Bad Brad's was not only doing solid business as a restaurant but officially catering barbecue to suites, parties and concessions at the Oklahoma

State home football games.

"When you can do barbecue for 1,500 people on a catering job, you begin to think you can do it at a place like this," Mike observes, logic squarely on his side.

The biggest change from Oklahoma, he says, is in the flavor demographic Bad Brad's tries to serve. In Oklahoma and much of North Texas, the customer base is dominated by cattle ranchers, who turn to barbecue as their default lunch or dinner out. Here in South Texas, there's hefty competition from Tex-Mex and seafood, especially among summertime tourists who flock to Corpus Christi and its miles of nearby beaches or among the winter Texans who take up the slack starting right after Thanksgiving. There weren't any "winter Oklahomans" to practice on, apparently.

Mike, Rusty Kelly and Joel Hoskinson do all the smoking over mesquite at Bad Brad's—that being the wood flavor locals and visitors seem to prefer. In the beginning, they went with three hulking black "farmhouse smokers" somebody sold them, but they now rely on a glistening silver Southern Pride rotisserie with a thermostat to control the fire. The guys vary cooking temperature a little and cooking time a lot depending on the meat, with briskets going 12 hours at 225 degrees and ribs going 3 hours at 250 degrees. All others among the nine meats (nine if you count bologna, that is) fall in there somewhere.

One of the neatest touches the Bad Brad's boys have picked up in their barbecue travels is having a fryer in the kitchen …thus, they report that home fries are their most popular side dish, along with great onion rings and crisp-tender fried okra. Another menu surprise is what's billed as (and actually turns out to be) a Cheddar Cheese Block. There it simply is—solid and yellow, not molten or batter-fried—waiting, explains Mike, to be spread on crackers. He says his customers eat a lot of these things.

The most popular desserts include four fruit cobblers, described as a kind of "cake cobbler" similar to what soccer moms whip up and call "dump cake."

And when all else fails, says Mike, there's always Bad Brad's bar. "They don't sell alcohol in Oklahoma," he says of the older outlets. "But the three of us like it. It's just like it goes with barbecue. Or Mexican food. Or seafood. Or Cajun. Whatever."

STEVIE LEW'S BBQ KITCHEN, ROCKPORT

ADDRESS: 5340 HIGHWAY 35 NORTH, ROCKPORT
PHONE: (361) 727-0866
ESTABLISHED: 2007
OWNERS: STEVE AND CARRIE MEINHAUSEN
BEST BITES: BEEF BRISKET, PULLED PORK, POTATO SALAD, CHILI (WHEN AVAILABLE), CHERRY COBBLER
PAYMENT: CREDIT CARDS

If Johann David Wyss had shipped in from the 19th century to eat brisket and ribs on the waterfront at Stevie Lew's, he might well have dubbed the proprietors "Swiss Family Barbecue."

Not that Steve and Carrie Meinhausen were shipwrecked on the Texas Coastal Bend with their four children. They chose the area deliberately, after considerable research. It's just the joyous, never-too-serious way all six of them work together, doing what needs to be done around the RV park that is home to one of the Lone Star State's quirkiest barbecue joints.

After more than 20 years running restaurants in Tucson, Arizona—including a 400-seater and a 200-seater at the same time, both open 24/7—the Meinhausens were ready for a change. And they certainly found one.

"What people don't seem to understand," says Steve, as the kids gather around him at the table, waiting for their turn to chime in, "is that barbecue is all about fishing." He nods to the cluster of rods leaning against the dining room wall, as though that should explain

everything. "Some people do barbecue to make a lot of money, I suppose. But we do barbecue...well, we're open four days a week for three hours a day. The rest of the time, we go fishing. If we're closed and you happen to catch us in here, we'll cook for you—whatever we have in the kitchen. But when we want to go fishing, we just go!"

Steve and Carrie homeschool their kids, so that removes one of life's biggest frustrations. And they live where they work, thus removing another. Still, that's not to say the work is easy. There are guests to tend to in the RV park, no doubt made easier by accepting only long-term rentals and getting a lot of visitors from Houston, Austin, Dallas and San Antonio who come to the coast only on weekends. And there's barbecue to be made every day, with Steve functioning as de facto pit boss. As for the standard difficulties of finding and keeping good help, Steve just smiles at the young faces around him.

"This is their Economics 101 class," he says of his children. "Sarah Makenna does the register. Matt waits tables, sometimes taking a skillet of cherry cobbler around and asking people, 'Y'awl want any of this?' Kasey does the sides and the salads. And Ellie just charms people."

Carrie Meinhausen keeps more than busy, with and without the demands of Stevie Lew's. In addition to handling some cooking and serving, she runs a wholesale coffee roasting business from the place, shipping her blend labeled Texas Thunder to clients all over Texas and into Louisiana and Colorado. Whenever she needs to make a fresh batch, she rolls the antique roaster out onto the front porch and fires away. The aroma, of course, is tantalizing.

For the Meinhausens, the big decision began forming in the early days of the new millennium, pressed along by the parental realization that their children wouldn't be little forever. The restaurant business in Tucson has lost its joy, and with Carrie being a fourth-generation roaster, the coffee business could be based anywhere. There was, all of a sudden, that dazzling yet intimidating freedom of being able to do anything you want wherever you want to do it. The research that led the Meinhausens to Texas and barbecue began.

"If you're a businessperson, you'd better do your homework," says Steve. "We wanted a double season, and the only way to get a double season was to stick to the I-10 corridor. You know, the Sun Belt. But water is the main draw of all camping vacations. We read about this place, came down here and just fell in love with it. So we sold everything we had, and here we are." He stops for a moment, probably picturing what they first laid eyes on. "This was nothing but a sandbar when we bought it, but we knew immediately it was home."

Gifted with his hands, Steve was able to build whatever was needed to open the Seaport Village RV Park in 2005 and the restaurant in 2007. After another round of research, he and Carrie settled on barbecue as their main product and set about perfecting ways to coax the best from the oak fire in the barrel smoker out front.

Brisket is their big seller, as well it should be after smoking 18 to 20 hours, but the Meinhausen kids tend to prefer Stevie Lew's pulled pork. Beef and pork have separate barbecue sauces, with what Steve calls "more zing" for the pork and something a bit "more savory and deep" for the beef—the latter secret recipe getting a definitive boost from Carrie's Texas Thunder coffee.

"We've carved out a lifestyle for ourselves," Steve says. "I've lived my life, and I've had a ball. Now it's all about the kids."

gate argued that his ex-wife was in the United States and he couldn't figure one good reason for making access any easier.

Tony Hiltzman probably takes considerable solace in his illustrious forebears. "Damn right I'm running away," he says. "You could say that, yes. I'm running away from Houston."

Before getting all up in arms, Houston lovers fearing the standard list of complaints—traffic, construction, lack of zoning, lack of respect for the past, heat, humidity, mosquitoes—should know that Tony's list won't be very different from the one they draw every time they gather. In his case, in fact, the exodus to the Coastal Bend was inspired less by such frustrations as by his disgust with life as a corporate chef. Tony will still hand you what seems his only business card, which identifies him as "executive chef" for Perry's Steakhouse & Grille and Perry's Italian Grille. Except those restaurants are in Houston. And he's not.

"Chef Tony is available to cater your event," promises the Texas Star menu. And then, with a flourish of substantial

TEXAS STAR BARBECUE ROCKPORT

ADDRESS: 2118 W. MARKET STREET, ROCKPORT
PHONE: (361) 790-7200
ESTABLISHED: 2006
OWNERS: CAROLYN RICHTER AND TONY HILTZMAN
BEST BITES: BEEF BRISKET, RIBS, COLESLAW, CREAM CHEESE CORN, APPLE-PECAN PIE
PAYMENT: CASH AND LOCAL CHECKS

The Lone Star State has a long and glorious tradition of running away. When this land was still part of Mexico, most of the Anglos who settled here were running away from something—or somebody. When Sam Houston's ragtag band turned to surprise Santa Anna at San Jacinto, until that moment they'd been running away. And when the Republic of Texas voted to join the United States, one dele-

understatement about a chef trained in Europe and paid over the years to cook virtually everything, "He is not limited to BBQ."

Still, the folks on this side of the country road don't want any confusion as to what business they're in: "No Bull, Just Beef" reads a sign out front.

As best a visitor can tell, the saga of Texas Star doesn't start with Chef Tony at all but with his sister Carolyn Richter. She had the earliest barbecue experience, helping her father run a joint in the nearby town of Poth when she was small. Then life and marriage and babies took over, moving Carolyn this way and that. With the death of her husband, however, in one of those connections that only Dr. Freud can explain, returning to the first thing she ever loved doing seemed the most logical move in the world.

"I would come down here to the coast when my babies were little to take them to the beach," Carolyn explains. "I never lived here before 1999, but it's like home to me."

After building a house next door to the building that became Texas Star—it had already served as a residence, a barracks and a gaming room full of slot machines—Carolyn embarked on building a restaurant with help from her son Jason. The place that evolved mixes a Texas country atmosphere with an unexpected dash of Jimmy Buffett tropical. There is a simple counter for ordering whatever you like from menus and chalkboards strewn about the walls, plus a smattering of tables for sitting down and enjoying your food.

When Jason got too busy with his own career, Carolyn's other son Gregory took over helping her. And while Carolyn figured out how she wanted the meats smoked and all the side dishes prepared, when business started picking up, she knew she could use some professional help. "So I called Tony and said, 'Get your butt over here.' "

Though Carolyn is his sister, Tony also understood that she was his boss—

better than many he's had in hotels and restaurants around the world, he's quick to add. Putting his skills in service of her recipes, Tony learned the ropes the way she wanted, tweaking things only when he could convince Carolyn his way was better. As a result, all the recipes served at Texas Star are essentially hers, except for a few Cajun things like gumbo and jambalaya he has added recently.

Typical of most chefs, Tony doesn't like to bake, so Carolyn handles that herself, turning out as many golden apple-pecan pies from a favorite family recipe as she can.

"She can't bake enough of them," says Tony. "I have eight of those going out of here this weekend."

"It's kinda like I took my two favorite pies," Carolyn says. "When I couldn't decide which one I wanted to make, I just made them together."

On the barbecue side of things, Tony uses nothing but mesquite to produce Texas Star's brisket, sausage, ribs and chicken. Two of the more interesting variations are called Buffalo Butt (boneless chicken thighs stuffed with jalapeños and wrapped in bacon) and Buffalo Boobs (boneless chicken breasts treated much the same).

Sides are notable, especially for a place that could just as soon buy them commercially. The potato salad is excellent, but even that pales beside the crisp, vinegar-kissed, no-mayo coleslaw or Carolyn's cream cheese corn.

On a whim, a visitor asks Chef Tony what dish he most likes to eat. "After 30 years in this business," he answers, ever the runaway, "I've made so much lobster and prime rib, nothing you put in front of me is going to excite me." He smiles. "Okay, maybe fried chicken."

MAC'S PIT BARBECUE ROCKPORT

ADDRESS: 815 E. MARKET STREET, ROCKPORT
PHONE: (361) 729-9388
ESTABLISHED: 1974 IN GREGORY, 1993 IN ROCKPORT
OWNER: DOMINGO HERNANDEZ
BEST BITES: BEEF BRISKET, PORK RIBS, BEANS WITH JALAPEÑOS, APPLE OR PEACH COBBLER
PAYMENT: CREDIT CARDS

When Domingo Hernandez was 16 and already accustomed to hard work, he took a job as a busboy in a barbecue joint in the town of Gregory. The food at Mac's was good, he realized in that adolescent sort of way. But mostly he had eyes for the pretty young lady at the cash register. It turned out she was the boss' daughter, and she was only 13 or 14.

Over the next three to four years, until the day he finished college, Domingo worked at Mac's—but not forever as a busboy. He took on additional responsibilities whenever they were offered, learning about smoking meats and preparing side dishes, educating himself in food safety, mastering the basic notions of customer service and satisfaction. And when his college degree was

firmly in hand and his barbecue apprenticeship more or less complete, he got the only promotion he'd ever really wanted. He married the boss' little girl.

"First I took the daughter," Domingo laughs today, "then I took the restaurant."

Still, Domingo's purchase of the Mac's location in Rockport was neither obvious nor inevitable. The young man and his bride had already established themselves in a restaurant enterprise of their own: operating several Burger Kings for the U.S. Army in Germany. And as anyone who's ever worked in fast food will tell you, the food may be only what it is, but the operational systems are inspirational.

In 1993, when his father-in-law called Domingo to ask him to bring his daughter home after five years, there was no easy answer. The couple had a new son, born in Germany. Indeed, they had a good life there, with so many details taken care of for them, thanks to their role serving Whoppers to Americans.

Mac was nothing if not persuasive, however, and Domingo knew that association with a barbecue brand that had spread from little Gregory to a total of five locations was an investment even Burger King would understand.

"I think of Mac's as one restaurant with five locations," says Domingo. "I've tried to

keep the restaurant the original way my father-in-law had it. Back when he started, all the recipes were trial and error. I remember him talking about a 'handful' here and a 'pinch' there, and in real food-service you can't measure like that."

With Domingo's corporate, multiunit experience, the recipes were fixed right out of the starting gate—perfected, stan-dardized and enforced, all to guarantee that things stayed through time and changing employees just the way Mac had intended them. There is mesquite, for instance, in the big rotisserie smoker that daily serves up tender brisket with a pink smoke ring, plus perfect pork ribs that show much the same. With the brisket in particular, for all the big flavors Domingo packs into other things like his pinto beans with jalapeños, the man is definitely a purist.

"We use no spices, no dry rub, on our brisket," he explains. "The only flavor is from the wood. We believe that if you're going to eat something, it should be good enough to eat all by itself, without putting a whole lot of sauce or seasonings on it."

Today, there are three other renditions of Mac's in the Coastal Bend area, run by different relatives under slightly different names: the original Mac's in Gregory, Mac's Barbecue in Aransas Pass and Mac's Barbecue # Fore (operated by an avid golfer, of course) in Corpus Christi. All four are related by recipe, by blood-line, and by the belief that hard work translates into both good food and good life. That's the message Domingo tries to get across to his 17-year-old and his 12-year-old, both of whom work at the Rockport Mac's.

"Just because we own a restaurant doesn't mean that money grows on trees," he says. "I tell them: This is what I'm try-ing to teach you. This is what you need to learn, no matter how many tears or cut fingers or burned hands you get."

THE BAR-B-Q SHACK FULTON

ADDRESS: 3114 HIGHWAY 35 NORTH, FULTON
PHONE: (361) 729-7676
ESTABLISHED: 2003
OWNER: PATRICK GARZA
BEST BITES: BEEF BRISKET, CHOPPED BEEF SANDWICH, PORK RIBS, SAUSAGE, ROASTED CORN ON THE COB (IN SEASON)
PAYMENT: CASH AND CHECKS

For some pit bosses, it's all about the meat ...while for others, it's all about the smoke. For still others, it's all about their special and secret dry rub. For Patrick Garza, it's about all of those things—and, in a sense, none of them.

"My whole thing is low overhead," says Patrick, gazing out through the ordering window of his tiny red shack on the side of the highway. Smoke drifts upward from a porch built onto the back, but even taken together, the two struc-tures add up to nothing much. "I think it's more cost-efficient. For a while, this building just sat here, and I kept think-ing there had to be something I could use it for. My brother used to sell snow cones out of it, but then he moved that inside the bakery."

For the Garza brothers and their mother, there is a close relationship between The Bar-B-Q Shack and the Rockport Bakery right next door. It's a kind of family compound, with Patrick living right on the property. And it was the bakery his mother owns that resulted in Patrick being persuaded to come home to Fulton in the first place.

"We're really in Fulton now," he explains, addressing the confusion in a visitor's eyes. "But nobody ever knows where Fulton in. And besides, this road used to be Rockport, back when the bak-ery started. But now it's part of Fulton."

That settled, it's time to talk about the business Patrick settled into in the shack that used to sell snow cones. He moved

home in 1998 after several years of working in the seafood business in Oklahoma. Apparently, for Patrick and his family, selling seafood in a state without a coast made even less sense than selling beef in a town right on the waterfront. At first, he worked in the bakery. But by 2003, he had stared out at that little red shack long enough. He brought in an old black barrel smoker, filled it full of oak wood and started dishing up brisket.

"It's been going real good," says Patrick. "In the next three or four years, I'd like to open a couple more of these. In some places, you have to rely on employees, and around here it's really hard to find good help. I'd rather do something with two or three employees than something that needs 10 or 12."

For most of the time The Bar-B-Q Shack has been in business, brisket smoked up to 14 hours has been the only meat. After considerable experimentation at home, however, Patrick has recently introduced pork ribs, and they've been coming out tender and full of flavor.

So far he has drawn the line at pulled pork, despite constant requests from winter Texans. There simply isn't room on the pit. On the other hand, during downtime, he has found space to accommodate local hunters who bring him ducks they've shot.

"We wrap them in bacon, put them on the pit and they turn out real good," Patrick says. "I guess these guys weren't going to take the ducks home and smoke them themselves. I guess they said, 'Hey let's see if Patrick will do it.' "

The bit about winter Texans and their desire for pulled pork caught Patrick by surprise. For one thing, in a summer beach destination, he initially expected to shut his shack down for most of the year. Instead, especially after he taught his winter Texans the joys of smoked brisket, he has kept the shack open year-round. Once introduced to real Texas barbecue, Patrick says, winter Texans come back two or even three times a week. And best of all, they stay for months at a time.

Beyond brisket, the addition of ribs and a bit of sausage from Prasek's Smokehouse in nearby Hillje, it's been a question of getting the most out of the pit. Turkey legs cook well over oak and sell wonderfully, especially in the transient, take-out world of the beach in summer. Corn on the cob comes away charred and sweet, being at the height of its season over the same months Fulton is at the height of its season.

Other sides are kept simple, just potato salad and beans, plus potato chips where the coleslaw might have been. There are no desserts, though Patrick is quick to point those with a sweet tooth a few feet across the grass to Rockport Bakery. You know, the one that's in Fulton.

"I have four tables in a pavilion out back, and my mom and my brother in the bakery," he says. "People say they eat over there every day for breakfast, then come over here for lunch and dinner. They tell us we've pretty much got the market cornered."

LITTLE JOE'S SMOKE N' GRILL
PORT ARANSAS

ADDRESS: 200 W. AVENUE G, PORT ARANSAS
PHONE: (361) 749-BEEF (2333)
ESTABLISHED: 2001, CURRENT OWNER SINCE 2006
OWNER: MARK ADMIRE
BEST BITES: BEEF BRISKET, PORK RIBS, PULLED PORK, HOMEMADE SOUPS (ESPECIALLY CHILI IN WINTER), SPICE CAKE, CARROT CAKE
PAYMENT: CREDIT CARDS

"Now *that's* a long story," says Mark Admire, asked how a smart guy like him, with 30 years in the restaurant business, ended up trying to sell meat to people who came to the coast looking for seafood. "Let's just say this was a playground of mine, had been for many years. The opportunity presented itself, and I decided to move here."

If the "story," as Mark puts it, is long, even longer is the list of restaurants all over the country and overseas he has worked in—"from fine linen to throwing pizzas." For the past 12 years, he has served as a "restaurant consultant," a

mysterious figure who researches, develops, advises and trains wherever a corporation or individual owner needs help. The result is a guy who knows a potential success when he sees one—though even when he *doesn't* see one, he does his best. And when Mark saw Little Joe's foundering under its original owner, he saw a place that he could grow, in more ways than one.

"This is a stepping-stone for me," says Mark, who grew up eating barbecue in the Hill Country's Kerrville as well as on his family's ranch west of Junction. "I'm using it mainly for recipe development." He thinks a moment. "Still, it would be nice if I can get it where it stands on its own."

Mark doesn't see selling barbecue to seafood eaters the biggest of Little Joe's challenges. Perhaps the biggest is dealing with the seasonality of Port Aransas, a town that fills to bursting in the summertime and empties out the rest of the year. Even some locals leave in the winter, those with other homes elsewhere. And the joys of looking for customers offseason are matched by the joys of looking for dependable staff.

"It's a big challenge," Mark admits. "I started in management, but I've been working around restaurants so long that I've become an avid cook. So I've been experimenting with steaks and seafood right along with barbecue, along with homemade soups—two every day—and salads. They're all cooked with a Texas twist. Basically, I'll only cook food that I'll eat. That may sound kinda narrow, but really there's no need to cook anything else."

This being Texas, even along the coast, beef brisket is the heart and soul of Little Joe's barbecue offering. Mark uses Black Angus beef, covers it with his own dry rub and smokes it 17 hours over oak. The old-time smoker Mark acquired with the building and the name also kicks out nifty pork ribs, which they cook covered with a dry rub but for far less time, only 6 to 7 hours. Like several other barbecue joints along the winter-warm Texas coast,

Mark has found a ready market for Memphis-style pulled pork as well, especially among the winter Texans most of the area's businesses live on through the off-season months.

Mark prepares traditional potato salad, coleslaw and beans to open each day but reports that his best-selling side dish is french fries. Partly this comes with the territory in a market accustomed to fried seafood; and partly it comes with his hand-cut potatoes dusted with another special seasoning blend. A lot of restaurants can't do what Mark does in recipe development—they have to hire a consultant, after all.

Desserts are made by a member of Little Joe's staff: homemade cakes and pies mostly, but also banana pudding.

Little Joe's has 40 seats inside, plus another 20 outside on a comfortable patio that shines even on a chilly winter day, at least when the sun is beating down and the winds have died down. The patio also offers the best view of something Mark alone might "boast" among Texas barbecue joints—a sand castle that changes throughout the year as though from visits by elves. Actually, every couple of months, a man comes out from Corpus Christi and builds a new sand castle. That was one tradition from the old owner of Little Joe's that Mark saw no reason to "consult" away.

As for his staffing issues, on this particular day, Mark is optimistic. He says he has arranged for two or more promising new employees—young, smart, motivated—to join the team through an arrangement with, of all places, Kazakhstan. After the struggle of relying on seasonal help, Mark is confident that even with exotic accents, these workers can add a lot to serving his "Best Beachin' Barbecue."

"We always tell people our barbecue is worth the trip for lunch," Mark laughs. "Well, I'd say that's quite a trip!"

RUSTY JEEP HICKORY PIT B-B-Q PORT ARANSAS

ADDRESS: 118 S. CUTOFF ROAD, PORT ARANSAS
PHONE: (361) 749-BARN (2276)
ESTABLISHED: 2000
OWNERS: B.H. AND DEBBIE COOK
BEST BITES: BEEF BRISKET, PORK RIBS, PULLED PORK SANDWICH, HOT LINKS, COLESLAW, CORN SALAD, HOMEMADE BREAD, FRUIT COBBLERS
PAYMENT: CREDIT CARDS

B.H. Cook and his wife, Debbie, looked at barbecue up close and personal before they headed south to the coast for a second career. For no fewer than four decades, they ran a cattle ranch about 80 miles southeast of Amarillo.

Still, customers searching for a serious business plan in their decision to become restaurateurs may be disappointed. Debbie was a schoolteacher, you see. When she took retirement from her school system, it just seemed the time was right to go where they'd always loved to go—and, quite frankly, to eat what they'd always loved to eat.

"We used to come down here to the coast each year for the whole month of July," B.H. says. In this latitude, he wonders if what he's about to say is heresy, then decides he's old enough not to care. "I'm not a big fish eater. I'd get down here in July and I'd get full of fish pretty damn quick. The way I saw it, I always used to barbecue at home at my ranch, and I'd gotten pretty good at it. Besides, it seemed like the barbecue I was tasting in places just wasn't as good as what I was coming up with. To me, barbecue is like that old cast-iron skillet. With time, it just gets better and better."

Like most Texans with successful lives on remote ranches, B.H. and Debbie knew how to make a lot with a little. The center of Rusty Jeep, from the moment B.H. envisioned it, would be an old-fashioned brick pit for smoking meats over hickory.

He built this pit one brick at a time, like a worshipper constructing his "holy of holies." Turns out, there was the pit itself, and then a host of adjustments and additions necessary to make a time-honored design more consistent with modern fire codes.

Then there was the matter of wood, no small issue to a guy who'd been cooking over it for most of his life. As the eatery's name implies, B.H. much prefers hickory over the mesquite popular in South Texas, or the oak and pecan favored in other parts of the state. But when he saw the cost of having hickory trucked from Rusk, north of Lufkin, to a barrier island on the Gulf, he decided it was time to do it himself. About once a year, B.H. gets a semi-truck and heads to Rusk to pick up 80,000 pounds of hickory. He has to deliver his load to Port Aransas the "long way" through Corpus Christi, since the loaded semi is too heavy to ride over on the ferry.

Rusty Jeep serves an entirely satisfying Texas-style brisket—how could B.H., a cattle rancher, not. But considering that Rusty Jeep gets some of its best business from winter Texans, the place has come to specialize in pork ribs and pulled pork as well. This seems appropriate in the end, since several non-Texas areas that specialize in pork tend to love to smoke it over hickory. For a time on his written menu, B.H. even offered a Memphis-style pulled pork sandwich with coleslaw between the buns, but he's reverted under "political pressure" to just do it by request.

"It was my wife that got me adding the coleslaw, and some people really like it that way," says B.H., in a kind of boast-meets-disclaimer. "But I got so dang tired of having to explain it to people. Besides," he wonders aloud, "why make anything more complicated when you want things as simple as possible?"

Sausage at Rusty Jeep comes in several flavors and forms, ranging from a spicy Tex-Mex link from San Antonio to a German-style "rope" from a producer between Fredericksburg and Boerne. The coleslaw, once rescued from the pulled pork sandwich, is exemplary—no mayo in sight, just the right crunch of fresh-cut cabbage and the right kick from vinegar —and so is the corn salad, bursting with kernels, celery and bell peppers in a sweet-tangy marinade.

B.H. even dabbles in baking, the farthest thing philosophically from being a pit boss. He bakes his own bread for the restaurant every day, and turns out enough cobblers on Tuesdays and Fridays to get him through the week. If he ever needs more, that could be a problem: "I've only got the one oven."

Finally, there's the business of the place's name, clearly linked in some fashion to the real-live rusty Jeep that sits outside B.H. and Debbie's red barn beneath the sign. Surely, this was picked up as some tongue-in-cheek part of the retro décor, perhaps purloined from some long-ago auction. Not on your life, says B.H.

"We had this old Jeep from our ranch," he says, warming to a story at the very heart of his life. "My father ordered this Jeep at the beginning of World War II, and with the military needing all the production, he had to wait six years for delivery, 'til the war was over. My father was so proud of that Jeep. He used to tell us, 'If the house ever catches fire, don't worry about that—just save the Jeep!' It's a '46 model." B.H. grins, loving the line that apparently always comes next. "I'm a '46 model, too."

JOE COTTEN'S ROBSTOWN

ADDRESS: 607 HIGHWAY 77 SOUTH, ROBSTOWN
PHONE: (361) 767-9973
ESTABLISHED: 1947
OWNER: CECIL COTTEN
BEST BITES: BEEF BRISKET, CHOPPED BEEF SANDWICH, HOMEMADE SAUSAGE, POTATO SALAD
PAYMENT: CREDIT CARDS

To hear his son tell it, Joe Cotten got into the barbecue business 60-plus years ago only to keep his clientele drinking and gambling.

"Back then," Cecil Cotten explains, "gambling was just a misdemeanor, so you paid a fine and went on about your business. My daddy always wanted to get rich without working for a living. That's why he got out of oil and opened a beer joint, you see. There was 14 Spanish beer joints on Avenue N, and then he was the only white guy. He started cooking cuz he noticed guys going home to have supper with their wives. This way he could keep 'em there all night, spending money. But then, they made gambling a federal offense, and my daddy didn't want to go to prison."

The gambling went. The barbecue stayed.

That original beer joint satisfied Joe and his customers from 1947 until 1969,

when a new location on the highway beckoned. Business patterns had changed, and he needed a place that wouldn't be so scary to women and children after dark. Plus, since word of Joe Cotten's barbecue had spread, the place needed to look and feel more like the tourist attraction it had already become. Strange decisions were made as a little beer joint became a huge restaurant capable of serving 385 in a trio of country-kitsch dining rooms. Waiters, for instance, ended up not costumed as Wild West cowpokes but dressed in jackets and bow ties.

"My daddy always had 'em in ties, once we moved over here," Cecil says. "I'm pretty sure he was one of the first to kinda dress it up a bit."

Today, Joe Cotten's is an intriguing collision of dressed-up and dressed-down. The customers *certainly* don't dress up to eat here, and nothing about service involving large hunks of meat on butcher paper would make them think they need to. There's not even a written menu, thus connecting the lowest country café with the finest of fine dining, where waiters often announce the evening's offerings verbally. Of course, within these dark wooden walls, offerings aren't complicated by weird sauces, accompaniments and presentations. In fact, if you've been working here as long as most waiters have—20 to 30 years—you long ago committed the simple list to memory.

"Nothing's changed," Cecil says. "I've been working here forever, and the only thing my daddy ever told me to do when I took over was to go up a nickel or a dime every six months." He laughs. "Now with inflation, we have to go up a quarter."

The Cottens, father and son, didn't stay in business this long without learning to delegate, especially with busy days of 1,500 restaurant diners and outside catering jobs serving even more. For a tour of the restaurant, Cecil turns things over to manager Tommy Rodriguez, an 18-year veteran, who in turn passes a curious visitor on to a head cook named

Mario for a detailed tour of the kitchen.

The kitchen is perhaps Joe Cotten's most impressive feature. According to Tommy, "We let anybody have a look who wants to, as long as they promise not to fall down." Though it's been smoking meat and turning out side dishes since 1969, the space is shiny and spotless enough to have been built yesterday. Mario shows the original black smokers that they had to walk into to turn meat. "It was real hot," he says, instinctively brushing a hand across the hair on his arms now allowed to grow in peace. "It's a lot better now."

These days, Joe Cotten's does all its meats on a series of huge, silver Southern Pride rotisseries. Brisket, sausage, pork ribs and sliced pork are the meats, and mesquite is the wood. In a hive of inter-connected little rooms, the kitchen not only turns out its few homemade sides but produces Joe Cotten's own sausage each day.

Meals are assembled in sequence between the smoker and the dining room, with each meat order on paper set in its own shallow tray, and all trays for a par-ticular table stacked atop a deeper tray holding all the sides. Waiters go forth into the dining room carrying, for the larger tables at least, a barbecue high-rise.

One of the strangest touches—one that, this being Texas, has become a beloved signature—is Joe Cotten's barbe-cue sauce. It almost *isn't*. Instead of the smoother, sweeter, thicker renditions that have become the norm, Joe's sauce is, well, chunky like Tex-Mex salsa. It's full of rough-chopped tomatoes, onions and jalapeños, plus mustard, Worcestershire sauce, salt and pepper. Cecil is proud to tell you, though, that the real secret is the "base" his father took to using, which, of course, his successors use faithfully to this day.

"It's drippings from the brisket," he reveals. "You gotta have some kinda base to put the other stuff in. My daddy said it took him eight years to get this sauce the way he wanted it."

Cecil stops to ponder the price of being a little different. "Hell, some people bring that store-bought stuff in here sometimes. Some people don't like our sauce, but I always tell them to bring their own if they want to. Some of our customers been comin' here so long— some of 'em 50 years—that they think this is their home anyway."

CB'S BAR-B-QUE KINGSVILLE

ADDRESS: 728 N. 14TH STREET, KINGSVILLE
PHONE: (361) 516-1688
ESTABLISHED: 1997
OWNERS: JERRY AND CYNTHIA MILLER
BEST BITES: BEEF BRISKET, PO'BOY OR RICH-BOY SANDWICH, PORK RIBS, JALAPEÑO CORN, BAKED BEANS, SWEET POTATO PIE
PAYMENT: CHECKS AND CREDIT CARDS

Jerry Miller has no illusions that his little barbecue joint in a bizarre geodesic dome will ever enjoy the fame of the 825,000-acre King Ranch that gives his adopted town its name. The empire Captain Richard King founded in 1853 on cattle and horses remains the biggest draw around these vast South Texas plains, whether for those who want to celebrate nature or those who want to hunt it down.

Still, between King Ranch visitors, incoming university students, posted military professionals and bird-watching tourists on their way to the Rio Grande Valley, Jerry and wife Cynthia have built a substantial fan club reaching very far away.

"We get people coming in to eat from Houston and Dallas, even from Oklahoma," he says, nestled at a no-frills table near the iced tea beneath his strik-ing off-white dome. "We get locals, of course, and a lot of hunters from the King Ranch, plus people passing through who've heard about us by word of mouth.

The military has been some of our best friends. Apparently everybody who's ever been stationed here has told lots of their friends about CB's."

For the first two decades of his adult life, Jerry was working on the railroad—just like in the old song. It was that job, in fact, that brought him from his home-town of Abilene to this corner of South Texas. He thought about doing barbe-cue—how could he not, with that being the chosen vocation of relatives in Abilene and Lufkin?—but it seemed a dicey career choice as long as he and Cynthia had a daughter under their roof. When their daughter got married, however, they felt a door swing open for a whole new life. Jerry left the railroad job to concentrate on the preaching he does on Sundays at the Peaceful Holiness Church and on the barbecue he serves at CB's every other day of the week.

"I started out barbecuing for our church," Jerry relates. "We've taken mesquite wood all the way to Hawaii for barbecue, or anywhere else the church had a convention. That kinda set things up for me to open a place of my own. I remember when I was first trying to get some insurance on this building, I still hadn't been able to think of a name. I mean, nothing worked...until my insurance agent told me, 'You Christian brothers sure know how to barbecue.' 'Christian brothers' became CB's. He gave us the name we'd been looking for."

Jerry is especially proud of what he cooks meat on. Positioned in a boxy room tacked onto the back of the dome, the L-shaped brick pit has a separate firebox for each leg. Though he cooks entirely with mesquite wood, the local favorite, and shortcuts with neither gas for heat nor lighter fluid to get his wood started, he did invent a quirky version of a fire starter. He ignites his mesquite with a five-foot pipe that runs off a backyard gas line and, in action, resembles a friendlier version of an old Army flamethrower. "We had to get a little creative, you know," he says.

Most of the usual meats sell well at CB's, starting with the beef brisket Jerry rubs first with his own dry spices and then bastes with his own marinade toward the end of 12 hours of smoking. Most days, he says, the chopped brisket sandwich is CB's biggest seller, though there's also a strong call for pork spareribs and whole barbecued chicken. Pork sausage is a winner here as well, working nicely on the segmented Styrofoam plate with sides ranging from jalapeño whole-kernel corn to something Jerry calls "cheese potatoes." If you mashed potatoes au gratin with a splash of cream, you'd probably end up with something like this.

The baked beans are a wake-up call, too, not only sweet with brown sugar but spicy with touches that might be nutmeg or allspice, giving these beans a strange reminiscence of holiday pumpkin pie. The journey isn't far, in fact, from the quirky spices in Jerry's baked beans to those underpinning Cynthia's wildly popular sweet potato pie.

"Yes," Jerry says, grinning a bit mys-teriously, "we use something like that." Apparently the Sunday exhortation to go into the world and give away all you own does not apply to secret recipes for some of the world's most unusual beans.

CROSSROADS BARBECUE
ALICE

ADDRESS: 406 N. JOHNSON STREET (BUSINESS 281), ALICE

PHONE: (361) 664-1157

ESTABLISHED: 1993

OWNER: FRANK TORRES

BEST BITES: BEEF BRISKET, PORK RIBS, SMOKED SAUSAGE, BARBECUED CHICKEN, CHILI, POTATO SALAD, COLESLAW WITH PINEAPPLE, SPICY BEANS, CORNBREAD

PAYMENT: CREDIT CARDS

During the years Frank Torres spent repairing auto bodies up in Austin, he specialized in Mercedes-Benz—a brand not associated with tolerating shoddy workmanship. Now, after nearly 17 years of cooking barbecue in Alice six days a week, Frank honestly can't say things have changed very much. "I guess I was raised to do things right," he says.

The place that gives Frank his second career doesn't resemble a high-end automobile—doesn't now, didn't then—but it

used to be an old Texaco gas station, for those diners who have to have an automotive theme. Actually, after one initial renovation that left barely a hint of the ser-vice bays and several expansions as the place caught on, few customers even notice the ghost of Texaco past.

"Everything that belonged to the gas station I took out to make it a barbecue place," explains Frank.

Frank enjoyed working in the state's capital, but when his wife started traveling regularly to Alice to help her brother's business with bookkeeping, the kernel of an idea began to sprout. Frank liked what he saw of this tiny town, a bit of a crossroads between San Antonio and the Rio Grande Valley, as well as between Laredo and Corpus Christi.

He made his case to his wife the best he could—starting, no doubt, with how she wouldn't have to drive so far, and probably describing his desire for a new career at the age of 48. "After you get 50," he says now, "who's gonna hire you?"

Instead of looking for a new job, Frank started a new business. And instead of leasing a place to serve barbecue, he bought one. It was all, good days and bad, about a man needing to be his own master. In Frank's case, this involved a great deal of smoke. All through his life, he had cooked barbecue at home for friends and family. He was yet another of those Texas guys who excelled with meat so often that just about everybody said he should open a barbecue joint. They surely figured they'd get to eat there. Little did they know he'd open that barbecue joint five or six hours away.

Things were hard for Crossroads at the beginning, even beyond the hard work of the renovation. Business was slow to build, reflecting the life of a sleepy Texas town. Habits resisted changing around Alice—a town first named Bandana, then Kleberg and finally Alice after the daughter of Richard King—and Crossroads Barbecue wasn't even a habit. Little by little, though, trying this and adding that, Frank found an audience among the locals, along with a healthy smattering of zealots who come here from the Valley, San Antonio, Austin and a great deal farther away. People regularly show up hungry from Oklahoma and Kansas, plus winter Texans from New York or Chicago. This very day, a couple had walked through the door and said they were from Ontario—they'd heard Crossroads had some excellent barbecue.

That it does, primarily because of the intense regimen Frank sticks to with the black steel smoker he built during the renovation. After reconstructing Mercedes after Mercedes, this smoker was probably a piece of cake. He built in no shortcuts for himself—no gas line, no rotisserie, no thermostat—figuring he would rely on instinct and experience. Briskets get a sprinkle of spice, then go into the mesquite smoke for 12 to 13 hours. Pork spareribs get a dash of the same spices before smoking about 2 hours. Barbecued chicken sells well at Crossroads, as does their version of smoked sausage.

At lunch each day, Frank knocks out some remarkable non-barbecue specials: from chicken-fried steak on Mondays through enchiladas on Wednesdays to a spin on the famous King Ranch casserole on Fridays. According to Frank, this dish combines chicken and cornbread with cream of mushroom and cream of chicken soups, plus hot Ro-Tel tomatoes and plenty of melted cheese. No wonder his customers keep coming back.

"Funny thing," says Frank, "they rerouted 281 a couple years ago, and everybody figured we were finished. Then McDonald's came in right down the street, and everybody figured that would kill us off for sure. But I told everybody it would help me, by letting people know we were here. If they come this far for McDonald's, a whole lot of them are going to see our place and decide they'd rather have barbecue. Besides, McDonald's has a big sign out on the new highway. I can't afford a big sign."

THE ORIGINAL WILLIE'S ALAMO

ADDRESS: 320 S. ALAMO ROAD, ALAMO
PHONE: (956) 702-1370
ESTABLISHED: 1990
OWNER: WILLIE GONZALES
BEST BITES: BEEF BRISKET, FAJITAS, PORK RIBS, TACOS, SPANISH RICE, CHARRO BEANS, PEACH COBBLER, COCONUT PIE
PAYMENT: CREDIT CARDS

Above the piano pressed against the wall of unpainted particleboard, amid paraphernalia ranging from old license plates to ranch equipment, there's an impromptu and surely unofficial shrine honoring three generations of Gonzales men.

The oldest photo belongs to Willie's grandfather—who died, Willie says, far too young after working all day in the hot sun. Next up is Willie's father, who lived a good bit longer while watching his sons open a barbecue place. Finally, there's a pencil sketch of Willie himself, happily still alive, kicking and working the pit, overweight and overworked, but very much carried along by his passion for barbecue.

"I'm here at 6:30 every morning, seven days a week," Willie reports. "That's a lot of hours. We're closed only three days per year, and that's my vacation: Thanksgiving, Christmas and Easter Sunday. Some people think it's easy to run a barbecue place. But it's not as easy to run as one of those Mexican places. At a barbecue place, if the food's no good, people won't ever come back."

Willie has been working hard to understand this dynamic, and, of course, to make it his own, since opening Willie B's with his brother Gilbert back in 1990. Despite the end of that partnership and the adjustment of the name to The Original Willie's, Willie himself works hard to understand it still. His son and daughter work beside him, both in their

20s and both balancing barbecue with the demands of college. And while finding good employees is always the hardest part, Willie has built a dependable team—dependable, he stresses, as long as he knows how to do every job and spends most hours there to keep a close eye on things.

Busy times, which include midday and an early dinner hour adopted by winter Texans, find Willie front and center, ringing up orders at the cash register while also answering the phone. On this particular day, most guests coming through the line speak English, while most of the calls are in Spanish. A true child of the Valley, Willie switches back and forth on a shiny linguistic dime.

"We have a lot of winter Texans who jam in here from October to March," he says. "They really go for that stuffed baked potato every Monday, since it's good food, it fills them up and the price is right. It's a 1-pound baked potato, that's why. I sell a lot of those."

Willie cranks up the Spanish to take a phone order, hands the slip down the line and returns to speaking English. "I always knew how to cook, even back when I was working in the oil field, but I had never run a restaurant. I mean, never in my life. Fifteen years ago, I didn't know anything about restaurants." He glances around the full dining room and smiles. "Now I do."

Along the way, Willie mastered the patient art of the pit boss, first and fore-most. He has three open-air smokers out back, their smoke curling into the sun from behind a high wooden fence, plus another four smokers in a separate shop he can use as needed for volume catering. Generally, he uses two different smokers at a time, loaded with two different types of wood: pecan for the beef brisket he slow-cooks for at least 8 hours, and mesquite for the chicken, ribs and fajitas that are a Valley pit master's stock in trade.

Willie's most popular side dishes are his Spanish rice and his glorious charro beans, perfectly balancing heat from jalapeño with cool from cilantro, a textbook lesson in how those two ingredients should work together.

As a business decision, Willie serves smoked pork butt to his winter Texans—a tradition largely unknown in this part of Texas—along with mesquite burgers every day and fried catfish on Fridays, with hand-cut french fries. The best desserts tend to be cobblers—peach, of course, but also apple and cherry. The pies are excellent as well, particularly the pecan and the coconut. Quite a few of this day's customers add those to their trays, "diet" being a four-letter word within these walls.

It's not precisely the popularity of Willie's that's causing the traffic jam outside his front door; it's the construction aimed at widening the street. Workers, their heavy equipment and their torn-up masterpiece-in-the-making force a food delivery truck to take several stabs at getting into the parking lot. Yet the same access problem that has put more than a few restaurants out of business only seems to heighten the frenzied devotion of Willie's fans. Each day they survey the latest construction/destruction, then pick out a path through dust, mud and rocks to Willie's door. Willie doesn't mention "mousetraps" as in the old aphorism, but he has apparently built a better one.

WILLIE B'S BAR B.Q. EDINBURG

ADDRESS: 114 E. LOEB STREET, EDINBURG
PHONE: (956) 318-1373
ESTABLISHED: 1990
OWNER: GILBERT GONZALES
BEST BITES: BEEF BRISKET, FAJITAS, BEEF RIBS, PORK BABY BACK RIBS, SMOKED SAUSAGE, CREAMED CORN CASSEROLE, POTATO SALAD, FRUIT COBBLERS, PECAN PIE
PAYMENT: CREDIT CARDS

In the sleepy hours between lunch and dinner, the long dining room leading back to the counter has the feeling of an Army supply depot about to be moved closer to the front. There are boxes of huge Idaho potatoes stacked high along one wall, joined elsewhere by bags of rice or sugar. Instead of lifting and moving these raw ingredients, the staff sweeps up calmly around them, as though they were beloved pieces of antique furniture.

"Nah," says Gilbert Gonzales, asked if today is delivery day. "That's just what we use."

The collection of movie cowboy photos, bits of ranch equipment, memorabilia from vintage license plates to advertising, and the way-oversized pair of red underwear has much the same feeling, surrounded as they are by plaster walls filled with customer inscriptions. Willie B's seems so impromptu, so unintended, that it's surprising it also feels so eternal.

"I started barbecuing out of my house in Sugar Land back in 1987," Gilbert explains, stepping past a barrier of straight-backed chairs to settle at a table with a Styrofoam cup of sweet tea and lime. "I had worked in the oil field way back, and then later owned a hair salon. But I was barbecuing from home and catering dinners of 500 plates or more. It just kept getting bigger and bigger, 'til I had to open a restaurant."

This realization launched Gilbert on a grueling multiyear, multistep migration from the bright, shiny-new Houston suburb home to the dusty Rio Grande Valley of his birth. That wasn't exactly his idea in the beginning, with possible locations in Richmond and Rosenberg presenting

themselves. But when his brother got laid off from an oil field job back home and then his parents entered their 70s, it seemed high time to spend more of his time in the rich, ethnic cradle of the far south.

Gilbert and his brother opened the original Willie B's in Alamo in 1990, with his brother remaining on-site while Gilbert commuted tirelessly from Sugar Land. At one point in the ordeal, Gilbert was leaving Sugar Land at 2 or 3 each Monday morning to be in Alamo to open Willie B's at 11. "This was very hard on my family," he remembers. "We all made a lot of sacrifices, and when you have kids, there's no way to ever get back the things you miss."

The welfare of his aging parents finally pushed business concerns aside. Gilbert sold the salon and moved his wife and four children to the Valley shortly after he and his brother opened a second Willie B's, this one in the increasingly suburban-looking county seat of Edinburg. "We could have grown a lot from here," says Gilbert. "I mean, a lot! We could have dominated the entire Valley, from Laredo all the way to Brownsville." Why the Gonzales brothers didn't has consumed much of their lives since 1999.

Working together full-time, they argued over just about everything, even the recipe for their mother's creamed corn casserole. In the spirit of Martin Luther, Gilbert drew up a three-page list of things he wanted to change. The end result was an even bigger change: the bitter breakup of their partnership, with Gilbert taking Willie B's in Edinburg and Willie getting the place in Alamo, which he logically renamed The Original Willie's.

Today, between the boxes of potatoes and the bags of rice and sugar, Gilbert presumably does everything on that three-page list. They were his rules, after all. He smokes his brisket at least 18 hours over pecan wood, an oddity in the mesquite-loving Valley, in a 22-foot tubular smoker with a firebox and four grates.

Gilbert uses no dry rub or marinade on his brisket, and none of the foil sometimes used to let steam speed up the cooking. "When you see that pink ring around the outer edge of the meat, you know you're smokin'."

Willie B's meat list takes in many things perfect for that old-fashioned smoker—whole chickens, pork butt, pork baby back ribs, beef ribs served as huge chunks of meat cut from the bone, turkey breasts. Gilbert also dishes up fajitas every day, along with oddities like beef sweetbreads—the acquired-taste organ meat known along the border as mollejas. These are fried and dropped into a taco with plenty of jalapeño-studded pico de gallo.

Despite the omnipresent rice and charro beans among the side dishes, not to mention the Texas-wide potato salad and coleslaw, there also is Gilbert's mother's sweet and savory creamed corn casserole, the dish that aggravated the tension between the two brothers. For obvious emotional reasons, it remains one of Gilbert's personal favorites.

"Thanksgiving and Christmas were the only times she made this," he says. "Now you can come to Willie B's and have it every day of the year."

UNCLE ROY'S BBQ PHARR

ADDRESS: 602 E. BUSINESS HIGHWAY 83, PHARR
PHONE: (956) 702-6967
ESTABLISHED: 2005
OWNERS: ROY AND MONICA PALACIOS
BEST BITES: BEEF BRISKET, PORK RIBS, BARBECUED CHICKEN, SPANISH RICE, CHARRO BEANS, MASHED POTATOES AND GRAVY
PAYMENT: CREDIT CARDS

For more than 50 years, Roy Palacios' grandfather barbecued cows' heads the old-fashioned way, digging a pit in the dirt, wrapping each head in moistened

burlap and burying it with hot coals overnight. By morning, the head was cooked—and the family could pick off the meat and serve it with warm tortillas for breakfast.

Roy offers no apologies that traditional barbacoa de cabeza is not on the menu of his barbecue joint. For one thing, health department regulations make it virtually impossible to cook barbacoa the way his grandfather did, with some version of roasting or steaming being the closest a restaurant can get. For another thing, it's really hard work. For a while, he and his wife, Monica, offered barbacoa on weekends, the way some Tex-Mex places offer menudo. But with the need to relax after a busy week, Roy—like many Hispanic pit bosses across the Valley—came to see traditional barbacoa as a case of diminishing returns.

"There'll always be barbacoa," he says, "but people are making it different, steam-cooking it and stuff. I don't know that I'll ever go back to cooking it with mesquite wood. Though I still do it once in a while for my family and friends, I think it's a tradition that's coming to an end. It was too much work for me and my wife. We had the business, but we didn't have the energy."

Ironically, the Tex-Mex joint right next door to Uncle Roy's promises precisely that—with "Barbacoa de Cabeza" written large on a big sign out front. Yet to Roy, who cooked barbacoa beside his grandfather from the age of 8 onward, the existence of something by the same name serves only to rub it in. Next door, barbacoa takes its exotic place on the buffet line with mollejas (sweetbreads) and tripas (tripe), having for most Valley residents fallen off the American menu to which it lent its name, barbecue.

Roy's grandfather retired from digging the pit after half a century (or, perhaps more accurately, retired from letting Roy dig the pit), and the grandson drifted naturally into the corporate version of what he'd been doing since childhood—foodservice. In particular, years spent with KFC taught him a treasure trove of lessons about quality, service and cleanliness—the mantra-like QSCs of a multiunit operator. Those years also filled him with nostalgia for the old ways, at least some of them, and especially the old flavors delivered by smoke.

"You need to find the right mesquite," Roy cautions, speaking with his two heroes, John Wayne and Hank Williams Jr., gazing down from the walls as solemn witnesses. "I've been chopping wood since I was 5 years old, and there's a lot of bad mesquite out there. No question about it, you need to know your wood."

As it turns out, Roy knows more than mesquite, and by the way, he likes only the red variety. While that is his pick for barbecuing chicken, he smokes with pecan wood for his brisket, pork ribs and sausage. It's the flavor of mesquite he's shooting for with poultry, which responds well to the hotter, quicker cooking. Slow-cooking with pecan, on the other hand, delivers a deeper, richer taste that Roy and his customers look for in the red meats. Pecan adds a nice red, or at least pink, color to these meats as well.

In the spirit of his foodservice experience, Roy has developed a two-part process for cooking his brisket in one of three giant metal pits behind his kitchen. After a sprinkle with seasoning, each brisket goes on the pecan smoke for about 4 hours, then gets wrapped in foil and moves to another pit with really low heat to finish cooking 10 hours more. As an overnight process, Roy makes the transfer before shutting down for the night, leaving the brisket in the loving hands of pecan wood all night long.

Monica handles the rice and beans, surely the most popular accompaniment at Uncle Roy's, whether the meat is brisket or chicken, spareribs or sausage. The potato salad is made fresh every day, a big seller right along with the indulgent mashed potatoes and gravy Roy perfected during his days with KFC.

Except at holiday time, desserts are mostly a no-show in Roy's kitchen. They simply aren't important enough to justify the effort. For most of the year, Roy simply offers whatever store-bought sweets he can get his hands on. During the holidays, however, his sister whips up one of

the lushest flans anywhere, complete with that golden caramel sauce that coats the dish beneath the custard, along with batch after batch of hot, fresh cookies.

"I'm not big on baking," Roy admits, and that's probably okay. How many other guys can say they spent their youths digging holes in the ground to barbecue cow heads?

THE RED BARN B.B.Q McALLEN

ADDRESS: 4701 N. McCOLL ROAD, McALLEN
PHONE: (956) 631-8332
ESTABLISHED: 1993
OWNERS: THE VILLAREAL FAMILY
BEST BITES: BEEF BRISKET TACOS WITH BARBECUE SAUCE AND/OR PICO DE GALLO, BARBECUED CHICKEN, SPANISH RICE, CHARRO BEANS, FLAN DE LA CASA
PAYMENT: CREDIT CARDS

If Tomas and Felicitas Villareal had a favorite show from TV's Golden Age, it should have been *My Three Sons*. It was their three sons, after all, who would assume the barbecue legacy they began in a small portable building in 1982 and carry into the 21st century.

Yet another son, by the way, would move that original building right next door to the former residence that became The Red Barn. He would run it as a casual Tex-Mex place called La Palmas—four brothers working in the same block, serving the two culinary styles that define South Texas and that, with numbing regularity, meet in the middle.

"Our brother Juan wanted to cook something different," observes Tomas Jr., taking a break from unloading mesquite wood into the open-air shed where The Red Barn's three startlingly different smokers reside.

"It's like a Mexican tradition here," brother Harvey calls down from the bed of the pickup, hardly missing a beat tossing thick pieces of wood to the ground.

"You go farther north, I guess, it's like different food."

In a sense, barbecue in the Rio Grande Valley is "different food"—at least as set against the standard menu at almost any-place else in Texas. While potato salad and coleslaw are prepared and offered, they usually take a backseat to Spanish rice. And instead of barbecued or baked beans with plenty of brown sugar, places like The Red Barn trot out spiced-up charro beans with more than a sugges-tion of jalapeño. Warm flour tortillas replace white bread, to no one's particular chagrin. Pico de gallo gives barbecue sauce a run for its money, while banana pudding definitely gets kicked to the side-lines by incredibly lush Spanish flan.

On this particular day, Noe Villareal is B.O.D.—brother on duty—something the restaurant wouldn't dare open without. That means he sprints for hours between the smoking pits and the kitchen, deliver-ing meats to the cooks as needed. Though he tends to defer to his brothers on the history of The Red Barn, he clearly feels no lack of expertise when it comes to smoking meats.

There are not one but three smokers in the shed, he explains, and, atypically, each is used for a different meat. The large barrel smoker at the center of things handles brisket, fajitas and sausage, while its smaller sibling takes on only pork ribs. At the outer edge, barely noticeable except for the thick smoke drifting out from a lid jerry-rigged from corrugated metal, is a low brick pit that smokes only chicken. The thing is downright rustic, or ancient, or both, suggesting less a cooking device in modern America than a thrown-together contraption used to jerk pork in a remote corner of Jamaica. Still, Noe doesn't want a visitor going away thinking things are merely quaint.

"The bricks hold the heat in better than any metal," he says. Noe smiles, tap-ping the side of his head with an index finger. "You know, there's a lot of science in what the old people used to do."

Over the years, as The Red Barn's rep-utation kept growing, a series of changes had to be made. The first was the move into this larger location, with only one room used for customers and all the rest as a family residence. All four brothers lived in this house with Tomas Sr. and Felicitas, each slowly being edged out by the need for more restaurant space and the desire for independence.

Now that every available inch of the brothers' former home is devoted to serv-ing South Texas barbecue, each can come to work and know he's carrying on a tra-dition. Besides, if Tomas Jr., Harvey and Noe ever get tired of eating their own barbecue, they can always pop over to Las Palmas and hit up their brother Juan.

LONE STAR BBQ McALLEN

ADDRESS: 3619 N. 10TH STREET, McALLEN
PHONE: (956) 664-9988
ESTABLISHED: 1988
OWNER: DARRELL MYSKA
BEST BITES: BEEF BRISKET, PORK AND BEEF SAUSAGE, SMOKED TURKEY BREAST, CORNMEAL-BATTERED FRIED CATFISH, FRUIT COBBLERS WITH HOMEMADE VANILLA ICE CREAM, GRAPEFRUIT PIE (SEASONAL, MISSION LOCATION ONLY)
PAYMENT: CREDIT CARDS

Darrell Myska was in the insurance business—happily and profitably, it would seem—when his father in the construction business called him and invited him to help open a barbecue place. Darrell had been cooking barbecue since the days he served up brisket for his fraternity brothers at Texas Lutheran in Seguin, so he had a grip on the culinary challenge ahead. Yet it was something apart from the cooking that reeled him in.

"I'm not a coat and tie kind of guy, but that's where I was at," Darrell recalls. "These days, if a dishwasher doesn't show up or the pit breaks down, I might wonder why I left insurance. But I love the people you meet doing this, and I love the freedom. I wear shorts to work every day, even if it's winter. I feel like it's summer, and I'm going to dress like it's summer all the time."

Darrell left one old career behind and pounced with both feet into a new one, working to master with consistency the skills he'd merely dallied with in college. His father bought the new business some time, staying in construction until Lone Star BBQ was able to consume and reward him. Before long, even Darrell's mother was involved, supplying the men with recipes for lovely side dishes and desserts like the cobbler made with peach, apple, blackberries or blueberries—whatever fruit is in season.

The beginnings of Lone Star were humble, a small location Darrell now describes as a "hole in the wall." Despite the lack of creature comforts, the food kept customers coming back. There were often more customers, in fact, than the original Lone Star could hold, but Darrell considered it a matter of pride to serve them with quality and friendliness. It wasn't long before the best customers were asking why he wasn't looking for a bigger, better restaurant.

"People kept telling us we needed to grow," he says. "But to be honest, the real reason we moved was the place was falling down around my ears. We got the new location, and while the parking is still bad, at least the place isn't falling down."

The Myskas, who point to their origins among the Bohemian Czech immigrations to Texas, found a previous barbecue place that was both larger and cleaner. With the construction expertise supplied by Darrell's father, it was no huge task to renovate, going so far as to encircle the dining room with fun house-wacky windows that are decidedly off-kilter. "My dad thought people would get a kick outta that," he says.

As for the pits that make the magic happen, Darrell started out with a

Southern Pride rotisserie but let that be trucked away when a second Lone Star opened in Mission with his parents in charge.

Borrowing the best elements from the Southern Pride and other touches from an Ole Hickory, he and a friend built two of their own rotisseries. Darrell burns only mesquite wood in his pits—"no mixing," he says, as though it's a law on the books somewhere—and boasts he can control the exact temperature and amount of smoke reaching meat at any time of the day or night.

Darrell's dry-rubbed brisket, fresh from the smoker after 12 to 14 hours overnight, is Lone Star's best-selling meat, followed by the tender pork spareribs with a sweet teriyaki-kissed sauce, sausage and barbecued chicken. Also wildly popular are the daily specials, such as slow-smoked beef fajitas on Tuesday, smoked pork loin on Wednesday, fried catfish on Fridays and baby back ribs on Saturday.

"No matter what they like, I'm going to get people in here at least one day of the week," says Darrell. "And if I feel like smoking a good prime rib, I can just offer it as a special that day. That's what's good about owning your own business."

Dessert gives Lone Star another chance for uniqueness, one that oddly sells well at the Mission store (from which his parents retired in 2006) yet not well enough to justify offering in McAllen. That would be the grapefruit pie, embraced in the heart of South Texas citrus country and filled with whole sections of the area's famous pink grapefruit. It's served only during citrus season, from just before Christmas 'til the first warm days of spring, and Valley residents drive from all over to enjoy it.

So why, everyone asks Darrell, doesn't grapefruit pie sell at the original Lone Star BBQ in McAllen when it flies off the shelf in Mission? "Don't ask me why," he says with the weary smile of one who's been there and done that. "I can't tell you why."

SMOKEY'S BAR-B-QUE SAN JUAN

ADDRESS: 608 W. HIGHWAY 83, SAN JUAN
PHONE: (956) 702-4127
ESTABLISHED: 1991
OWNER: JUAN SALINAS
BEST BITES: BEEF BRISKET, GRILLED FAJITAS, BARBECUED CHICKEN, SPANISH RICE, CHARRO BEANS, PECAN PIE
PAYMENT: CREDIT CARDS

As most Americans have come to understand, fast food is all about systems—simple, no-fail ways to do things that let consistent food be prepared by employees of finite training and little imagination. As any pit boss will tell you, barbecue is the opposite of fast food.

For one thing, it's excruciatingly slow. Perhaps more important, barbecue is a culinary art built as much on reaction as on action. When the meat does this, you do that. When the meat does that, you do this. It's all in the eye of the maker, and in the way meat feels when poked with a finger or prodded with a fork. The accurate answer to any barbecue question, whether anyone will tell you or not, is always: it depends.

Still, having cut his teeth in fast food—managing Church's fried chicken stores in the Valley and as far north as Houston—Juan Salinas tries every day to wrestle an ambiguous, intensely fickle form of cooking into something he can legislate by way of an employee handbook. For the most part, with an original location in San Juan, an expansion store in Pharr and almost certainly more to come, he seems to be succeeding.

"I was always doing barbecue for free," he explains, "volunteering for just about any fund-raiser anybody had. I decided I might as well get paid for it. It wasn't so much the barbecue business I wanted as the chance to own my own business. I knew how to barbecue already, so this made the most sense."

As Juan learned long ago frying chicken, the key to doing barbecue his way was to break difficult and complex tasks requiring a master's touch into brief steps that virtually no one could mess up. This way, he says, he can "duplicate" himself, whether that means consistent food cooked and served at multiple locations or simply taking a day off. Surely the most controversial of these moves is the way Smokey's cooks brisket...usually the litmus test for the "low and slow" crowd that glares at a rotisserie with a thermostat as though it's an instrument of the devil.

"My brisket is 80 to 85 percent broiled in a gas oven, then finished the last 15 to 20 percent in the smoker for flavor," says Juan. In terms of time, this means a process expedited from the Texas norm, each brisket spending about 4 hours in the oven and $1\frac{1}{2}$ to 2 more in the smoker. For that last step, a purist in his own fashion, Juan goes along with the local love of mesquite, using it for smoke even when he's knocking out 800 to 1,000 plates at a time for the school and church fund-raisers that remain a backbone of his business.

In terms of sales, Smokey's serves beef fajitas in amounts right behind brisket, and barbecued chicken not too far behind that. Side dishes include items expected in barbecue joints all over Texas, but built out with the Spanish rice and charro beans demanded by customers in the Valley. Juan's best efforts to take that dynamic duo off his menu have never lasted long. "This is the Valley," he says, "and you just gotta have 'em."

Though tourism has grown in the cities along the Mexican border in recent years—with visitors from both sides of the international bridges—this is not a market that strikes Juan as promising. Neither do the winter Texans who improve other restaurants' bottom lines between October and March. He sees his customers as almost entirely local, particularly those who first sample his food at charity events. And having been in business since 1991, he's known a lot of his best customers from the days they came in with their parents.

"They started out as kids 16 years ago, eating a chopped beef sandwich for 99 cents," Juan says. "Now they're married and bringing kids of their own."

SONNY BRYAN'S
DALLAS

....

ADDRESS: 2202 INWOOD ROAD, DALLAS
PHONE: (214) 357-7120
ESTABLISHED: 1958, WITH ROOTS IN 1910
OWNERS: WALKER HARMAN AND PARTNERS
BEST BITES: BEEF BRISKET, PORK RIBS, FRIED
ONION RINGS, FRENCH FRIES, POTATO SALAD,
TWO-MEAT PO'BOY
PAYMENT: CREDIT CARDS

The investors who bought Sonny Bryan's Barbecue from Sonny the man and turned it into Sonny the corporation in the years since his death have 10 locations now, including a predictably glitzy one at Macy's in the Galleria. Yet pilgrims from across Texas and around the world continue to forgo creature comforts at these other stores and make their way to the original, where barbecue comes out on banged-up plates arranged on even more banged-up trays that can be carried to one of 26 weathered wooden school desks.

It was in this setting that Sonny Bryan built his reputation and what presumably was his fortune. The year 1910 proclaimed on various printed materials actually points back to his grandfather's barbecue joint, while many around Dallas still remember his father's place known as Bryan's. Yet the fame enjoyed by William Jennings Bryan, known universally as Red, proved nothing compared to that garnered by his son, William Jennings Bryan Jr., known to his family and eventually to the world as Sonny. What else can you say of a barbecue place honored with a James Beard award and chosen to feed Julia Child on a visit that also showed off food by Dean Fearing and Stephan Pyles?

"We're on the Travel Channel and the Food Network," says Dave Rummel, general manager of the surprisingly tiny original Sonny's. "When people come in, they have all these questions about what Rachael Ray ate, so we get slowed down

trying to answer them. Some people get mad because we're not taking orders fast enough or getting their food out fast enough, but all this stuff takes time."

No way around it, Sonny Bryan's is—in the hearts and minds of some locals—a victim of its own success. Ever since Sonny discovered he was dying of cancer and started talks with an investor group led by Walker Harman, an equal legend has been growing that Sonny's isn't the place it used to be. Few people factor in that the corporation preserves the original as it was, even as it expands the brand elsewhere. And few factor in that Sonny's sons grew up to be a famous dentist and a well-known Methodist minister who now heads the theology department at SMU.

"They sure didn't want to get in here and serve barbecue every day," explains Dave. "Sonny worked so his boys could go to college. If they wanted to sign up or not after that, either way was fine with him."

Sonny launched the place in 1958, with no indoor seating. It was the '50s, after all, so for the first few years he had pretty carhops lifted straight from the frames of *American Graffiti*. Equally in keeping with the times, he sold as many hamburgers and milk shakes as orders of barbecue. Over the years, the carhops and their signature foods faded from popularity here, though not the notion of eating in your car. Most days at Sonny's, during the hours considered lunch, there are pickups parked all over the lot with their tailgates down and hungry workers with legs dangling and mouths munching.

At some point, Sonny closed in a new section up front and installed the now-signature school desks. During weekday lunchtimes, every desk tends to be taken… with quarters so close it's hard to not think of cribbing off your neighbor's exam paper. According to Dave, thanks to these desks, he has been a personal witness to America's obesity problem, since more and more of his customers try and fail to squeeze in. "There's a lot of people," he lets on, "who say they want to eat in here but end up at the tables outside."

The menu at Sonny Bryan's is presented on a series of signs posted above the line. Beef brisket and St. Louis-style pork ribs, which make up 80 percent of Sonny's meat sales, are cooked without any dry rub or mopping sauce on an old brick pit fueled by hickory. In a world that seeks more and more complicated ways to apply smoke to meat, at Bryan's the meat sits pretty much atop the fire, which therefore must be kept low to cook slow. That about does it for each brisket, which is then sliced or chopped to order. Ribs, on the other hand, get smoked first, then dunked by the rack in barbecue sauce and allowed to marinate in the refrigerator. For service, racks are sliced into ribs, covered with more sauce and finished on a hot grill—thus the delightful, brown-sugary-crisp caramelization around the edges.

Side dishes at Sonny's are limited and mostly traditional; even the potato salad that's omnipresent everywhere else had to be added here when the new owners took over. Still, nothing outsells the favorite side: fried onion rings with batter engineered by Sonny himself to taste incredible with his barbecue sauce. There's even a sign on the wall encouraging diners to make this counterintuitive pairing.

Every day that Dave comes to work, he knows he's going to meet one or more customers who knew Sonny way back when. And every day, he knows, there are people around Dallas who stopped being Sonny's customers the minute the place was sold. Dave wishes people would let their taste buds be their guide, instead of some mixture of perceived wisdom and unjustified nostalgia.

"The legend has grown, and people love to complain by saying how Sonny wouldn't allow this or wouldn't have stood for that," he offers. "It's almost like Sonny was a saint-type person. Come on: Sonny drove a Mercedes. He liked to bet on horse races. He always had plenty of money, and he put his sons through college paying cash. It's not like he was Mother Teresa."

PEGGY SUE BBQ DALLAS

ADDRESS: 6600 SNIDER PLAZA, DALLAS
PHONE: (214) 987-9188
ESTABLISHED: 1989
OWNER: MARC HALL
BEST BITES: BABY BACK RIBS, BEEF BRISKET, CHOPPED BRISKET QUESADILLA, MASHED POTATOES, STEAMED BROCCOLI, COLESLAW WITH BOILED VINEGAR DRESSING, FRIED APRICOT PIE
PAYMENT: CREDIT CARDS

Because barbecue is such a tightly focused, obsessive-compulsive cooking style, the number of barbecue guys who've enjoyed success with other types of food is actually quite small. Yet Marc Hall is serving up barbecue at Peggy Sue today precisely because his previous Amore and Cisco Grill had already proven to be knockouts in the neighborhood.

"This place was a barbecue joint for 50 years before it closed in the '80s," Marc says of the space known long ago as Howard & Peggy's and later as Peggy's Beef Bar. "Since we have two other restaurants here, the owners approached us about taking this over. I mean, we kinda looked at it and at each other and said, 'No thanks.' Finally, the guy said he'd give it to us rent-free until we figured out what we wanted to do with it. That time we couldn't help but say yes."

Marc, who looks like he should play charming, salt-and-pepper college professors in the movies, was smart enough to keep "Peggy" from the place's original name...especially after he found some of the old porcelain letters lying around. By adding a wise tribute to his wife, Susan, he not only could reference the hit song "Peggy Sue" by Buddy Holly of Lubbock but the Francis Ford Coppola nostalgia fest *Peggy Sue Got Married*, starring Kathleen Turner and Nicolas Cage. Clearly, something '50s was going on here, with all those shimmering memories of two-straw milk shakes at diners. So that's the look Marc went with for *his* Peggy Sue, made specific to Texas at every opportunity. It's a bit like *The Last Picture Show* before the sadness set in.

Still, if the '50s was very much on Marc's mind as atmosphere, in terms of food he was thinking both older and younger than those cream-and-butter-besotted days of Eisenhower optimism. "Sometimes people say we're New Age barbecue," he laughs, clearly amused by the kinds of things people say. "Come on, all we wanted to do was have some fresh, colorful vegetables with our traditional Texas barbecue. We realized it would be very easy to compete with what we saw out there. Things here are fresh. We don't buy things in bags."

In preparation for opening Peggy Sue in 1989, Marc did what any college professor should do: plenty of research. Leaving his Italian and Mexican restaurants in capable hands, he packed Susan and their two young daughters off to discover the best Texas barbecue had to offer. This he found, to his taste anyway, in the Hill Country. Though he was more familiar with the hickory beloved in North Texas, he was seduced entirely by the oak he saw being used in the state's center—he liked that it wasn't so sweet. Of course, he talked tirelessly with the pit bosses about those twin barbecue fetishes, time and temperature. "Low and slow" he was told repeatedly, and like a young apprentice (despite his years of restaurant success), he took it all in.

Along the way to opening day, Marc acquired a J&R rotisserie smoker from the nearby town of Mesquite that cooks up to 700 pounds of meat at a time, a smoker capable of handling the brisket that Peggy Sue's current pit guys cook overnight for about 15 hours. Still, Marc ventured out on his own on one to-him significant point. Instead of the tradition of all meats being finished before the day's first customer walks in, Peggy Sue keeps meats cooking all night and all day—barbecue's closest proximity to the French *à la minute*. Timing to cook brisket to-the-minute isn't exactly easy when it takes 15 hours.

"On our smoker, the fire is never out," says Marc. "We're serving stuff as fresh as we can."

With a vision of full dinner service more front and center here than at the typical barbecue joint, Marc started with the meats—buying top-quality beef, baby back ribs, Polish kielbasa sausage and even whole turkey breasts, the latter as opposed to "those glued-together things that taste like Jell-O."

With the foundation solidly built, he turned his eyes to everything around it: from appetizers like chopped brisket quesadillas and griddled artisan bread to updated sides like fresh spinach or squash casserole, to dessert. For each meal's final flourish, Peggy Sue concentrates on the one thing every Texan knows is better than a freshly baked pie—a freshly *fried* one. This required caloric research as well, but Marc and his girls finally tracked down the perfect combination of thick, flaky, buttery crust with sweet-but-not-too-sweet fruit filling. Apricot seems to be the favorite of all concerned.

"It's all high quality and it's all extremely consistent," Marc says, speaking as someone who knows the restaurant drill. "And it's all full service. We wanted to be not a cafeteria."

BIG AL'S SMOKEHOUSE DALLAS

ADDRESS: 3125 INWOOD ROAD, DALLAS
PHONE: (214) 350-2649
ESTABLISHED: 1973
OWNER: AL PLASKOFF
BEST BITES: BEEF BRISKET, HOT LINKS, RIBS, COLESLAW, FRUIT COBBLERS, PECAN PIE
PAYMENT: CREDIT CARDS

Each December, as mainstream barbecue joints across Texas give themselves over to Christmas trees, Christmas lights, Christmas carols and even the occasional cowboy-themed Christmas Nativity, "Big Al" Plaskoff makes a somewhat different holiday statement. You see it there in the front window, not jumping out at you, but definitely not hidden either. Al, a former butcher who got drawn up the Texas food chain, must be just about the only barbecue guy in the Lone Star State to welcome his holiday diners with a menorah.

Beyond that graceful symbol of the Jewish Festival of Lights, however, Big Al and his ideas about barbecue are Texas all the way.

"It's great food with great service, and Al wouldn't have it any other way," says manager Scott Collard, a veteran of the company when it had as many as four locations scattered around the Metroplex. "Pedro back there's a great guy, the cashier's a great girl, and you got me usually walking around. A whole lot of people come in that I consider my friends, even though I never see them outside of here."

Only one Big Al's remains from the days of eateries in Richardson, Garland and Irving, but in some ways the place is where its heart always was. The Dallas location was once Loren Brown's BBQ—until, that is, Al bought it in 1973 and renamed it for himself. Odds are good, says Scott, that Al knew the folks at Loren Brown's from his days selling them meat. Other than barbecue joints back then, he primarily sold to school districts—something he happily felt no inclination to buy. The popularity of the first Big Al's led to inevitable expansion, something Al has backed away from as he has grown older. Focus seems to be the key, relates Scott, focus and concentration.

"Like most things," he says, "restaurants come and go. Somebody walks in and offers you a lot of money, it's time to sell."

Though Texas plays a significant role in the décor of Big Al's, so does a lot of personal entertainment and sports memorabilia. Signed T-shirts and other rock concert swag have come Al's way over the years, all to end up papering his walls. Other displays come from catering gigs in the distant and not-so-distant past, decades marked by the odd haircuts seen on Al and his many guests. Everyone in the party montages seems to be having a very good time. Beyond that, Big Al's is pleasantly utilitarian, with a selection of booths and tables spreading out from the cashier and iced tea dispensers at the end of the cafeteria line.

Over his years of tasting barbecue (a lot of it surely made with meats he supplied), Al came to prefer the taste of

hickory smoke over that of any other wood...so, of course, his customers now prefer it, too. The smoke goes on by way of two rotisseries in the back—one inside that's used daily, the other loaded on a truck outside the back door for lighting whenever Big Al's gets too busy. "If it's a little cold outside," Scott instructs, "it's going to take a little more wood."

Briskets go on about 3 p.m. and stay on over super-low heat for 18 to 20 hours, one of the longer cooking times around. That means they come off about 9 a.m., letting the ribs have the smoker to themselves for a while. Other meats get added throughout the morning: turkey breasts, chicken breasts and a dynamic duo of sausages. The hot links at Big Al's are definitely heat-driven, while the German-style pork-and-beef blend is all about the smoke.

As far as side dishes are concerned, the smokehouse offers a nice, predictably mustardy potato salad and a surprising version of coleslaw that's light, sweet and tangy. The same pinto beans come in two flavors: spicy Old West with jalapeño, chili powder and cumin, or sweet-smoke barbecue ladled hot from a pot that spent hours beside the meats in the smoker.

Most popular desserts are the cobblers—peach, cherry or apple; but a definite fan club has formed around the carrot cake, German chocolate cake and time-honored pecan pie. Even through the festive days and nights of December, the menorah in the window is by no means the only tradition embraced at Big Al's Smokehouse.

JASPER'S GOURMET BACKYARD CUISINE PLANO

ADDRESS: 7161 BISHOP ROAD, PLANO
PHONE: (469) 229-9111
ESTABLISHED: 2003
OWNER: KENT RATHBUN
BEST BITES: PROSCIUTTO-WRAPPED SHRIMP AND GRITS, GRILLED CHICKEN MASA SOUP, SLOW-SMOKED BABY BACK RIBS, ALMOND-CRUSTED RAINBOW TROUT, TEXAS PEACH BARBECUED PORK TENDERLOIN, BANANA PARFAIT, ROCKY ROAD ICE CREAM SANDWICH
PAYMENT: CREDIT CARDS

Kent Rathbun, who came to Dallas to cook at the Mansion on Turtle Creek, bristles when asked why a trained, experienced and now-famous chef with his own destination restaurant called Abacus would go slumming and learn how to barbecue.

"I was a young pit master who later learned how to be a chef," he says with emotion, that of a man who's finally come to understand his life story, "not vice versa." He stops, as though wondering how much his visitor really wants to know. "As long as I can remember life, my dad was barbecueing. He was a total, 100-percent backyard grill guy. I never had better brisket anywhere, and I say that as a professional chef.

"This menu represents many dishes from my mother, my father and my grandparents. And from the time I was 8, I'd stay up with my dad on Saturday nights to put the brisket on the smoker. He had me basting those things 'til I couldn't keep awake anymore. Even then, Dad would nudge me every so often and say, 'Go down and baste the brisket.' "

The father who raised both Kent and his brother Kevin (of Nava and Rathbun's in Atlanta) to be famous chefs belonged to perhaps the greatest barbecue fan club that ever existed—the brotherhood of touring jazz and blues musicians. From

Louis Armstrong to B.B. King to Wynton Marsalis, the arrival routine for such artists has changed not one bit: find the gig, find the hotel, find some barbecue. Inspired by what he tasted in his travels, as well as by what he tasted at home in Kansas City, Kent's father perfected his own skills to the point of asking to cook for his buddies in hotel kitchens on the road. Back home, he made sure his sons knew their way around not only a smoky backyard pit but the classics of Kansas City's barbecue scene, especially the legendary Arthur Bryant's.

"It's one of my earliest memories," Kent recalls. "I was standing by this counter while my dad was talking to somebody, and I was too little to see over it. So I kinda pressed myself up on my arms 'til I could see, and there was Arthur Bryant himself talking barbecue with my dad. And there was this big old pit with a stack of wood on it. And there on top of this wood was a very mean-looking Doberman, who looked up and growled at me. I guess he decided I was too small to be much of a threat."

The single most intriguing thing about Kent's concept for Jasper's, beyond its tagline "Gourmet Backyard Cuisine," is the absence of a true smoker in the kitchen. At the original location in Plano, as well as in expansions to The Woodlands and then to the Austin area, Kent has not only installed the "next best thing" but has, in a sense, carried barbecue even farther back to its roots.

The smoker-grill he's designed for Jasper's starts out each day as a rotisserie, with chicken, turkey, baby back pork ribs and even rainbow trout turning slowly high above a fire of oak and hickory. At this point, the grill man pushes the burning wood and glowing coals forward under a low grate, adding more wood as the evening progresses, to create a high-heat grill for finishing smoked meats as well as cooking flat iron steaks. There's no time-honored 18 or 20 hours of cooking beef brisket at Jasper's, but there is the tradition and the taste, delivered by a man who remembers the boy who loved nothing better.

A perfect example of what a chef-artist does with old-fashioned barbecue is what Kent does with his baby back ribs...even before he dishes them up with New Age/Old World "creamy baked potato salad." You have to start, he says, with a great product—which is chefspeak for "expensive meat." Each rack gets rubbed with olive oil and a spice blend created for the occasion, then allowed to marinate with those flavors for 12 hours or more. These racks are then cooked over a low fire until medium-well-done, being flipped often and basted with a citrus barbecue sauce. Once they reach that desired status in life, they are transferred to a pan, covered with foil and chilled. When ordered, the racks are cut into "bricks" of three ribs each and finished on the by-now super-hot grill.

As though in response, Kent's version of traditional Texas potato salad starts out as a baked potato, gets cubed and flash-fried, then mixed with sour cream and spices where the mayo normally would be. Even to a potato salad lover—or, indeed, to a baked potato lover or french fry lover—Kent Rathbun's spin on this classic is an epiphany.

One of the joys of Jasper's, seldom seen in other, far simpler Texas barbecue joints, is first-rate appetizers, soups and salads. Best starters include the prosciutto-wrapped shrimp and grits, direct from the Carolinas by way of polenta-crazed northern Italy...the jumbo lump crab cakes, made a textural wonderland by tomatillo-poblano cream and jicamatortilla slaw…and (for blue cheese fans) a freshly fried order of perfect potato chips doused with creamy-crumbly Maytag blue. The best soup is the grilled chicken masa, a bit like Tex-Mex "tortilla soup" that's died and gone to heaven, while the single best salad wanders far from Texas barbecue. It features red chile-seared ahi tuna, with rice noodles and a heat-infused Thai vinaigrette.

Happily, desserts at Jasper's come as "minis," not so much so you can eat less as so you can eat more of them. Customer favorites based on childhood memories include the banana parfait with home-made Nilla wafers (the pudding whipped 'til air-light, garnished with banana slices and a sprinkle of crushed vanilla wafers), the rocky road ice cream sandwich with chocolate and caramel sauces and "gooey marshmallow cream," and Rick's Rockin' Chocolate Cake, a celebration of both dark and light—like barbecue itself.

DAVID'S BARBECUE ARLINGTON

ADDRESS: 2224-H W. PARK ROW, ARLINGTON
PHONE: (817) 261-9998
ESTABLISHED: 1910, THIS LOCATION IN 1988
OWNER: JIMMY HARRIS
BEST BITES: BEEF BRISKET, PORK RIBS, POTATO SALAD, FRIED OKRA, FRIED PIES
PAYMENT: CREDIT CARDS

Before he went off to serve several terms as constable beginning in 1992, David Harris wanted to be sure his son, Jimmy, was ready to take over a barbecue business with links back to the same 1910 family enterprise that gave birth to Sonny Bryan's. So he put Jimmy to work peeling and chopping 50 pounds of onions…when the lad was all of 8. By the time David and Jimmy had trouble fitting through the same narrow passageway behind the counter, father knew that son was ready.

"Those onions took me about four

hours that first time," David says, clearly not remembering the incident at all. "Now I can do it in 15 minutes." He thinks about what the story from childhood might mean, other than the tears caused by all those onions, of course. "It's very difficult working with your dad, but now I have one of the greatest relationships with him. We're best friends. If there's ever any kind of problem, I can call him or he can call me."

Turns out, there was nothing weird about David Harris running for constable, since he'd spent seven years as a sheriff's deputy earlier in his career. Yet barbecue had always been in David's blood. How often, growing up, had he listened as relatives regaled him with tales of his uncle, William Jennings "Red" Bryan, who had founded the Red Bryan's barbecue chain after starting out with *his* father, Elias Bryan. And how often had he heard about Red's son, William Jennings Bryan Jr.—known as Sonny, in the Texas way—who eventually left home and hearth to launch the restaurant chain that still bears his name today. Both ancestors were, naturally, named after the great American political orator, of the "Cross of Gold" speech and the Scopes "Monkey Trial." Obviously, both were more interested in smoke than in mirrors.

At Uncle Red's insistence, David let

himself be lured away from law enforcement and into the barbecue business, ending up the owner of one Red Bryan's restaurants starting in 1965. He was waiting for Jimmy through the years, however, pouncing as soon as the young man finished college. Jimmy opened the only surviving memento of Red Bryan's back in 1988, by which time the chain's name had come off and his dad's name had gone on. David's Barbecue was a lesser-known entity without so much as a glancing reference to Red or Sonny Bryan, but it was a business Jimmy could live with. And he has, every day since.

"Look, I'm now a fourth-generation pit man," Jimmy explains. "In this business, it's all about consistency, which is why you try to keep the same help. I wouldn't know any other way to cook this stuff." He smiles with self-deprecation. "I'm very scared here in my little box. But I can't see my way to branching out. We use only wood to smoke our meats, for instance—no gas, no electricity. We don't even use any spices. If you start out with a good piece of wood and a good piece of meat, the smoke will create a great flavor."

At David's, the great flavor comes exclusively from hickory, which applies the wonderful taste to about 1,200 pounds of brisket each day. There are also some serious pork ribs and even turkey breasts coming out of this pit, along with ham and sausage. The barbecue sauce is thinner than most—"It's a sauce, not a gravy," Jimmy laughs—but full of rich, sweet, smoky flavor.

A place with this much tradition probably sees little reason to look for side dishes past potato salad, coleslaw and terrific barbecue beans (also smoky from the pit), but that does limit the public's eternal preference for fried. French fries are offered, along with fried okra and fried onion rings—three things nobody will ever hate you for serving them. There are only two desserts here, but both are super: banana pudding for the purists, plus Mindy Lu's fried pies.

Still, for all the satisfaction of carry-ing on a family business that cites its beginning as 1910, Jimmy looks at today's foodservice industry and sees many forces at work against old-fashioned Texas barbecue. Not against him personally, mind you, but against a segment of the industry that draws its greatest strength and identity from small mom-and-pop eateries.

"I sometimes think we're an endangered species," Jimmy says, "because of all the outside influences. Government controls make the cost of doing business these days just incredible. When my great-granddad started out, he couldn't even afford to give customers napkins. He just hung an apron by the door, so customers could wipe their hands on their way out."

D-TWO BAR-B-Q PANTEGO

ADDRESS: 2503 W. PIONEER PARKWAY, PANTEGO
PHONE: (817) 460-7427
ESTABLISHED: 2004
OWNER: PATRICK JONES
BEST BITES: BEEF BRISKET, PORK RIBS, HOT LINKS, GREEN BEANS, FRIED OKRA, CHERRY COBBLER
PAYMENT: CREDIT CARDS

Patrick Jones, with roots deep in the Texas Hill Country and 29 years of cooking barbecue in northeast Texas, is one big mass of aphorisms. If he ever stops smoking meat for a living, he might consider coming up with slogans for bumper stickers—except then they'd have to make *bigger* bumper stickers.

"Three of us opened a barbecue place," he quips about his past, "but that ended up bein' three *too many*." Surrounded by the red, white and blue that is D-Two's color scheme, Patrick smiles and chats about his food some more, then feels another aphorism coming on. "You see a barbecue place with some pit guy walkin' in at 9 in the morning, then you'd better not go there. There's a whole lotta stuff

two months old. In later years, when he finally got serious about barbecue, he would return to those Hill Country towns to learn everything he could, watching and asking questions. "You got guys there been cooking barbecue for 40 or 50 years," he says. "I truly believe that kinda guy is a dying breed."

Patrick himself is a good argument that the breed isn't "dying" entirely. He learned barbecue the old-fashioned way, by doing it. He spent many years cooking for the popular Spring Creek chain around Dallas, finding his single greatest mentor in a guy named Londel. As a young man, it seems, Patrick wasn't just looking for a cooking teacher but for a father figure in the business to teach him how to live.

"I just wanted to be a bum, at least for a while," Patrick smiles. "But Londel said: 'No, man, you *gotta* do barbecue.'" It was this relationship that led Patrick to eventually open Stagecoach Bar-B-Q with Londel and another partner—the now-gone team he describes as "three too many." But Patrick learned from that adventure, too, and still gets a little misty-eyed talking about the lessons taught by Londel. And when he needed another job after Stagecoach went away, Patrick found his second great hero—a Greek-American named George Deonis, who hired him to cook barbecue at Danny D's.

George took Patrick under his wing, kept him cooking and paid for nine long years, until it was his turn to retire. As a son of Greece in America, George knew there was nothing better for a man than owning his own business, being the master of his own fate. And George wanted that dream to come true for Patrick. Making it possible for him to purchase Danny D's and reopen it in 2004 (as D-Two's) was George's contribution to the goodwill fund of the cosmos.

Like a good Greek-American but in disguise, Patrick comes in early every day and works late, putting the Southern Pride rotisserie through its paces with pile after pile of hickory wood. Brisket is

comin' from a can."

Patrick walks in at 7 or earlier each day, and not just to check on the brisket that, as usual in Texas, has been cooking over low heat overnight. He also comes in to whip together D-Two's incredible side dishes, which merge the barbecue place gently with a soul food restaurant on the old side of town in any other part of the Deep South. He does things this way, he says, because he's never done them any other. And he's done things this way long enough to know that most shortcuts—especially the ones taken by the barbecue chains—extract a high cost in terms of flavor.

"I understand this old barbecue thing," says Patrick, "and people don't want it too fancy. I want you to sit right here in my little place surrounded by red, white and blue, thinking of Texas and America." He himself thinks for a moment, perhaps seeing a long parade of mentors, many now dead, pass before his eyes. "Barbecue is a slow-paced cowboy thing. You start trying to speed up barbecue and you in trouble."

The same idea offers a general description of Patrick's life. He was born in Austin of parents who knew great barbecue, having themselves come to the capital from Welder near Lockhart, where smoke was definitely in their eyes. All that became a no-show memory fast, though, as Patrick's family moved north to the Arlington area when he was just an 11- or 12-hour thing to Patrick, allowing him just enough time to put it on, go home at night and come back in to take it off. By the time the briskets are done, the St. Louis-cut ribs dusted in dry rub, the chicken halves and turkey breasts, the ham and sausage are going strong.

And by the time the first lunch customer walks in to take one of the seats in the original Danny D's or in the newer section Patrick closed in, the Big Three barbecue sides as well as the green beans, corn on the cob, french fries, fried okra and beer-battered onion rings are ready to roll. For dessert, D-Two's has fried pies, plus a more old-fashioned version of the same thing: peach or cherry cobbler.

"The saddest thing about being in the barbecue business all these years is not being able to smell it," Patrick observes, allowing that tragedy to hit home. "You know, it takes me up to 14 days away from this place before I start being able to smell smoke the way everybody else who comes in here does. So now, whenever I get to where I can smell barbecue again, man, I just *take...it...in!*"

HOBBI'S BBQ
IRVING

ADDRESS: 5459 N. MACARTHUR BOULEVARD, IRVING
PHONE: (972) 870-1227
ESTABLISHED: 2002
OWNER: EUNKYUNG KIM
BEST BITES: CHOPPED BEEF SANDWICH, PORK RIBS, HOT LINKS, SMOTHERED TURNIP GREENS, SWEET POTATOES
PAYMENT: CREDIT CARDS

In the first five years of its life, Hobbi's had four owners in quick succession. And it had one Tony.

More days than not, Antonio White comes in around 5 a.m.—and not because some owner has posted a schedule that says he has to. To Tony, coming in before dawn is the only way he can get a jump on the beef brisket in the smoker, or on

the pork ribs he puts in for a tenderizing few hours, or on the flavorful soul-food vegetables that pack in the crowds for lunch. It's also, he says, the only way he can make sure he'll have the time to share at least a quick laugh with each and every customer.

In an age that sees trained chefs demonstrating every step and nuance of a dish in hopes of getting a TV show—of being the next Emeril or Mario or Bobby—Tony is a cook full of secrets. They represent his job security, of course, as they have since Hobbi's opened its doors with a name that means "Home Of the Best Barbecue International." But they also represent his personal touch, his daily ritual of self-expression, his way of making certain that no matter who owns Hobbi's as a business, as a restaurant it's absolutely "Tony's place."

"I'd really hate to tell you any of my secrets," he grins, "cuz I'd really hate to have to kill you."

Ironically, the native of West Monroe in north Louisiana grew up in a culture that shared few to no cooking secrets with anyone male. Boys and men were not encouraged to cook; and in the case of Tony's grandmother, "not encouraged" would be putting it mildly. "She wouldn't let any man in her kitchen," he remembers from his childhood, a time filled with those wonderful Deep South cooking smells womenfolk mysteriously had in their power. "The men just sat around on their butts until it was time to come eat."

Another irony is that Tony neither cooked nor even ate barbecue until he moved to North Texas going on two decades ago. Once he arrived, though, his learning curve was impressive—quickly becoming a pit boss for local chain Spring Creek and later for Sonny Bryan's. He had just left Sonny's when he spotted an ad in the newspaper: a brand-new place was looking for a pit boss who could also cook sides and indulge in a bit of baking. No stickler when it comes to job descriptions, Tony signed on with Hobbi's and began creating most of the foods the place's customers would come to love. When Eunkyung Kim arrived from Nashville and decided to purchase the restaurant in stylish Las Colinas, she knew enough about the business to leave Tony front and center.

"The places where I used to work might do more business," Tony says, "but I get better customers here. A lot of families come in, and a lot of people from offices during the day. Plus we do some catering, if people will come and pick it up. I love to talk and joke with them even when we're busy. I have a blast. That's why I haven't left here. I get new customers. And I got customers from the first day we opened."

Tony slow-cooks his meats over pecan wood in a small Southern Pride rotisserie—letting the briskets go for 13 to 14 hours, starting around 7 each night. The ribs, naturally, have to cook far less, 4 to 5 hours, as do the spicy Earl Campbell hot links.

While Hobbi's cafeteria line features the greatest hits of barbecue accompaniments, including excellent potato salad and coleslaw, on the right side of the cash register, the left side has all the signs of being Tony's playground. He's convinced, in fact, that the fresh vegetables he cooks every day—smothered turnip greens, smothered cabbage, lush and savory creamed corn, secret-recipe sweet potatoes with a soft kiss of brown sugar and cinnamon—are a major part of what keeps customers coming back. In addi-

tion, Tony wields a mean fryer, putting out Texas-traditional chicken-fried steak with cream gravy and even crunchy, golden catfish that would make any cook in the Mississippi Delta proud.

"A lot of people don't understand that the longer and slower you cook most things, the better they're going to taste," says Tony, stepping up to his cutting board and smiling at the approaching wave of customers before completing his thought. "You'd put the love in this food at home. That's why I put the love in it here."

FRED'S BAR-B-Q IRVING

ADDRESS: 808 E. IRVING BOULEVARD, IRVING
PHONE: (972) 579-7655
ESTABLISHED: 1953
OWNERS: LEON AND QUEENIE BROWN
BEST BITES: SLICED BEEF BRISKET, STUFFED BAKED POTATO, PORK SPARERIBS, POTATO SALAD, SMOKED BARBECUE BEANS, BLACKBERRY COBBLER
PAYMENT: CREDIT CARDS

The huge brick pit still hunches where it has for 55 years, challenging anyone in his right mind to try and move it. The bricks that make up the outer wall and the iron grates that hold the meat inside are so crusted with grit and smoke they could

probably keep on smoking without any wood, and the temperature gauge stopped functioning years ago. Happily, after spending 25 of those 55 years reaching into this pit, Leon Brown wouldn't be relying on any temperature gauge anyway.

"It's just from experience now that I'm cooking," offers Leon, in between interactions with customers who keep him slicing and chopping. "The old smoker does a wonderful job. I think it steals the show many times when it comes to the flavor of the meat. It's a well-seasoned pit, all right. I think that after so much hickory over the years, I could throw a piece of oak in there and the meat would still come out smelling like hickory." Leon giggles at the line he knows is coming next: "I usually come out smelling like hickory, too."

After a quarter century at the same cutting board, you'd think the folks who frequent Fred's Bar-B-Q—some since the day Leon bought the place—would know this guy's name *isn't* Fred. Yet to the contrary, during a recent busy lunch, several people waiting to place their orders assured a visitor the place is good because *Fred* himself is always working. "Hi Fred," they say as they reach his meat station. "Hello," Leon says right back, nodding as though his name is Fred for all the world to see.

There *was* a Fred, Leon explains in a brief lull, the guy who started the business and built it into a small barbecue chain more than half a century ago. It was at one of those other locations that Leon Brown first signed on to help cook, a whim while visiting a cousin in Dallas from his hometown of Texarkana.

"I was once a schoolteacher back home," says Leon. "I enjoyed that all right, and coaching at the junior-high level, too. But it looks like cooking took over all that. I've been here 25 years and everybody associates me with the name on this building. I just answer to the name Fred's Bar-B-Q. So not only is my first name 'Fred' now, but my last name is 'Bar-B-Q.' If I see folks at the mall or just out and about, they may not remember me as Leon, but they sure remember me as Bar-B-Q."

Leon bought the original location (and endless years of being called Fred, apparently) when the chain decided to disband. Still, his commitment to the business he operates with his wife, Queenie, faced its most serious challenge 17 years ago, when Leon discovered he needed a kidney transplant. In the beginning, there were no kidneys available at all. Even after Leon had spent more than a year on the waiting list, the best his doctors could come up with was a kidney not expected to last more than two or three years.

"It looked hopeless for a long time," he recalls. "I've had that kidney 17 years now, and it's working perfect. God and I had a conversation, you see. I told Him if He could maintain that kidney, I could maintain my service to Him. Today, we offer not only the food we serve but a word of consolation to anyone who might need it."

Leon cooks his briskets 16 to 18 hours in that old brick pit, longest whenever the weather turns cold enough to affect the temperature of the hickory fire. Weather is only one of the many variables Leon has learned to factor in, another being the intensity of heat based on where the meats are placed. As he describes the situation, there are two doors in to high heat and one in to low heat. It's essential that the man in charge understand which is which. But since the *only* man in charge of the pit is Leon, that has never been a problem.

Best bets at Fred's include Leon's brisket and his wonderful pork spareribs that go into the smoke after a dusting of dry rub. Repeat customers prefer the potato salad and the smoked barbecue beans over any other side dishes—all prepared in small homemade batches by Queenie each day.

As for dessert, there is the standard peach cobbler, although Leon has been pleased to see old-fashioned blackberry come to dominate that sweet side of sales.

Still, when asked which single item has kept customers coming back for more than 25 years, there's absolutely no hesitation: Fred's larger-than-life stuffed baked potato.

"It's a huge deal," Leon says with a smile. "When you order this stuffed baked potato, just don't order nothing else with it. And it's *grown* over the years. People started out with just your regular baked potato, but then they kept adding stuff. Before long we had people adding two or even three meats, plus butter and cheese and sour cream and our smoked beans. Some people coming in now are adding rice, corn, grilled onions. I mean, it's a gigantic situation."

TOMMY'S BAR-B-QUE IRVING

ADDRESS: 2840 IRVING BOULEVARD, IRVING
PHONE: (972) 986-0559
ESTABLISHED: 1991
OWNER: TOMMY KIM
BEST BITES: BEEF BRISKET, PORK RIBS, BARBECUE BEANS, PEACH COBBLER
PAYMENT: CREDIT CARDS

The world of barbecue has no idea how close it came to losing Tommy Kim—or to what business it almost lost him.

"My mother and I were trying to find a business that everybody needed," the energetic Korean-American explains, and it's tough to disagree with his logic. "We thought of maybe opening a sock store, since everybody needs socks. But then we found our way into barbecue."

In the traditional Texas version of "guns or butter," Tommy and his mother chose barbecue over socks. And for the past 20-plus years, the barbecue lovers of the Irving area have been very happy they did. At a recent busy lunch, the line has been steady for more than an hour—a wide array of suited business types and dirt-encrusted construction workers.

Many of the signs around Tommy's are written in both English and Spanish. Not a single sign is written in Korean.

"Mine is strictly Texas barbecue," Tommy says, dismissing any suggestion that there might be soy sauce or ginger or some other Asian touch enlivening his flavors. "I took straight, plain, classic Texas barbecue and started cooking that." He smiles. "The only thing I added from my Korean heritage was my work ethic."

Watching Tommy blur through a lunch rush, chopping and slicing meats before passing plates down the line for side dishes, you see exactly what he means. And you understand how a kid who started serving barbecue in a poor neighborhood while still in college became a man with one of the most popular barbecue joints in town.

Tommy was a student at University of Texas-Arlington when he and his mother opened Soul Man's Bar-B-Que on Dallas' south side in 1985. At times, he may have felt the need to apologize for *not* being the least bit black, but business prospered anyway. As anyone who's sold any type of food in a poor neighborhood will attest, you learn quickly to keep your prices low. Even then, profits were decent enough that when Soul Man's lost its lease after four years, Tommy could open something he called BBQ Barn in Plano and operate that for six years. And when a Burger King in Irving came on the market, he turned the Barn over to an uncle and started a place under his own name in a

longtime Home of the Whopper.

Today, only the most discriminating fast-food scholar would guess at this restaurant's previous life. Yes, the building remains more or less a box, with the entrance leading straight to an ordering counter on the left and tables spread around the sides (a case of BK déjà vu if there was one). But the hulking presence of the brick pit right behind the counter should wash away any doubts about Tommy's barbecue seriousness.

Even the boxiness of the building is muted by wave after wave of Texas ranch memorabilia strewn about the walls. Some pieces even have a story Tommy loves to share, having once belonged to World War II hero Audie Murphy, who came from this area and later starred in a series of movies about the Old West. Other accents include tributes to Tommy's all-time Hollywood hero, James Dean.

The stone pit at Tommy's holds up to 300 pounds of meat at a time, subjecting beef, pork or chicken to smoke from the hickory Tommy brings in from Oklahoma. He prefers his wood fresh and green, not dried or "seasoned," since this way it produces more smoke and keeps burning longer. Brisket always goes into the smoker overnight, cooking between 7 and 12 hours depending on the amount. When he comes back the next morning, Tommy adds dry-rubbed pork ribs, chicken and sausage—along with oversized pots of his spectacular barbecue beans. Smoking the beans is one of Tommy's big deals, he says, since they take on the sweetness and flavor of the hickory. As a result, they typically outsell coleslaw and even Tommy's tangy, bright yellow, almost mashed potato salad.

Tommy Kim has traveled a long road to success since his days as an unlikely Korean "Soul Man" selling slabs of ribs. But the hard lessons learned two decades ago continue to guide him in a no-nonsense pursuit of profit by offering customers of many races and languages excellent value.

"The biggest challenge in the barbecue business is making money, with meat prices always going up," he says matter-of-factly, as though uttering a truth that has mysteriously eluded poets and sages. "I have to keep giving the same amount of meat, and I can't adjust my prices every six months. This is a local place. And I want it always to stay a local place."

ANGELO'S FORT WORTH

ADDRESS: 2533 WHITE SETTLEMENT ROAD, FORT WORTH
PHONE: (817) 332-0357
ESTABLISHED: 1958
OWNERS: THE GEORGE FAMILY
BEST BITES: BEEF BRISKET, PORK RIBS, POLISH SAUSAGE, HOT LINKS
PAYMENT: CREDIT CARDS

Ask any veteran of eating barbecue at half-century-old Angelo's and the most likely question you'll be asked is: Do they still have that bear? Truth is, three generations of the George family—Angelo, his son Skeet and now *his* son Jason—have run the pits and the cash register at this

Fort Worth landmark, but the most important face longtime customers want and even need to see is the furry one rising from the T-shirt just inside the entrance. Ironically, Angelo George by all accounts foresaw *his* national fame as a barbecue guy about as clearly as that bear understood he'd someday have a job in a restaurant.

"This was mainly a beer joint," explains Skeet, glancing around at the dozens of full tables that stand where only four used to be. "It was real small and easy in my dad's time, and there was a lot of money to be made in beer in those days. I mean, that's why Dad started putting more seasoning on all the meats, so people would drink more beer. I guess it just kinda backfired."

Angelo started a much smaller version of the business on this location back in 1958, getting considerable help from his brother Orville until his death just over 25 years later. And for all Skeet's insistence the place was a beer joint—and the prominence on the menu of an ice-cold mug—Angelo had been a butcher on Fort Worth's north side before venturing out on his own.

By doing so, he followed in the footsteps of many in Texas before him, taking the meats they had butchered to the next level, literally and figuratively. Along the way, Angelo's became a favorite of many who can "make" a restaurant: entertainers, sports figures and a healthy dose of journalists. It wasn't long before the humble place serving frosty beer had become a barbecue joint that attracted customers from around the world.

For the first three decades of his place's life, Angelo George tried to accommodate the growing numbers through a series of additions than can only be described as "patchwork." In 1988, though, the restaurant went seriously under the knife. At the time, Angelo said colorfully, "The people pushed the walls out themselves." If only it had been so easy. By the time the job was done, Angelo's had new restrooms, air-conditioning, raised ceilings, more freezer space to hold those beer mugs, and two new rooms to raise the guest capacity to 300. By the time Angelo passed away at age 71 in 1997, he had not only built a Fort Worth destination but a barbecue dynasty, with two generations doing virtually no other job their entire lives.

"I wouldn't know any different," says Jason, flanking his father as they show off the two 15-by-8-by-12-foot brick pits that are the business end of Angelo's. "The hardest part is trying to live up to their legacy, but then again, I was part of it every day of my life. The best I can do is keep it going in the same direction."

Like a lot of the oldest Texas barbecue families, these two generations of Georges reject the "advances" offered by modern rotisserie smokers. Though they'll assure you the old way makes better barbecue, they can't exactly explain why...and that's probably okay. It's their comfort zone, doing things just the way Angelo did, and it's their expertise.

That very expertise is what chooses briskets with "just enough fat and marbling to not dry out," covers it with a proprietary dry rub and smokes it for 8 to 14 hours. Cooking time depends on where meat is in the pit, since the racks are, by definition, stationary. And since the racks don't move, it's up to Jason as pit master to move meats around to achieve optimum cooking. Ribs and a surprising variety of other meats—salami, ham, chicken, turkey, Polish sausage, hot links, braunschweiger—go on for much shorter times, each for its carefully chosen season in the smoke.

Lunchtime at Angelo's is all about going through the line, getting your choice of one, two or three meats and building out with simple side dishes like potato salad, coleslaw and beans. As though understanding its place in the universe right along with its limitations, Angelo's invests in no homemade desserts, offering a few outside pies for those customers with a hopeless sweet tooth. At night (beginning at 3 p.m., when any good beer joint should start its "night"), there are waitresses to serve up domestic brews and even a few imports, plus the frozen margaritas Angelo George probably wouldn't have seen coming either.

"Heck," says Skeet, "this was all sawdust on the floor into the late '70s, when the health department got around to putting a stop to that. I think this place is a kind of legend, and it's unique. There's a few items we've added over the years, and we might add a few more. But mostly we'll serve the basic barbecue stuff. We'll try to keep it the best we can—and hopefully the best around."

RAILHEAD SMOKEHOUSE BBQ, FORT WORTH

ADDRESS: 2900 MONTGOMERY STREET, FORT WORTH
PHONE: (817) 738-9808
ESTABLISHED: 1987
OWNER: CHARLIE GEREN
BEST BITES: BEEF BRISKET, PORK RIBS, CHOPPED BEEF SANDWICH, SAUSAGE, FRENCH FRIES, FRUIT COBBLERS
PAYMENT: CREDIT CARDS

Some Texas barbecue places are shacks just for the neighborhood. Some are wholesome, family-friendly theme restaurants already turned into chains or begging to be at any minute. And others are sports-bars-by-way-of-pickup-joints-by-way-of-honky-tonks. By all the telltale signs on a busy night with a Cowboys game about to start on TV, Railhead is definitely the latter.

Fact is, for all the casual tables spread around and filled with families devouring barbecue, it's impossible to tell where the restaurant ends and the bar begins…if, indeed, they do. People greet each other across open spaces, laughing and waving longneck beers as though in salute. Men and women lean against the bar in casual disarray, making sweet eyes at people who may or may not be their spouses. The only thing standardized about this room is the uniform: many shades of blue jeans and denim separating boots at the bottom and cowboy hats at the top. Everybody is here for the barbecue. Except maybe those here to meet somebody. Except maybe those here to watch the Cowboys and drink beer.

"We've got cold cheap beer in frosty mugs and great food," says night manager Jason Sturgis, taking a short break by letting someone else handle the growing line to order barbecue. His eyes seldom leave the line. "That's a pretty good recipe, I think." He ponders a question about nomenclature. "I don't rank it quite a sports bar, cuz we have a good family atmosphere. But you'll always find people here watching a game, watching the waitresses and drinking beer."

As Jason tells it, that recipe and all the others used at Railhead were the creation of one Harry Pitcher, who started a little beer and barbecue barn just up the street back in 1987. Railhead was an immediate hit with two separate constituencies: students at nearby TCU, who also brought their parents during campus visits, and denizens of the adjacent reserve military bases. Within five years or so, the barn simply wasn't big enough to hold everybody, so a new location was found. When Pitcher passed away, ending a life spent in this and several other Fort Worth barbecue joints, his main financial partner, State Rep. Charlie Geren, found himself the sole owner.

Busy year-round, with plenty of regulars to smooth over changes in sports season and academic calendar, Railhead keeps its meats smoking on three huge rotisseries fed with hickory. Brisket is left to cook overnight over very low heat, 12 to 14 hours, with ribs and sausage joining it when the first guy arrives in the morning. Meats are sold by the sandwich, the sandwich plate, the dinner plate and the pound; but thanks to the casual, stand-up nature of a lot of Railhead's business, sandwiches and other finger foods are incredibly popular.

Sides include traditional mustardy potato salad and a sweeter-than-usual version of coleslaw, but also sports-bar nibbles like french fries, cheddar peppers and something less than functional called a "cheese boat." There's always a nightly special, plates composed from familiar pieces in a bigger, better setting, with iced tea flowing like, well, beer.

During the summer months, Railhead becomes as much an outdoor venue as an indoor, especially when things start to cool off in the evening. For one thing, Jason says, there are 50 or 60 official seats on the colorful patio, and on nights that a country radio station broadcasts live in what must be dubbed a "redneck karaoke" format, people bring their own chairs. Inside and outside, there's the feeling of alcohol-inspired free-for-all, with large groups grabbing any table in sight and pulling it and others into truly inconvenient configurations. In the end, nobody seems to mind when they can't get a table at all; they just head for the bar, the waitresses and the nearest TV.

"I think that early in the evening, people eat a little to soak up the beer," explains Jason, a Railhead behavioral scientist after six or seven years. "But then they get more to eat when they've been drinking awhile. I've seen a lot of strange stuff here, but just the kind of drinking people stuff. There've been a few fights here and there, but I wouldn't say that's typical. At the bar, you'll have a whole group of bikers right next to a whole group of businessmen, just mingling. I've never had to call the cops."

RISCKY'S BARBECUE
FORT WORTH

ADDRESS: 140 E. EXCHANGE AVENUE, FORT WORTH
PHONE: (817) 626-7777
ESTABLISHED: 1927
OWNERS: THE RISCKY FAMILY
BEST BITES: CHEESE GALORE APPETIZER, BEEF BRISKET, BEEF RIBS, SMOKED CATFISH, FRIED CORN, PECAN CREAM CHEESE PIE
PAYMENT: CREDIT CARDS

Mary and Joe Riscky, newly married and here from Poland just over a decade, thought they were opening a simple little grocery store not far from the stockyards that gave Fort Worth what little fame it had. The year was 1927. Descendants of Mary and Joe still own and operate

Riscky's, except now they've got three barbecue restaurants, three delis, a steakhouse and a burger joint. The center of it all remains that "simple little grocery store," since that's where the Riscky family smokes *all* the meat for *all* their locations every single day.

Of course, Fort Worth's Historic Stockyards has risen quite a few notches in terms of daily tourist traffic—and especially in terms of entertainment value. "You get a cattle drive two times a day," offers manager Brad McClendon, realizing just how much this must sound like Disney World, "and gunfights on weekends. You can't get a better deal than that."

Brad takes a moment, thinking about the Riscky's story as he surveys the huge platter of red meat on the table, each dark slab offset by smoked turkey or a surprising fillet of smoked catfish. "The thing is, when people come to Fort Worth, they want to come to the easier side of the Metroplex and look back at the way things used to be. It's always a little slower here. Riscky's is a Fort Worth tradition, and when people come from out of town, their hotels always suggest they come see us. Riscky built that reputation doing only one thing: busting his hump *every* day."

As a manager working for Joe Riscky's son Pete and *his* son Jim, running the busy location on Sundance Square, Brad is well aware of the family "voice" emanating from that 1927 location. It emanates in the form of all the smoked meats, rushed over from the smokers after many KFC-style secret touches not shared with anyone outside the family. It emanates in the hush-hush Riscky's barbecue sauce, arriving from the mother ship daily and mysteriously in 10-gallon containers. And it emanates in the décor of all the restaurants and delis that have grown from that single Polish-American grocery, a heavy-handed serving of the wood-floored, animal-skinned Wild West kitsch at the heart of the Stockyards "experience," mixed with modern neon saying silly things like:

"Warning: Our Ribs May Be Habit Forming."

At Riscky's, even the smoker is a kind of secret, having been designed and patented by Pete Riscky's son with a bit of Rube Goldberg, mad-scientist panache. According to Brad, the trick to this smoker is that the pit guy never has to *decide* when the meats go on. Everything is lined up on various conveyor belts, with various timers all over the place. Different meats go on, and different meats come off—literally, like clockwork. And based on the flavors you find on your plate, Jim Riscky deserves every crossed "t" and dotted "i" in his patent registration.

It's all a bit hard to picture, though, a sort of Willy-Wonka-Does-Barbecue scenario, especially to those who know the old Texas tradition. Even without being shown this wondrous machine, you already miss the all-powerful, virtually inerrant pit bosses who operate *themselves* by a clock and, in obsessive solitude, make all things smoky work for the good.

Naturally, Riscky's wasn't always this way. It was just a grocery for years, with Mary and Joe at some point building a shack outside to make barbecue from whatever fresh meats didn't sell. Everybody involved seemed happy. But then a huge construction project took root nearby, employing hundreds of men who tended to get hungry. At first, Joe Riscky sold the developers fresh meat, which they then cooked for their workers. Inevitably, even that effort got old, and the Risckys were contracted to serve barbecue to the multitudes. Requests for adding barbecue sauce, potato salad and coleslaw were answered with a smile and a ring of the register. The family enjoyed this so much they never really stopped. As it turned out, many workers from that construction project chose to remain in the Fort Worth area. Riscky's Barbecue had its first fan club.

Over the decades, those initial fly-by-night efforts have become gospel truth, as they always tend to do with success.

The wood used for smoking, for instance, is an odd but delightful proportion: 80 percent mesquite, the other 20 an equal split of hickory and pecan. With the help of all those secret recipes and that patented monster of a smoker, the Riscky family turns out terrific brisket and chopped beef so good that other barbecue chains and concession stands buy it to sell as their own, plus pork ribs and mastodon-like beef ribs the regulars love to attack.

"A lot of football teams come in just for these," Brad says, "and they compete on how many they can eat. We put a big bucket out for the bones."

Appetizers are a kick at Riscky's, especially the irresistibly named Cheese Galore, a Tex-Mex-Italian fantasy of cheese sticks gone to heaven. Side dishes are first-rate, all the usuals plus something the family dubs "fried corn." Definitely a case of "what's not to like," this is a quick-fried and crisp Old South hush puppy with whole kernels of sweet corn inside. These get dipped (and dunked and dabbed) into some way-better-than-average ranch dressing for a treat as euphoric as it is artery-clogging. And…they happen to go superbly with the smoked catfish, delicate and clean-tasting farm-raised fillets that have their own spot on the conveyor belt, smoking $2^{1}/_{2}$ to 3 hours.

Riscky's is a large enough operation these days to hit desserts out of the park, by one means or mad machine another; this they do with their carrot cake and pecan cream cheese pie. If pecan pie married cheesecake, you might get a happy marriage like this. If you were lucky.

Still, despite all the food-borne euphoria at the table, Brad has something he wants to say. "The hardest part," he struggles, "is having a family member with his name on the building." A veteran of big, national, TV-advertised chains with corporate ownerships far away and often distracted, the man knows whereof he speaks.

"This isn't like working for a major corporation. You're never going to person-ally upset Mr. Chili's or Mr. Bennigan's. Riscky is a real man who'll travel around in his pickup with a hammer and try to fix something before he'll call somebody to fix it." Brad shrugs, brushes aside a thought and smiles. "There's a lot of character in a family business."

FEEDSTORE BBQ & MORE SOUTHLAKE

ADDRESS: 530 S. WHITE CHAPEL BOULEVARD, SOUTHLAKE
PHONE: (817) 488-1445
ESTABLISHED: 2001
OWNER: BILL LAFAVER
BEST BITES: SOUTHLAKE-CUT PORK RIBS, BEEF BRISKET, GREEN BEANS WITH HAM, DIRTY RICE WITH CHOPPED BEEF, POTATO SALAD, FRENCH FRIES AND FRIED OKRA COOKED TO ORDER, PEACH COBBLER
PAYMENT: CREDIT CARDS

For 41 years, Bill Lafaver was a man with a mission: sell as much Jack Daniel's whiskey in Texas, in America and in the world as humanly possible. Throughout most of those same years, the ramshackle old building in the farm community

where he chose to live had a similar mission: sell as much gas and groceries, and then as much animal feed, as humanly possible. At some point, as this farming community became Southlake—the home of mansions and millionaires—the two missions became one.

"As this place started to develop and the houses took over the horse farms, the feed business went to pot," Bill explains. He laughs quietly at the irony. "We used to feed the animals. All we did here was change what we was feeding."

Feedstore BBQ, opened by Bill with his son's help in 2001, carries on—more or less—the retail tradition it enjoyed in what seems another place and most assuredly another time. To understand either, you have to look out from Feedstore's front door and pretend all those sprawling brick-and-marble edifices don't exist, and you have to pretend that your next-door neighbors don't include football broadcaster Pat Summerall or *Laugh-In* comedienne Ruth Buzzi.

You have to insist on seeing only the land, covered in trees, cattle and horses, with only old-fashioned fences to keep the ownership halfway straight. That's the "Southlake" Bill moved into with his wife, Phyllis, and their children. He was a Texas country boy whose mother came from Leonard and whose father came from Lane…a Texas country boy who would travel the world with whiskey in his briefcase but love nothing better than coming home.

"This store was here before Southlake was here," Bill remembers. "It was a little country store with two old-timey gas pumps out front. It was just a little country store on a little country road. When I moved out here, a guy named Bill Miller

had bought it and worked it all by himself. Bill died musta been about 1977, and a lady took it over and ran it as a feed and tack for seven or eight years. Then someone bought it from her and expanded it, ran it up to 1997. It did fairly well. I bought it then, and my son ran it."

More than running a feed and tack store for a customer base increasingly disinterested in feed and tack, Bill started mulling over another idea, especially after he retired as Brown-Forman's vice president of the southwest division in 2001. You see, one of Jack Daniel's most successful promotions had always been barbecue cook-offs. In addition to cooking the stuff himself as a native Texan, Bill had often served as a cook-off judge. He'd listened as the pit masters boasted about this or that trick or secret, heard their tireless mumblings about time and temperature, low and slow. And he figured, quite frankly, that if *these* guys could enjoy success cooking barbecue, then he and his kids could, too.

Of course, as the "feed store" morphed into Feedstore BBQ & More, there was the little matter of all those well-heeled imports, Bill's new Southlake neighbors.

"We've been through so much controversy about what we've done here," Bill says, as though he'd been opening a Wal-Mart next to the White House. "In the beginning, a lot of people in these multimillion-dollar homes didn't know *what* they thought. Everybody has kinda embraced us now." He glances over at the signed celebrity portraits on the wall, nodding to a couple in particular. "Pat Summerall and Ruth Buzzi both live in the neighborhood, and they come in here to eat sometimes."

Away from the frozen gaze of celebrities, away from a customer's gaze in general, Bill, his general manager and their crew operate a traditional Texas barbecue joint, doing the vast majority of the right things right, from fresh-cut french fries and fried okra at the start to amazing peach cobbler at the end. They rely for smoke on two Southern Pride rotis-

series, one holding 500 pounds of meat and the other 700. Their preferred wood is hickory, applying it for 12 to 14 hours overnight to beef briskets and for shorter times to the ribs that actually outsell the Texas beef favorite more days than not.

As though to make his point, Bill looks down and carefully sketches a rack of pork ribs on his small order pad, slicing through with lines where the knife might go. "Officially, they're called a St. Louis cut," he explains, "but here we call them the Southlake cut, of course, and they're the most expensive ribs on the market. They're $2^{1/4}$ pounds per rack, and they have a lot less fat than ones that are $2^{1/2}$ pounds. You see?"

Glancing at the penciled-in lines on the notepad, a visitor has no choice but to nod. Bill has been nothing for most of his life if not a great salesman. And before he sold barbecue, even before he sold Jack Daniel's for more than four decades, he was a Marine drill instructor. There's simply not a lot of promise in trying to tell this man no.

CLARK'S OUTPOST TIOGA

....

ADDRESS: 101 HIGHWAY 377 AT GENE AUTRY DRIVE, TIOGA
PHONE: (940) 437-2414
ESTABLISHED: 1974
OWNERS: JAMES HILLIARD, JEFF WELLS AND STEVE GRESSETT
BEST BITES: BEEF BRISKET, PORK RIBS, POLISH SAUSAGE, POTATO SALAD, BARBECUE BEANS, JALAPEÑO BLACK-EYED PEAS, DEEP-FRIED CORN ON THE COB
PAYMENT: CREDIT CARDS

The hometown of singing cowboy Gene Autry has a population of 754...except when Clark's Outpost gets really busy.

This is horse country, the ranches large and spread out, with more than a few crowing about their champions around their grandiose entrances. That means money is changing hands, for the animals themselves as well as for stakes in their futures. And there isn't a better place to talk horses and the money to

157

own them, race them or breed them than the rough-hewn barbecue joint that Warren Clark built.

"People come in from Germany. Or Australia. Or Oklahoma," reports Steve Gressett, one of the three Tioga natives who worked here for years and committed themselves to keeping it going when Warren died in 1999. "They sit out at those tables, making their horse deals and eating our barbecue. We have a helicopter fly in every once in a while." He nods toward the window. "It sets down right over there."

"It's kind of a destination," adds business partner Jeff Wells, "with an old building and good food." He smiles. "And the chance to get outta Dallas."

Considering how far people come to eat at Clark's Outpost, there has to be more to it than getting out of Dallas, no matter how great that sounds to three guys from Tioga. Nearly every day, somebody walks in from Arkansas or Oklahoma or Colorado, mentioning that he or she has read about Clark's in one of those glossy gourmet magazines. At such moments, the boys can only shrug, smile and lead the folks to a table. It doesn't make sense, entirely. It doesn't make sense unless you knew Warren Clark.

"Warren was real popular," Jeff says, clearly aware of his understatement. By all accounts, Warren could sell just about anything to just about anybody, whether working in the garment industry in his youth or putting in profitable time later in oil and gas, radio and television.

"He was a pretty good showman," says Steve, "and he sure could sell some barbecue."

When Warren retired, moved to the country and opened Clark's Outpost in 1974, he wasn't all that serious about it. After all, how much business was he going to do with just one room holding nine tables? But when you're a salesman, even when you're retired, you can't help yourself. The Outpost started to gain a local following when it served only hamburgers. Within a couple years,

Warren bought a smoker and started selling barbecue.

As word about Clark's spread as far as Dallas and Fort Worth, and finally with the media far beyond, Warren needed help. The place was barely open when James Hilliard signed on, followed by Jeff in 1976 and Steve in 1982. The table count grew along with the employees, with a four-table bar added in 1983 and an old grocery store becoming a dining room in 1989. Today, Clark's Outpost has 23 tables.

On days when all 23 are filled, it's bound to be because of Warren's genius for promotion. But since many of these customers have been to Clark's Outpost dozens of times, the food deserves credit, too.

According to Steve, the place tries to smoke its meats with 100 percent hickory but occasionally has to blend in some oak. More notably, the Outpost cooks its beef briskets "lower and slower" than just about anybody else in Texas. When a listener questions his own hearing over meat cooked for "two, two and a half days," Steve comes at the number another way: "48 to 60 hours," he says. "It just gives it more tenderness. The faster you cook brisket, the more it turns rubbery or turns to mush."

The perfect meal at Clark's Outpost should include as much of this brisket as possible—cut thicker than usual because it's so tender—plus some St. Louis-style pork ribs smoked for 8 to 9 hours. Unless you detour for an order of smoked rainbow trout (from Idaho, of all places) or any of the Tex-Mex dishes, simply accompany your meats with potato salad, brown-sugary barbecue beans, jalapeño-kissed black-eyed peas and one truly bizarre idea: deep-fried corn on the cob.

No one here will mind if you eat and run, or if you sit back and visit all day. Whatever you do, you won't be the most unusual customers Clark's Outpost ever had.

"The freight trains used to slow down or even stop for a couple minutes right across the highway there," Jeff recalls. "The guys in the engine would run in and place their order and run right back. Then the train would move on, and the guys in the caboose would jump off to pick it up." Jeff thinks back to those days in the only place he's ever worked. "It was kinda funny, just watching 'em."

COUNTRY TAVERN
KILGORE

ADDRESS: STATE HIGHWAY 31 AT FM 2767, KILGORE
PHONE: (903) 984-9954
ESTABLISHED: 1939
OWNER: TOBY PILGRIM
BEST BITES: PORK RIBS, SAUSAGE, BEEF BRISKET, POTATO SALAD, BEANS, COBBLER (PECAN, PEACH OR BLACKBERRY)
PAYMENT: CREDIT CARDS

Toby Pilgrim knows three things with relative certainly about the history of Country Tavern, other than the fact that his family has worked here for nearly half a century.

First, Toby knows the Tavern is one of the few places in all of Texas that sells more pork ribs than beef brisket—at

times in the past, not bothering to cook brisket at all. Second, he knows that 1939 is the most likely year the joint opened its doors, though no one in town remembers and certainly no one can supply any evidence. Kilgore was still enjoying its boomtown years, being what someone called the largest oil field in the history of the world up until Saudi Arabia. And third, Country Tavern's initial success had less to do with food—even with its now-famous ribs—than with being a bar pressed up against a dry county.

"You should see the old pictures," says Toby, who has clearly spent hours piecing images together. "The highway all along here was just liquor store and bar, bar and liquor store, crammed right up to the county line. You can imagine how it was back then, with folks coming over from Tyler to get their beer and whiskey, and, of course, the workers from the oil fields around here. There were fights all the time, the older customers have told me, and guns fired here and there." Toby smiles and glances around his shadowy dining room, which seems merely an extension of his bar. "Of course, it's not like that anymore."

In the 1960s, presumably before Toby's grandmother and mother came to work at Country Tavern as waitresses, the old

place on the highway burned down. The owner at that time rebuilt using steel, apparently all the rage back then, and sure to appeal to anyone who'd just watched fire take his business. He rebuilt on the same footprint, Toby reports, keeping the bar at the same end and installing booths and tables outward from there. At some point, the dance floor faded to make room for more seats, but there's still a colorful jukebox at the opposite end from the bar, ready to spin platters from the past. And on the way to their tables, guests still must move beyond a sure sign of the Tavern's misspent youth—a brightly illuminated pool table.

"I used to play when I was a kid," says Toby. "I remember I was barely tall enough to see over the edge. And when I shot, I usually used the thick end of the cue. It was just easier for a little kid that way."

By the time two generations of Pilgrim women had gotten busy waiting tables here, the owner decided he'd had enough. Toby's grandmother decided she'd had enough, too, and she talked the man into letting her take over the lease. After several years of success, she bought the building and land from the real estate company. It was a true family business throughout those years: the family's job, the family's recreation and the family's social life. "I worked with both my grandmothers, plus aunts and uncles from both sides," Toby recalls. "Every one of my birthday parties, and my dad's and my mom's and everybody else's, was held right here."

Culinarily, one of the key moments in Country Tavern's history was the day Toby's father took over the kitchen. He convinced the old cook, described as a wonderful African-American man named Maxie Thomas, to teach him all his secrets. These included smoking meats on the old pit, the generational and cultural mastery of making perfect pork ribs.

Country Tavern's ribs became so popular that the Pilgrims served them for years with only potato salad. Brisket was an afterthought at best. Often they had none in the kitchen. Other times, Toby confesses, they'd smoke up a brisket or two, slice it and freeze it to reheat in barbecue sauce whenever anybody ordered some. He stresses that today, Country Tavern has raised Texas brisket to the respect it deserves.

Like so many cooking "secrets," the secret to Country Tavern's exquisite ribs is mostly no secret at all. Toby starts with better-quality meat than just about anybody. They're not spareribs, not the omnipresent St. Louis cut, but something called "pork loin back ribs"—like tender "baby backs" except larger, each rack weighing $2^{1}/_{2}$ to 3 pounds. These marinate in a dry rub the family makes with upwards of 20 ingredients, many tending toward the sweet. Maxie taught Toby's dad, and Toby's dad taught Toby, to reapply more of the rub once the ribs have been smoking awhile. The seasonings stick better that way, once the sugars on the ribs have begun to caramelize.

If you've come to doubt words like "best-ever," if you've come to question every such exuberance you've ever read in newspapers or magazines or heard on the Food Network or the Travel Channel, just take a bite of Country Tavern's ribs.

The total cooking time is $3^{1}/_{2}$ to $4^{1}/_{2}$ hours in one of three big new rotisseries that sit alongside the abandoned old smokers that Toby's father used, delivering modern quality and consistency in an age quite different from a generation ago. Toby understands these differences, having worked here since near-infancy and later opening Country Tavern's only outreach to date, in Shreveport, Louisiana. In his tavern-like setting on a highway with a history outside Kilgore, however, he knows that every one of his customers is waiting to pay for a sweet-spicy blast from the past.

"My dad knew how those old cookers worked," Toby says, "and he never left their side. He listened to those ribs."

SHEP'S BAR-B-Q
PALESTINE

ADDRESS: 1013 E. PALESTINE AVENUE, PALESTINE

PHONE: (903) 729-4206

ESTABLISHED: 1978, REOPENED IN 1985

OWNER: BRUCE BARRETT

BEST BITES: BEEF BRISKET, PORK SPARERIBS, SMOKED SAUSAGE, POTATO SALAD, GREEN BEANS, COWBOY BEANS, FRIED OKRA, PEACH COBBLER

PAYMENT: CREDIT CARDS

In 1978, the same year Joe Sheppard opened a small, tacked-together barbecue joint under a sign bearing his nickname, he hired a 12-year-old boy named Bruce Barrett to help clear tables and wash dishes. With 20/20 hindsight, for the sake of Shep's legacy, this would have to be considered an excellent hire.

Bruce already was spending time with a grandfather who operated a soul food restaurant in Palestine, watching the man cook pork chops, mashed potatoes and gravy, stewed beans and smothered turnip greens. So when an uncle called Bruce to say that Shep's could use help as much as a 12-year-old could use spending money, the boy was inclined to say yes. Bruce understood at the time, or at least he understood later, that his uncle was feeling old and tired and thought someone younger could take over. At 12, Bruce was imminently qualified for that task. By the time he reached junior high, he was assistant manager. By the time he was in high school, he was running the whole thing.

"By then, I guess, Shep was kinda spoiled from having me around so long," Bruce says of the time after he finished high school and left Palestine to seek his future. "Six months after I was gone, I heard they closed the business. I came back to town after a year and half, and somebody contacted me about buying the place. I called him up and worked a deal with him."

Most old-timers insist Shep's hasn't changed a bit since Joe Sheppard first opened the doors, but that's a bit of self-delusion. In 1988, for instance, three years after Bruce reopened the place, a fluorescent light on the ceiling shorted out and sparked a fire that destroyed much of the interior. Bruce did his best to re-create the feel of the original, though entirely with new décor. Happily, he was able to easily resuscitate the line that passed his cutting board, leading toward the cash register by way of side dishes and peach cobbler. Just before the bill is rung up, there's a canister of sweet tea—some of the sweetest brewed anywhere. "There are people who come in just for the sweet tea," asserts Bruce.

From the beginning, Bruce saw catering as an important part of his business plan. On any given day that he's slicing brisket and ribs at Shep's, he might be just back from or just about to travel to Houston, Dallas, Austin or San Antonio to serve barbecue to the multitudes. In light of this volume, Bruce began the purchasing process that led to his owning three different rotisserie smokers, the largest capable of cooking 500 pounds of meat. Hickory is his wood of choice, a flavor he loves all by itself (with no dry rub) on the beef briskets that slow-cook 13 hours before ending up sliced or chopped on plates and sandwiches.

Ribs are another story. Bruce uses pork spareribs and marinates them in his dry rub overnight, then smokes them about 4 hours, until they're pull-apart tender with a crust resembling candy. Smoked sausage and hot links are also solid sellers, followed by smoked chicken and turkey. The increasing popularity of turkey, whether for health reasons or simple great taste, is one of the changes Bruce has adjusted to over the years.

Beyond doubt, the two best side dishes within these walls show a debt to Bruce's youth spent serving soul food. Instead of the boring green beans that are the barbecue norm, Bruce cooks his with plenty of salty ham, raw onion and onion salt. And instead of the often-boring pinto beans, he serves "cowboy beans" that not only have a hint of heat but memories of time spent in the pot with the end pieces cut from Shep's spareribs.

Completing the circle in a way that should surprise no one, Bruce has refused to let his soul food love affair fade away, no matter how much time he spends smoking meats. He operates a restaurant called Triple A in Palestine, a home-cooked soul food eatery whose best-selling dish is the Thursday night special—oxtails in gravy served over rice. Asked if there's crossover between the two menus, Bruce simply smiles and shakes his head. Each cuisine is its own tradition, he seems to be saying, and it's best to keep such traditions pure...even if you love both to distraction.

"I love meeting people every day," says Bruce. "I love to cater and go out to different places, whether it's a barbecue or a fish fry. You just learn the basics from everybody's recipe, then you change it up a little and make it your own. You find what people like and you stick with it."

BODACIOUS BAR-B-Q MOUNT PLEASANT

ADDRESS: 100 W. FERGUSON ROAD, MOUNT PLEASANT
PHONE: (903) 572-7860
ESTABLISHED: 1973, THIS LOCATION IN 1979
OWNER: BOB ADAMS
BEST BITES: BEEF BRISKET, PORK RIBS, SAUSAGE, BROCCOLI-CAULIFLOWER SALAD, HOMEMADE SOUPS, STUFFED BAKED POTATOES, CORNBREAD
PAYMENT: CREDIT CARDS

Before Bodacious had exploded into a chain with something like 25 locations in different parts of Texas, it was just one little joint in Longview. So when a bank that held the note on a struggling barbecue place in Mount Pleasant decided to foreclose, it called in the couple who gave every indication of knowing how to make the thing work.

The couple took over the Mount Pleasant location and worked in it for about a week before selling it to the woman's brother. And when that brother was ready to sell after five years, he called his brother in Dallas. Bob Adams had spent several years selling fountain drinks to restaurants for Dr. Pepper. He figured that if some of the people he sold to could operate a restaurant, then he could, too. He packed up his family and headed east out of Dallas on Interstate 30.

"That was November of 1979," says Bob. "I still buy my meat from the same guy, and I still get my wood from the same guy, who has a bunch of land with trees all over it. These days, that's mighty unusual. Most places shop around. But I don't."

Considering the familiarity of the Bodacious Bar-B-Q brand, it's fascinating how little Bob's place looks, feels, acts or smells like a chain restaurant. It all goes back to the beginning, of course. When Bob bought in, there was no chain. It was his responsibility to figure things out, either from what his brother told him or simply using his head. To this day, while he uses barbecue sauce and seasonings

made at the Bodacious plant in White Oak, he puts on his menu whatever he wants—and cooks it by whatever recipe he wants. For Bob Adams, there are no Bodacious Police.

"I'm not really a part of all that," he says. "I don't go to their meetings or go by their handbook. I'm sure they got rules, but I don't know anything about that."

What Bob does know about is making barbecue, and making a pretty good living doing it. For his meats, he goes exclusively with oak wood, dividing it between a rotisserie smoker that cooks nothing but 30 briskets at a time and an old-fashioned flat smoker with racks for pork ribs, sausage, turkey and chicken. Bob smokes his briskets 13 to 17 hours, with the outside temperature having a lot to say about how long, and his ribs about 6 hours. The briskets are plain—not so much as salt and pepper, and definitely no sauce. The ribs get a dusting of that official Bodacious seasoning before they go into the smoker.

For being in Texas, Bob does a brisker-than-usual business in pulled pork. At some point, the Pilgrim's Pride company moved lots of employees from elsewhere to Mount Pleasant—elsewhere in this case meaning places where pork barbecue was popular. Bob got a little tired of these Texas immigrants asking why he had no pork, so he watched a show on the Food Network about cooking the stuff and added it to the menu. As for the Memphis tradition of dressing a pulled pork sandwich with coleslaw, however, Bob figures it's important to draw that line in the sand somewhere. "This is Texas," he says, shaking his head. "That's not the Texas deal."

As the menu at Bob's Bodacious makes clear, a lot of his customers like vegetables. Beyond the standard-issue potato salad, pinto beans and coleslaw (which people from Memphis can use any way they see fit), there are green beans and whole-kernel corn and black-eyed peas, the latter exceptional with the homemade cornbread that seldom lasts beyond lunchtime. Perhaps the most popular vegetable strays a bit from the "healthy" concept, though: chopped broccoli and cauliflower studded with cubes of cheddar cheese and drenched in ranch dressing. It's vegetables for people who really hate vegetables.

Stuffed baked potatoes are exceedingly popular, particularly topped with plenty of chopped beef. Presumably, Bob makes sure he always has leftover baked potatoes, for these get turned into a huge and happy surprise: a potato soup many a chef would be proud of. This is one of two homemade soups set out for ladling each day, the other being a knockout tomato and vegetable.

Bob glances around his dining room that seats 88 and anticipates the next question: What schizophrenic genius was in charge of décor? All the usual hunting trophies are mixed up with old signs for products and photos of country music stars. Most eye-catching is an impromptu series of framed newspapers and other documents, detailing everything from 1930s politics to the JFK assassination, with stops for the deaths of Bonnie and Clyde and of Sheriff Buford Pusser of *Walking Tall* fame.

"Everybody wanted to hang their deer horns and their hogs and their fish," Bob shrugs, a man who knows when to stop fighting back. "I just cleared the walls and let them at it."

TEXAS BAR-B-Q CORRAL MOUNT VERNON

ADDRESS: I-30 SOUTH SERVICE ROAD, MOUNT VERNON
PHONE: (903) 537-4848
ESTABLISHED: 1996
OWNER: ROYCE DIMSDLE
BEST BITES: BEEF BRISKET, PORK RIBS, SMOKED TURKEY, STUFFED BAKED POTATOES, COWBOY BEANS, LBJ SALAD, PECAN PIE
PAYMENT: CREDIT CARDS

When he isn't cooking or serving barbecue with the recipes his father perfected almost 50 years ago, Royce Dimsdle likes to repair musical instruments and dream he had more time and talent for playing them. Some of his handiwork, highlighted by a refurbished 1939 Epiphone acoustic guitar, hangs on the walls of his barbecue joint.

"Here," Royce says to a visitor, carefully lifting the Epiphone from its hook. "You owe it to yourself to strum on this a

little bit. It's the wood. Guitars just aren't made with wood like that anymore." He notices the look he's getting, even as the visitor cradles the guitar and takes a few reverent swipes at the strings. "I wanted to be a musician, but God wanted me to be a cook," relates Royce. "You see which one I'm doing now, don't you?"

Between God and his father, Royce figures his fate was sealed. As far back as 8 years old, he was working in his family's barbecue joint in downtown Dallas—clearing tables, washing dishes, making change the old-fashioned way. "You had to add it up in your head," he recalls, "or do the math with a pencil and paper. Those old registers didn't do any of the work for you the way they do now."

Despite the intense apprenticeship in barbecue, Royce wanted a career and a life of his own, going to work in various factories before ending up in the tree business. This went well enough, until he fell and seriously injured his back. Forced to choose a new way to make a living, Royce found his way back to the old way. Looking around the historic town of Mount Vernon, Royce stumbled on a barbecue place from the 1970s right on Interstate 30. He knew it was the place to cook his father's recipes.

"I'd like to take credit for them, but sure as I do, he'll be standing right there listening," says Royce. "There's nothing written down. You just had to watch him make 'em. The only reason I can come so close is that our hands are about the same size."

In the spirit of a man who prefers old guitars to new ones, and even old cash registers to new ones, Royce definitely prefers his old camp-style freestanding pit to any of those modern rotisseries with gas burners and digital thermostats. The pit at Texas Bar-B-Q Corral is nearing 40 years old. "My dad had it in one of his places, and it's about wore out," Royce laments. "I'll probably have to fix it pretty soon."

Using either hickory or pecan wood— he prefers pecan, but hickory is sometimes easier to get—Royce smokes his meats with no sauce and no seasoning. He fits up to 30 briskets on his pit, letting them smoke for a mysterious amount of time somewhere between 18 and 28 hours. "It depends on the brisket," he insists, "even if you have two side by side. When I stick a fork in it and it feels right, I pull it off. It doesn't matter what the clock says. You just have to cook 'em 'til they're done."

Sausage, pork ribs and smoked turkey are other popular meats at the Corral, sided with some deliciously spicy "cowboy beans" and something Royce calls the LBJ Salad. Most customers ask if it's named for Texas-born President Lyndon Baines Johnson, but if pressed, he'll admit it stands for Little Bit a' Junk. Actually, it's nothing of the kind: a wonderful mix of crunchy raw vegetables in a sprightly vinaigrette.

Though Royce's repaired guitars, fiddles and other musical instruments are the most expensive bits of décor on the wall, they are hardly the most numerous. That honor goes to inscriptions scribbled by diners from across the United States and from as far away as London and Cairo. Best wishes turn up in many penmanships and several foreign languages, all honoring a man who sometimes wishes he were playing music onstage rather than making his own kind of music on a battered old smoker.

"I only meant to do one little section," Royce says of the signatures. "I guess it got out of hand."

FAT BOY'S BBQ PITTSBURG

....

ADDRESS: 413 S. GREER BOULEVARD, PITTSBURG
PHONE: (903) 856-0000
ESTABLISHED: 2007
OWNER: KEITH WITTEBORT
BEST BITES: BEEF BRISKET, PORK RIBS WITH MAPLE COATING, SMOKED SAUSAGE, BAKED POTATO SALAD, PINTO BEANS, BANANA PUDDING WITH VANILLA WAFERS
PAYMENT: CREDIT CARDS

Everybody knows the traditional Olympic progression: you trade childhood for practice, compete until you win one or more gold medals, and then turn pro. Much the same progression exists for amateur barbecue cooks, even though they're seldom the same shape as Muhammad Ali, George Foreman or Sugar Ray Leonard...or, for that matter, Cathy Rigby, Mary Lou Retton or Nadia Comaneci.

Competing for barbecue's gold medals takes a lot out of you—or puts a lot on you, more to the point. And with a new barbecue restaurant named Fat Boy's, Keith Wittebort is clearly a man who's walked the walk.

"I spent seven years doing competitive barbecue, traveling just about everywhere that had some kind of cook-off," says Keith, slipping carefully into one of his wooden booths along the front window. "Quality was definitely an issue for us. I wanted to provide the same quality I was doing at competitions, but here it had to be for a reasonable price. In the beginning, I tried to buy out a guy doing barbecue here in town, but I just couldn't afford what he was asking. So I started looking around, and one day when I was heading over to Gilmer, I saw this old Laundromat."

For Keith and the Laundromat, it may have been love at first sight. Yet so much work went into the transformation, much of it done by Keith's own hands, that nobody would spot mementos of the place's previous life without Keith pointing them out. This, in fact, the man loves to do. He takes pleasure in describing the cedar accents on either end of the corrugated metal that decorates several walls, and in describing how he and a few helpers constructed the booths of stained pine. "I've touched nearly every board in this place," Keith says with pride, "including that bench you're sitting on."

Still, the renovation story he enjoys most concerns the long, communal table that runs along one side of Fat Boy's dining room, seating a maximum of 17. That was once a row of washing machines, he says, and when he ripped them out he discovered a deep trough in the concrete to drain away any possible overflow. Smoothing out the concrete, using the good stuff he was committed to using, would have cost $600 he didn't exactly have. So Keith built the long wooden table right above the trough and only filled up to the edges with concrete. Today, he says, his customers love that strange table, especially for business meetings and birthday parties when everybody wants to sit together. He seldom reminds such customers that necessity can, indeed, be a mother.

As you'd expect of a longtime and successful cook-off competitor, Keith takes the art of barbecue seriously. In fact, you'll seldom find a professional restaurant guy who's half the stickler for obsessive detail that one of these amateurs tends to be. As a restaurant owner himself now, Keith is charged with taking these same obsessions and molding them to fit commercial reality. After all, you're not just pleasing a table of judges once—you're trying to please a "table of judges" many times a day, every day, for basically the rest of your life.

If cedar and pine are the woods of choice in Keith's dining room, pecan rules in his Ole Hickory smoker visible behind the counter. "You can cook with pecan start to finish," he explains, "and not overflavor your meat." Keith likes a special maple-kissed dry rub on his pork ribs, but he uses no seasoning at all on his brisket, which he cooks for about 12 hours at 225 degrees.

At Fat Boy's, ribs get the same multi-step handling Keith perfected as an "impractical" competitor and believes in too fully to change now. They smoke for 3 hours, then get covered in that maple rub, then get wrapped in heat-resistant plastic and returned to the smoker, where they finish cooking for 1 more hour in their own juices. "The wrap keeps the moisture in," he says, "and it makes the rub caramelize and cook on as a coating. People from around here don't always know what maple is, but they love it."

The choice of side dishes is no work at Fat Boy's: the baked potato salad, made with red potatoes and sour cream to mimic a "loaded baked potato" with plenty of ranch dressing, and the pinto beans slow-cooked in porcelain pots. The trick with the beans, Keith lets on, is cooking them in jalapeño juice. The top dessert is homemade banana pudding with vanilla wafers.

Still, true competitor that he is, Keith knows that some days you just get out of bed and do what you do, fully aware there are a thousand others guys doing something a little different. "This is just something we've always done," he says.

WILLIE'S BAR-B-QUE
PITTSBURG

ADDRESS: 417 S. TEXAS STREET, PITTSBURG
PHONE: (903) 856-1103
ESTABLISHED: 1992 AS WILLIE'S
OWNERS: WILLIE AND LURLEAN SUGGS
BEST BITES: BEEF BRISKET, PORK RIBS, CHOPPED BEEF OR PORK PIE, HOT LINKS, POTATO SALAD, FRIED CATFISH, POUND CAKE
PAYMENT: CREDIT CARDS

Sages through the centuries have noted the circular quality of many human lives. After a full career with the U.S. Government, Willie Suggs would like to add his personal testimony to the body of evidence.

"I've been doing this for 30 years, give or take," he says matter-of-factly, not continuing 'til he has greeted three bundled-up workmen stepping in from the rainy cold. "I learned about barbecue right here, on this spot. My grandfather had a barbecue place at this location for 40 years. You know how it is, with the first grandchild always spending time with his grandparents. Well, I hung around this place with my grandfather all the time."

In one of life's mysteries, to hear Willie talk, you'd think he'd never left, that his 30 years flowed uninterrupted from his grandfather's 40. Yet like more than a few barbecue guys who tried to escape the inevitable, Willie tried to do something else. In fact, he succeeded—spending two decades as a mechanic at the nearby Red River Ammunition Depot, repairing tanks. When the time came to think about retiring, however, Willie found himself dreaming more and more about those years he spent working beside his grandfather.

"His pit was just laid in the ground out there with bricks, with the fire right under the meat." Willie gestures out through the door, to the piece of lawn now filled with the parked trucks of his customers. "He showed me the whole nine yards." Another customer walks in, another familiar first-name greeting. Then, "It's a good feeling, that your grandfather can hand something down to you and you keep it going. Now I have a 9-year-old grandson. I tell people this is his place. I just work for him."

Considerable work it has been, too. Using his skills as a mechanic, Willie built the metal building that now houses his spartan six-table restaurant. He also brought the cooking inside, replacing his grandfather's open pit with first a small and now a large barrel smoker.

"I don't use gas, I use wood," he says simply. And to Willie, wood means red oak, which gives the flavor he loves (and almost certainly remembers) to the brisket, ribs, hot links and chicken served at Willie's Bar-B-Que. He definitely uses his grandfather's seasoning recipe for his brisket, slow-cooking for 7 to 8 hours until it's tender. The same rub goes on Willie's ribs, which cook about 4 hours. While he's heard of all kinds of complicated processes for ribs—wrapping them, letting them steep in their juices—he insists that's making way too much of a really simple thing.

"You just talk to your fire," says Willie, "and you'll get it right."

In a turn that would mystify most barbecue places in Texas, all of Willie's tender meats take a backseat in sales to a main dish they probably don't even serve: fried catfish. Between the straightforward batter of seasoned cornmeal and the crispy french fries on the side, this is enough to make less of a carnivore out of just about anybody.

Those french fries, by the way, return in one of Willie's greatest hits, something he calls the "chopped beef pie." For this, Willie fills the bottom of a paper-lined basket with fries, then covers them with chopped beef (or pork), cheese and bacon bits, then with another layer of fries beneath a blanket of ketchup. Chopped beef pie at Willie's is a solid reminder that ketchup really does have a place in the universe.

Dessert couldn't be more straightforward: pound cake baked by Willie's wife, Lurlean. It's plain pound cake, the way they used to make it on the frontier using a pound of each ingredient. Not orange-macadamia pound cake or Meyer lemon-poppy seed pound cake. Just pound cake,

with the simplest sugar glaze spread across the top. Lurlean can't bake enough of them.

"We don't do nothing fancy," Willie says, nodding to several customers who've taken up residence during the pound cake course. "We just do what we know, what we've been taught."

RAMAGE OLD FARM MARKET BBQ, HOOKS

ADDRESS: 901 MAIN STREET (I-30 EXIT 208), HOOKS
PHONE: (903) 547-6187
ESTABLISHED: 2000
OWNER: BRENT RAMAGE
BEST BITES: BEEF BRISKET, PORK RIBS, FRIED OKRA, COWBOY POTATOES, SMOTHERED GREEN BEANS, PECAN PIE, BLUEBERRY CHEESECAKE
PAYMENT: CREDIT CARDS

Attacking the problem like the engineer he was, Brent Ramage tried to "engineer" a way for people to remember his place when all other businesses along Interstate 30 had served their purpose and faded behind the mile markers.

"I knew they'd never remember Ramage, and they'd probably never remember Hooks, Texas," observes Brent, gazing around at his 6,000 square feet of hyper-rustic space divided between retail and a barbecue joint—a kind of Texas-crazed Cracker Barrel. "But I figured they'd never forget 'that place with the silo.'"

Yes, alongside the main building Brent built a silo, an architectural tribute to one of the few things that Ramages haven't seriously farmed: dairy cattle. They've raised just about everything else since they started farming in central Texas in the early 20th century, moving to the far northeast corner in the mid-1950s.

Pecans were their first cash crop, followed closely by blueberries when the Texas Department of Agriculture was heavily promoting that. Along the way, there have been other things, all adding

up to a farm tradition that Brent both takes pride in and strives each day to exploit.

"My family was hunting moisture when my dad moved us up here," he explains. "You know how dry it can get in central Texas. Fact is, we would have moved here sooner if we weren't waiting for my mom to give birth to me. So she did, and we moved here when I was three weeks old."

Although Brent is in the restaurant and retail businesses now, the link between those and the family farm has always been well-defined in his heart. Early on, the family built a market to sell its pecans to locals and passersby, and once they started turning their blueberries into jelly, the retail side got serious. For a time, the Ramages even ran a steakhouse in one of their barns, which taught young Brent a good deal about customer service and a great deal about cooking meat. Lessons learned on both counts still guide him in the endeavor beneath the Texas flag-emblazoned silo that he designed, constructed, decorated and opened with the new millennium.

"I kinda consider this place to be a liaison for all those Yankees coming south," he says. "And when those lost Texans see my flag, they know they're home. I'm selling Texas the second they see my billboards and my storefront." He thinks for a moment, his mind caught somewhere between the state's patriotism and the state's favorite cuisine. "I like something that when you put it in your mouth, it sinks its teeth into you."

Like most things for this family, their barbecue venture began on the farm. In fact, even the huge black pit Brent designed was constructed on the farm and then moved to a place of honor behind the restaurant—all 7,000 pounds of it. The distance was less than five miles, but for someone without the right skill set, it might as well have been 2,000.

"I have this engineering background, and I wouldn't be much of an engineer if I couldn't figure a way to move 7,000 pounds from my farm to here," he laughs. "But still, I like to tell folks that if anybody wants to borrow it for a backyard barbecue, they're welcome to come and get it."

Looking a bit like a medium-sized submarine, Brent's smoker is old-fashioned to the max, though its maker did build in a thermostat and a small electric engine to turn the rotisserie. He loves to use pecan wood exclusively, since he has upwards of 30 acres of pecan trees, but he'll toss a little oak on the fire in a pinch.

Brent's pit can cook as many as 60 briskets at a time—each of the 60 covered in a salt-popped dry rub that, of course, he has engineered. He cooks the brisket for 10 to 11 hours, knowing that some of the seasoning will drip off in the pit or get sliced off later on the cutting board …thus the extra salt. The rub for Brent's ribs will mostly stay on, so its recipe is different and its application more precise. The ribs cook only $1\frac{1}{2}$ to 2 hours, just until the meat starts peeling back from the bone at the tips.

The serving line at Ramage Old Farm Market BBQ features a delightful array of vegetables—both fried like okra and stewed or smothered like green beans, corn and black-eyed peas. The "cowboy potatoes" are a special thing here. They're small red potatoes, boiled, chopped and sautéed with onions, bell peppers, the family's signature steak seasoning and a final flourish of "garlic spray." Lest you think that last step is some hush-hush engineer's secret, Brent will happily sell you a canister of the stuff on your way out.

And Ramage's wouldn't be Ramage's if you didn't have dessert. They're always making peanut or (even better) pecan brittle in the back, but that's more of a souvenir. For dessert, get both the pecan pie and the light, whipped cheesecake made from Brent's mother's recipes. The latter is a square cut from a sheet pan, turned unforgettable by the pecan crust on the bottom and the blueberry sauce on top.

"It's like my whole family history is in that cheesecake," Brent observes with a satisfied smile.

SMOKEY JOE'S BARBEQUE NASH

....

ADDRESS: 300 E. NEW BOSTON ROAD, NASH
PHONE: (903) 334-8227
ESTABLISHED: 2005
OWNERS: ERIC HILLIARD, JOE HACKLEMAN AND EDDY HACKLEMAN
BEST BITES: BEEF BRISKET, PORK RIBS, STUFFED BAKED POTATOES, BBQ FRIES, SWEET POTATO FRIES, BLACKBERRY OR PEACH COBBLER
PAYMENT: CREDIT CARDS

Eric Hilliard knows how his business cards should describe him, if he ever has time to get some printed: "owner, manager, pack mule, dishwasher."

"It depends," he says, "what day it is."

Still, after 15 years working in the barbecue business for others or being in situations that turned out to be dead ends, Eric takes considerable satisfaction in having his own shop poised for expansion. You can just tell, especially when an owner without a business card has invested time and money in a super logo. Here's a logo, you say, that deserves to be on more than one restaurant. Eric gets up every day to make sure his is a restaurant worthy of its logo.

As joints go, Smokey Joe's is large, squeaky clean and family friendly. There are even Bible quotes on the wall, but that's another story. The place can seat 110 in its brightly windowed dining room, plus another 30 in its game and party room, plus a full 130 in the banquet room Eric and his partners built alongside. This space has become a major hit, and not just for office parties. Meetings are held in the room regularly, making full use of its hotel-quality audiovisual equipment complete with a screen that rolls down automatically. Even in Texas, how many barbecue joints can boast of offering that?

"You bring in everybody with a banquet room," says Eric. "They come in whether they want to or not, if they've got a meeting. You do some good food and you've got yourself a customer."

Eric has spent his entire working life figuring out what a customer is and how to keep him or her happy. He started out with that northeast-Texas powerhouse Bodacious, helping the chain keep growing in Gilmer, then Gladewater, then Longview. In fact, for most of those years,

the plan was for Eric to get a Bodacious store of his own. As he tells it, though, the problem was that he had the know-how and his parents had the money, which was not how Bodacious liked to do things.

Taking his parents' money elsewhere, Eric opened the Texarkana barbecue joint that became Big Jake's in a former Dairy Queen. But at some point, his parents wanted out and, after a couple of painful steps, Eric and his wife found themselves running a tiny, mom-and-pop barbecue joint far out on a stretch of country highway.

"We did that five days a week for three years," he recounts, feeling the disappointment all over again. "The building was wore out, and the roof leaked. It was rough. And it was far out of town, which meant it was out of sight, out of mind."

The breakthrough that gave the world Smokey Joe's came through conversations with two brothers he met at church. They became convinced God wanted them to build and own a restaurant, and since they were in the construction business, that made a certain sense. All they needed was a guy to operate the place for them, a guy who had worked in barbecue. The word "coincidence" is unlikely to turn up in such a narrative.

"My partners said it was God's will to open this place," Eric says.

Able at last to have a major say in his future, Eric went to work in a frenzy. With his experience cooking barbecue large and small, he pulled together a couple of Southern Pride rotisseries that hold 1,000 pounds of meat each. He committed himself to using hickory, which he loves, but also knew he could compromise using red oak, post oak, pecan or mesquite whenever supplies ran low.

Smokey Joe's brisket goes on the smoke for about 14 hours, the St. Louis-cut pork ribs about 4. Both meats get a coating of Eric's dry rub at the start. And while those meats and Smokey Joe's popular sausage can be enjoyed with standard barbecue sides (especially the potato salad, made with skin-on red potatoes), insiders know better. They get one or more orders of Smokey Joe's hand-cut sweet potato fries, dusted with a spicy-sweet seasoning that includes powdered sugar.

On many days, derivative products are the biggest sellers, whether it's the baked potato stuffed with chopped beef and cheese or the so-called BBQ Fries, pretty much the same notion except with the ever-welcome Texas addition of being deep-fried. All things stand ready to be covered with Smokey Joe's barbecue sauce, made in 15-gallon batches from Eric's recipe by the same employee every morning.

"The biggest challenge in this place is making sure the employees do things my way," he says, perhaps wondering how to express that on a business card. "They have to do things as you would, whether you're there or not."

BIG JAKE'S SMOKEHOUSE TEXARKANA

ADDRESS: 2610 NEW BOSTON ROAD, TEXARKANA
PHONE: (903) 793-1169
ESTABLISHED: 1998
OWNERS: MATT AND JESSICA PALMER
BEST BITES: BEEF BRISKET, CHOPPED BEEF SANDWICH, PULLED PORK SANDWICH, PORK RIBS, SMOKED CHICKEN, SMOKED TURKEY, SPICY PINTO BEANS, FRUIT COBBLERS
PAYMENT: CREDIT CARDS

At the risk of sounding biblical, a man had two barbecue joints. And even though the two barbecue joints offered identical menus, in one place the biggest seller was beef brisket and in the other it was pulled pork. The distance between the two barbecue joints?

"Oh, maybe four or five miles," says Matt Palmer, owner of Big Jake's. "Of course, this is Texas, and that over there is Arkansas. In this place, we can barely give away pork shoulder most of the time, cuz here it's all brisket and sausage. You

go a few miles into Arkansas and all they eat is pork shoulder. They love our pulled pork sandwiches, with the coleslaw on top like they do in Memphis…well, that's optional."

Big Jake's isn't the only thing that goes a few miles into Arkansas—so does Texarkana. Originally thought to sit as a settlement in Texas, Arkansas and Louisiana (thus the name), the city finally realized that maybe two of the three ain't bad. Besides, the entire area is part of a four-state crossroads, weaving Oklahoma and its different tastes into the tapestry. Matt opened the first Big Jake's on the "Texas side" in 1998 and ran that for three years before adding the other store on the "Arkansas side." In 2007, a third location came around, in Hope, Arkansas, made famous as the home of former President Bill Clinton.

For Matt, owning three restaurants with his wife, Jessica, before he turned 30 is a bit of a dream come true. Of course, he's been working in the barbecue business since he was 15, washing dishes and cleaning the dining room while also struggling to master the mysteries of the pit. He worked at several locations of Bodacious spread around East Texas before moving to Texarkana to help open Big Jake's. Before long, like that guy on TV with the razors, he found himself owning the company.

"I've been doing this so long, I could do it with my eyes closed," says Matt, his eyes checking on customers in every part of this renovated Dairy Queen. "And I've got staff that's been with me since the day we opened the doors."

The DQ memory remains at Big Jake's, if you're able to picture where the entrance used to be and realize you're eating barbecue inside where the outside used to be. Matt's smoker is where the kids' playground used to be, a fine investment in the future of America all the same. Back in his teenage years, Matt trained on the old-fashioned flat pits powered only by wood—trained just enough, that is, to convince him his business needed two rotisseries that used gas for heat and wood for smoke.

Matt smokes his ribs 12 to 15 hours with no dry rub or sauce, while his ribs get a hit of seasoning before going into the smoke for 3 hours. Arguably better than either, though, are Matt's smoked chicken and turkey breast. Go for the thinner pieces around the edges, which seem to absorb more smoke and take on a crusty, caramelized sweetness.

"As far as consistency and training employees, these pits are obviously the way to go," he says of his modernization. "On my catering trailer, I still use an all-wood pit, but that's a lot of work." Matt smiles. "I guess I've gotten a little bit spoiled."

For all the firepower in the back, Big Jake's isn't one of those modern barbecue places that want to be more than a barbecue place. As in the best of such settings, the menu is impressively lengthy, but nearly everything on it is a different combination of the same basic things. The standard side items are here, and not a whole lot more. Matt is especially proud of his pinto beans, however—cooked with chopped onion and whole jalapeño peppers. The fruit cobblers with ice cream are the main desserts, though Matt does bring in some pecan pie and double-fudge chocolate cake.

With barbecue, he's learned—whether he's making it beef for Texas or pork for Arkansas—it isn't so much about venturing forth as it is about staying home. "To me, barbecue is a rustic brick building with concrete floors," says Matt. "That's what we work at here. I try not to have any flat-screen TVs."

THE WEST

HAROLD'S PIT BAR-B-Q ABILENE

ADDRESS: 1305 WALNUT STREET, ABILENE
PHONE: (325) 672-4451
ESTABLISHED: 1956
OWNERS: HAROLD AND DRUCILLA CHRISTIAN
BEST BITES: BEEF BRISKET, PORK RIBS, SAUSAGE, TURNIP GREENS, GREEN BEANS AND NEW POTATOES, HOT WATER CORNBREAD, BLACKBERRY COBBLER
PAYMENT: CASH

Everyone has good days and bad days at the office. But on this particular day, after 53 years of serious barbecue, Harold Christian clearly believes he and his wife, Drucilla, have earned a better day than this.

"I love this place, and I love to work," says Harold, relaxing in a booth moments before the lunch crowd starts banging on the latched front door. "But I can't take it anymore. When it stops being fun, it's time to go. All I do now is holler and scream and tell people what to do, and I usually end up doing it myself anyway. And I'm tired of it."

Harold's complaints are a grab bag of old and new, predictable and unexpected, from unreliable help to customers with attitude to a worn-out back. Yet it's clear from the depth of his frustration that Harold isn't merely having a bad day at the office. It's equally clear, chatting with him in the dining room and later with Drucilla in the kitchen, that neither of them has known any other life.

Harold was born in northeast Texas near Tyler, a hotbed of African-American barbecue tradition. His father, Tobie Christian, brought him west to Abilene in 1956 to work with a man who had a barbecue joint—*this* barbecue joint, as it turned out. Within a couple years, that man gave up and sold the business to Tobie, whose son had been working there since Day 1, since he was 10 years old.

The place called Tobie's Bar-B-Q caught on right away, becoming known throughout the African-American community and eventually to all of Abilene as a haven for good, consistent food and what Harold now calls "good relationship."

"You wanna know what that is?" he asks, then proceeds to craft an essay in the air. "When people come in our place, they don't come in as a number. That's not the way we do it. We know their grandfather, their mother and their children. We know when they're sick and what hospital they're in. That's the relationship we have with our customers. We're for real. We have nothing to hide, nothing to cover up. And we've never had to advertise, like in the newspaper or on the radio. Everything for us has been mouth-to-mouth."

In the beginning, the dining room seated only 35 people; half a century later it seats twice that. In the beginning, there was sawdust on the floor; today the sawdust is gone and the floor shines not with affluence but with attention.

A major change occurred in 1972, when Harold was 27. By then his father had fallen into trouble with the government over taxes. Harold took over the business and, for any number of strategic reasons, Tobie's became Harold's. One thing that didn't change was Tobie's presence alongside his son. He worked at Harold's until he died in 1984.

Even after 53 years of cooking meat, Harold's kitchen is one of the cleanest

you'll find anywhere; that's one of the many things he "screams and hollers" about all day. His black box of a pit keeps the meat amazingly close to the oak wood, cooking and smoking at the same time. He doesn't specifically season his meats—no top-secret dry rub, in other words—clinging to the belief that each wood carries a "spice" of its own. Oak carries a pepper taste, he theorizes, just as surely as pecan tastes like sugar and mesquite tastes like salt.

Harold likes to smoke his brisket fairly fast, he says, 12 to 15 hours, drawing his inspiration from cowboy days of cooking on a stick over an open flame. Other wildly popular meats at Harold's include pork sausage, pork ribs and smoked turkey.

While all the traditional side dishes are offered, Harold's has at least three signature extras: turnip greens so good some people think they must be spinach, the green beans and new potatoes he added to the menu recently and now can never take off, and a spectacular spin on a Southern classic called "hot water cornbread."

While revealing how the batter is made, the name misses the most striking touch. Drucilla forms each oblong cornbread piece in her hands and drops it carefully into hot oil for frying. Available in regular and even-better jalapeño, hot water cornbread is both like and unlike anything you've ever tasted. It is, without a doubt, the world's largest hush puppy. It just might be the world's best as well.

There is something bittersweet about watching Drucilla fry up another delicious batch, just as there is something bittersweet in the way Harold points out all the things his employees haven't done today…talking about them as though they're not standing three feet away. He's pondering exit strategies, he says; and if all of them fail, he and Drucilla just might lock the doors one of these days and walk away.

"I'm not saying it wouldn't bother me not to come up here," says Harold, who in his prime could be counted on to sing gospel standards like "Amazing Grace"

and "How Great Thou Art" in the dining room for any customer who asked him to. "But I feel like I could have a life, getting up every morning and just drinking coffee." He smiles, more than a little wearily. "I'll have to take a pay cut if I don't have this place. But for my happiness, I need a pay cut."

SHARON'S BARBEQUE ABILENE

ADDRESS: 849 E. HIGHWAY 80, ABILENE
PHONE: (325) 672-3330
ESTABLISHED: 2005
OWNER: SHARON RILEY
BEST BITES: BEEF BRISKET, PORK RIBS, PORK LOIN, BONELESS CHICKEN THIGHS, GREEN SALAD, JALAPEÑO CORN, GREEN BEANS AND NEW POTATOES
PAYMENT: CREDIT CARDS

Sometimes it's a couple getting together that gives the world another terrific barbecue joint. But sometimes, this being the real world, it's a couple breaking up—or, as Sharon Riley puts it with considerable gentility, "parting company."

For 22 years beginning in 1980, as Sharon *Allen*, she was the unnamed but hardly inactive or invisible partner in Joe Allen's, one of Abilene's biggest barbecue success stories. When Joe and Sharon divorced—OK, "parted company"—in 2002, Sharon discovered it left a bigger chasm in her life than she'd expected. A chasm about more than a job or an income, and having something to do with her soul.

"Before I was in the barbecue business, I was a registered nurse," she relates, putting the pieces together. "And that makes me a caregiver. I want to please people. I love good food, and I love to cook. I was proud to be part of Joe Allen's. I feel like I had a lot to do with its success, and I know I worked really hard. I got down to 90 pounds at one point. In the split, Joe kept the barbecue place and

I kept the steakhouse. But I found that I really missed the barbecue business."

By 2005, Sharon had a barbecue business of her own. Officially the place was called Sharon's, but it was known locally as "Sharon Allen's" for a good long while. This became harder to justify after Sharon remarried and became Sharon Riley. But since only her given name had ever been on the sign, no major change was required.

"I don't know how this sounds, but I think people liked me and missed coming to see me," she explains. "I guess I wanted to give them a way to come see me."

The "way" Sharon built is fresh and clean—like many a modern steakhouse concept, not so exclusively masculine as in the past. At heart, Sharon's is a comfortable family restaurant that *happens* to serve Texas barbecue. Its owner thinks in terms of masculine and feminine, going so far as to call "feminine" her commitment to having more meats than brisket, ribs and sausage and many more vegetables than potato salad, coleslaw and beans.

Of course, Sharon had a lot of years to clarify what was important before putting her own name over the door. She was familiar, for instance, with those old-fashioned, labor-intensive pits, difficult and sometimes dangerous devices more about romance than efficiency. She knew their pluses and their minuses too well, she laughs, so all the meats at Sharon's come out of a modern rotisserie.

Following West Texas tradition, Sharon is a big believer in mesquite and smokes with no other wood. She uses an exceedingly simple dry rub—just salt, pepper and granulated garlic—before putting her briskets in the smoke overnight for 12 to 13 hours. As in many other barbecue places, it's the efficiency of this process that wins out, producing a consistently good product in time for the staff to pull in the morning.

As promised, there's plenty of variety among the meats set out in a display case right inside the door. Brisket finds itself wrestling for shelf space with not only sausage and pork ribs but smoked turkey, pork loin, half chickens and something Sharon describes as boneless chicken thighs. These last are lovely, moist and bursting with flavor. "I've always loved the dark meat," she lets on.

More "femininity" is obvious in the placement of a big bowl of mixed green salad front and center—what guy would ever think to do *that*?—plus an array of vegetable side dishes well beyond the norm, from green beans with new potatoes to the best side of all, jalapeño corn. As Sharon narrates with affection, this is made by sautéing onions and jalapeños in butter, then adding drained corn kernels followed by cream cheese. A little salt and pepper, and you're tasting a secular miracle.

Sharon serves up two kinds of barbecue sauce: the traditional tomato-meets-brown sugar of Texas for beef and a thin, "almost Carolina" vinegar-based liquid for pork. Yes, you're allowed to mix and match. Sharon's actually bakes its own breads—white and wheat, plus regular and jalapeño cornbread—and offers peach and cherry cobbler for dessert.

The place seats about 80, and it often has to during the lunch or dinner rushes. That seating, Sharon insists, is only the tip of the iceberg. "I would never put in any kinda place that doesn't have a drive-thru," she says, almost giggling. "That's the best thing ever."

BETTY ROSE'S LITTLE BRISKET, ABILENE

ADDRESS: 2402 S. 7TH STREET, PLUS TWO OTHER LOCATIONS, ABILENE
PHONE: (325) 673-5809
ESTABLISHED: 1981, CURRENT OWNERSHIP 1996
OWNERS: KYLE AND CHERRY JOHNSON
BEST BITES: BEEF BRISKET, PORK RIBS, MASHED POTATO SALAD, FRIED CATFISH (FRIDAYS AND SATURDAYS), STEWED CABBAGE, SEASONED SPUDS, BANANA PUDDING
PAYMENT: CREDIT CARDS

When Betty Rose Stokes opened her barbecue joint in an old gas station in 1981, she kept things all in the family. She brought in two aunts as partners to help out. And she brought in her grandmother exactly as grandmothers should always be: laden with great recipes.

Today, after not one but two changes of ownership since Betty Rose retired in 1992, quite a few things have evolved.

Most significantly, the place has gained enough respect from barbecue lovers in its quirky original location to open two others far less quirky. But those grandmother's recipes remain the coin of the realm. Or as Irving Berlin once put it, the melody lingers on.

"We still use their exact recipes," boasts Kyle Johnson, who started as a part-time dishwasher for extra income here in the early '90s when he was stationed at Dyess Air Force Base. "We cook on the same pit Betty Rose used at the original location, and the pits at our new locations were built for us by her son. We don't try to do a whole lot of different things here. We don't do a lot of chicken and Mickey Mouse ears and stuff."

With all due respect to The Mouse, those ears clearly represent for Kyle and his family (for Betty Rose's remains all in the family) a shopping list of things the place just isn't *supposed* to do. And like most people who've enjoyed a bit of success—he since acquiring the business from the buddy who hired him in 1996—Kyle feels his approach validated by broad customer acclaim.

The former gas station remains the flagship of Betty Rose's, a breath of fresh air in a world more accustomed to look-alike eateries in strip centers. The bay

doors marked for auto services remain visible from the outside, though just inside them sit happy families devouring barbecue without fear of their table rising up like a '57 Buick on the rack. In one of the more colorful blasts from the past, the doors to the restrooms also remain outside—just the way they always were in old gas stations.

Internally, Kyle and kin have rejected the notion of modern rotisserie smokers, despite any advantages they might have. He is content with the old black barrel smoker that still works well in the original Betty Rose's...content enough to install new ones in each new location. Though he considers himself and indeed Betty Rose's something of "the new young kid on the block," he feels it's important to stay close to the barbecue traditions that gave him those all-important recipes.

"We use mesquite," he announces, as though it were dogma. "That's just what we use. It doesn't matter what other people use. It's the only kind of wood to ever cook brisket on."

And cook brisket Betty Rose's does—upwards of 30,000 pounds of it per month, to be sold sliced or chopped up for saucy sandwiches or even whole. Any barbecue place would probably sell you a whole brisket if you ask, says Kyle, but his place is one of the few to put such a thing on the menu. Betty Rose's brisket gets a fairly typical dry rub and goes into that dogmatic mesquite smoke for 18 hours. Still, according to Kyle, that's not their big secret.

People love the brisket here, he insists, because it's trimmed of fat both before and after it's smoked. Under interrogation, Kyle admits they leave some fat on to keep the meat moist through those 18 hours, but after that, all bets (and just about all fat) are off. That makes, clearly, for meat that's juicy and flavorful yet still surprisingly lean. Pork ribs are the other top seller among meats, sporting the same rub and emerging tender from the smoke after 4 to 5 hours.

Side dishes (the forte of any grandmother worth her, well, salt) are exemplary. With additions and adjustments by Kyle's family along the way, these include stewed cabbage with butter and jalapeños—a longtime employee meal that a customer finally tasted, and that was that—and something known as "seasoned spuds." These are baking potatoes cut in large wedges and baked in butter with mushrooms, onions, Parmesan cheese and a healthy dose of brisket rub.

With Kyle's wife, Cherry, running the original and he operating a second, the future seems bright for the legacy of Betty Rose Stokes. But if you think this thing will go national at any minute or at least pop out more restaurants in different sections of Abilene, that's not what Kyle is thinking on this particular day.

"Five or eight locations?" he asks, echoing the question. "Probably not. We've got all our families and wives and cousins running it. To do this right, we're probably about as big as we can get."

JOHNNY'S BBQ & DINER MIDLAND

ADDRESS: 316 N. BIG SPRING STREET, MIDLAND
PHONE: (432) 683-4581
ESTABLISHED: 1952
OWNER: ROY GILLEAN
BEST BITES: BEEF BRISKET, PORK RIBS, SMOKED TURKEY, RICKY SAUCE, POTATO SALAD, COLESLAW, BUTTER BEANS, PEACH OR CHERRY COBBLER
PAYMENT: CREDIT CARDS

Nobody seems to remember what year this was, but there came a time while Johnny's and its owner, Johnny Hackney, were flying high that a dozen or so Midland movers and shakers told him they were coming in on Sunday.

Well, all right, offered Johnny, but we're not open on Sunday.

That's OK, said the group, we're coming in anyway. And they did, cooking

their own food on Johnny's stove or in a ragtag assortment of devices they imported with them. Best of all, for the true birth of a West Texas legend, they brought plenty of whiskey.

"This went on for years and years, with the group including a lot of local business leaders, oil executives and even a few ex-mayors," says Roy Gillean, who bought the place shortly before Johnny Hackney's death. "Laura Bush's dad used to be one of them. I mean, this was the place to be on Sundays, and all these guys knew about the key Johnny kept for them out in the flower bed. They'd eat, drink whiskey and watch the games on TV. One guy, well, he even broke his arm falling off the roof. I'm sure there was no alcohol involved in that."

Until he died in 2007, Johnny Hackney was a Midland original, a barbecue guy who came of age as a Marine in the Pacific Theater of World War II. Despite being in his barbecue restaurant every day starting in 1952 (and for a time, fronting an Odessa location as well), Johnny also dabbled successfully as a real estate agent, a travel agent and, in the early 1970s, a stockbroker. Somehow, for Johnny, all these other businesses fed into his central barbecue enterprise. It got where Johnny knew everybody in town and everybody knew Johnny. It was a great way to keep a restaurant full, even on the one day a week it was closed.

"We made the deal with Johnny," Roy remembers, "and I told him he had to come up here and eat barbecue every day for the rest of his life. He was 83 at the time, and unfortunately, he got real sick. We didn't see much of him after that."

"Johnny was amazing," chimes in Daniel Ruiz, the remarkably young general manager who's worked for Roy at other restaurants since he was a teenager. "He was a character. Everybody loved him. And you know, he never had a computer or anything, but anytime you asked Johnny, he could tell you how much the place had taken in that day, to the dime."

Fact is, Roy has done a lot of work to the Johnny's building, a former gas station when Johnny first laid eyes on it but now something of a destination theme restaurant with a '50s diner décor. One thing Roy wisely has *not* changed is the first guy customers talk to when they walk in, meat cutter Ricky Bowers. For more than three decades now (getting the job when his predecessor passed away), Ricky has been on a first- or at least last-name basis with most of Midland's financial and political elite. They all, of course, call him "Ricky." People especially like to talk to him about his two favorite sports, football and dice.

"Some of these people come in every other day," he relates, "and I know what they want when I see 'em comin' in. They don't gotta speak. I just make it for 'em." Ricky thinks back to what must be one of his favorite things. "Johnny's buddies took me to Las Vegas once. They gave me

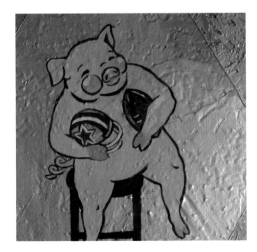

about $1,000 to go gamble on." How'd you do? "Shucks, I came back broke. But I had fun."

Part of the renovation carried out since Roy took over in 2006 has affected the smoking method, but so little, he says, that no one has noticed. The old pit (built and installed in the kitchen by one of those ex-mayors) had acquired a really bad habit of catching fire, and the fire department was less sympathetic now that it wasn't dealing with Johnny the local icon anymore. The shiny new rotisserie, like the kitchens for antebellum Deep South plantations, is separate from the building in its own concrete-walled space.

Johnny's pit crew sprinkles upwards of 40 briskets at a time with a little bit of dry rub, then puts them on to smoke over oak wood for 8 to 9 hours. Pork ribs are the next most popular meat, Daniel says with Ricky nodding enthusiastically, followed by sausage, turkey breast and ham.

Potato salad is probably the biggest-deal side at Johnny's—"Man, they *love* that potato salad!" Ricky editorializes—plus the sweet-and-sour coleslaw and the butter beans simmered with bacon and ham. Best desserts are the peach and cherry cobblers, with pecan pie for those wishing a change.

Longtime customers, of which Johnny's has no shortage, know to load up on Ricky Sauce before they take their trays and sit down to eat. No, not the place's homemade *barbecue* sauce, which is wonderful enough. They go straight for the *Ricky Sauce*, to be used judiciously on meats, beans and anything else, like a spicy chow-chow. A brief description by its creator makes a visitor wonder about his recipe: Does it have a vinegar base, like Tabasco and its many sweat-producing kin?

"Vinegar?" Ricky exclaims, like he's just heard the dumbest idea ever. "No, man, it sure *don't*. Everything I put in it is hot!"

HOG PIT PUB & GRUB MIDLAND

ADDRESS: 7500 W. COUNTY ROAD 116, MIDLAND
PHONE: (432) 561-9301
ESTABLISHED: 2004
OWNER: QUATRO AARON
BEST BITES: PORK SPARERIBS, BEEF BRISKET, GRILLED BRISKET CHEESE, HOG BITS, JALAPEÑO "BOTTLE CAPS," SPICY "SOUL SLAW," MASHED POTATOES AND GRAVY, BAKED BEANS
PAYMENT: CREDIT CARDS

Quatro Aaron is larger than life. Happily for the roughnecks and cowboys who fill his tables at lunch or dinner and cover his bar stools the rest of the time, so is his barbecue.

Quatro (born Glen Aaron IV, thus the numerical nickname) has apparently taken to heart the notion that everything is bigger in Texas. With his shaved head, close-trimmed beard and mast-like apron on a body that's tall as well as wide, Quatro resembles nothing as much as what he's been from time to time: a barroom bouncer. You know, the kind who, even if he can't beat you up, can at least sit on you for a while. Barbecue, it seems, has appealed to his calmer, gentler and more creative side...not to mention his sense of life's irony.

"I figured I'd have a bar that served a little barbecue," Quatro says between drags on his cigarette and swigs of his longneck beer. "Instead, pretty quickly, I ended up with a barbecue place that has a little bar."

Before he turned to owning the Hog Pit on a remote plot of dusty land close to Midland's airport, Quatro broke up his nights as a bouncer with work as an office manager for lawyers. Well, he admits, most of *that* was for his father, for 13 years. And when his father decided to retire from law, Quatro looked for a new line of work. What he came up with was one of his oldest.

He'd learned to slow-cook meats from his grandfather when he was a little boy—OK, a larger-than-average little boy—helping with the fire but eventually seasoning and turning the ribs, brisket or chicken. Like so many in Texas with similar childhood experiences, he'd evolved into a better-than-average Sunday pit master. To hear his friends tell it, he was a *lot* better than average.

"People seemed to like what I made," the man says with some modesty. "Still, I didn't know anything about cooking in volume. A guy who worked here early on showed me how to do that. Now it's just second nature."

Quatro figures he and his guys have cooked 35,000 slabs of ribs in their first four years of operation (and since he's a former office manager who looks like a bouncer, you're inclined to take him at his word). In fact, Quatro's barbecue joint is one of the few in all Texas to sell more pork ribs than beef brisket. Thus, the name Hog Pit over the door, on the roof for planes passing overhead, on his pickup for catering jobs and on a huge sign that blew down in 95-mile-an-hour winds, seems more than a little prophetic.

Quatro says he couldn't afford one of those fancy rotisseries that cook with gas or electricity, all kept nice and uniform with a thermostat. The best he could do was talk a buddy into building him a strange-looking stand-up pit with doors for meat. And then, when business at the Hog Pit went through the roof, he went back to that buddy and had him cut off the top and enlarge it. Quatro uses only

mesquite and a simple dry rub on his meats, cooking brisket and his oversized, meaty, fall-off-the-bone ribs for 12 to 13 hours.

"As we're smoking, every couple hours we'll go outside and rotate the meat," he says, a not-entirely happy poster child for barbecue done the old-fashioned way. "Rainy days are harder than sunny. Windy days are harder than not windy. And cold days are harder than hot ones. Cooking this way, you just have to adjust to everything."

As barbecue places go, the Hog Pit has a large menu, with burgers, country-fried steak and fried catfish, plus many items drawn from the general tradition of "bar food" (a.k.a. stuff that makes you drink more). This seems only fair, since Quatro claims that all his best new recipes were invented while he was drinking. Things like the word-scrambled "grilled brisket cheese" (a Lone Star version of Philly cheese steak, outfitted with Swiss cheese and onions) and "hog bits" (sliced sausage that's battered and fried) give every indication Quatro is telling the God's truth.

"I just had a few beers and thought about it some," he recounts of that last epiphany. "Then I had a few more beers."

In addition to the restaurant seating 250 and the bar seating as many as are thirsty at any given time, the Hog Pit doubles—or to be precise, triples—as a live music venue. There are bands playing here every weekend, many of them local or from Abilene or Lubbock, but some big names too like David Allan Coe and Leon Russell.

"Doug Moreland played our grand opening," says Quatro, glowing with admiration and definitely knowing a kindred spirit when he sees one. "He's just nuts. We have so damn much fun with him."

KD'S BAR-B-Q, MIDLAND

ADDRESS: 3109 GARDEN CITY HIGHWAY, MIDLAND
PHONE: (432) 683-5013
ESTABLISHED: 1997
OWNERS: DWIGHT AND KATHY FREEMAN
BEST BITES: BEEF BRISKET, PORK CHOP, JALAPEÑO-CHEESE SAUSAGE, "MIXED SAUSAGE" IN BARBECUE SAUCE, POTATO SALAD, PINTO BEANS, JALAPEÑO-TOMATO RELISH (CALLED "HOT SAUCE")
PAYMENT: CREDIT CARDS

Like that candy mint that's also a breath mint, KD's Bar-B-Q is two, two, two joints in one.

In 1997, Dwight and Kathy Freeman moved from the Hill Country to Midland with their son Dustin to be near Kathy's ailing father. And if that generational saga weren't enough, they invested their futures in the most generational thing in the whole state of Texas: barbecue.

Finding a location where a lot of roads and reasons came together, they built a 300-seat restaurant and filled it with everything everybody's attic used to have in it. And when they got the chance to

buy the gas station right next door, they built a second location only a few steps from their first.

"That thing cost so much, I figured we'd better do something with it," Dwight says simply. "I'd thought it would just give us some more parking, but it sure didn't work out that way."

"We have arrows everywhere," Kathy adds, addressing the issue of customer confusion. "We just call it the Big One and the Little One." She smiles. "We're gonna get 'em, one way or the other."

The two side-by-side KD's may share a color scheme—"red" about covers it—but they actually have different personalities and purposes. A method in the madness. The Big One is about as full-service as Texas barbecue is likely to get, following the Llano Method of customers ordering meat from the pit as soon as they come in the door, then passing through a cafeteria line for side dishes, desserts and drinks. There's a quirky island in the center of the dining room, where bread, onions and jalapeños await, along with four different styles of barbecue sauce.

The Little One is decidedly different, a case of function following form. As a former gas station, it had serious drive-thru potential, so that is what it became. Cars pull in for and out with barbecue all day long. Once the Big One closes after lunch around 2 p.m., focus shifts to the Little One until 8 or 9. And for people smart enough not to eat food dripping with sauce while driving, the second location has 40 seats and just enough kitschy décor on its own.

"I wanted it to be real comfortable for everybody," Dwight says of KD's, named after his wife and son—not, as almost everyone assumes, himself. "We used to have a full-service steakhouse on Lake LBJ, before we moved here, and I wanted this to be less labor intensive. That's why you see so much paper and Styrofoam."

Dwight considers a typical lunch in the Big One. "It's still hard, though. At five minutes to 12, you have nobody here. At 12, you have 400 people."

As the de facto pit boss, Dwight cooks all his meats over mesquite in a big rotisserie, before transferring it to the low-lying serving pit by the front door. He says the place averages 400 to 500 pounds of brisket per day, with the rest of the meats bringing the total to 700 pounds. And if you need help doing the math, that means KD's goes through as much as eight cords of mesquite every single month.

"That's a lottta wood," Dwight sighs. "But my dad is the one who taught me how to barbecue, and mesquite is all he ever used."

Brisket goes into the smoke for 18 hours at a mere 200 degrees after a dusting of dry rub—secret, naturally, and featuring no fewer than 12 herbs and spices. Pork ribs get a different rub, one built more around brown sugar, before turning in the rotisserie for 3 to 4 hours. Also popular are KD's jalapeño-cheese sausage and super-lean smoked turkey, plus a pork chop introduced only recently. The popularity of this chop keeps on growing, with all 60 minus one selling out today. That one had to be set aside and guarded, in order for a visitor to get a taste.

Additional touches at KD's include a rustic live music stage out back with shows a couple times a month spring and summer, chopped beef that's done in chunks with a knife rather than reduced to mush by a food processor, and a wondrous jalapeño-tomato relish (a kind of hopped-up Tex-Mex chow-chow) that customers spoon over their pinto beans, potato salad and almost anything else that strikes their fancy.

Kathy loves to mix this relish 50/50 with their sweet barbecue sauce. But as a business owner (she and Dwight have a running comedy routine about figuring her percentage), she's afraid to spread this idea around. Everyone will surely go through a lot more sauce.

SAM'S MESQUITE COOKED BAR-B-QUE MIDLAND

ADDRESS: 1113 E. SCHARBAUER DRIVE, MIDLAND
PHONE: (432) 570-1082
ESTABLISHED: 1983
OWNER: LEE HAMMOND
BEST BITES: BEEF BRISKET, PORK RIBS, HOMEMADE SAUSAGE, MASHED-UP POTATO SALAD, CREAMY PINTO BEANS, BANANA PUDDING
PAYMENT: CREDIT CARDS

As an infantryman, Lee Hammond had obeyed, endured, survived and generally put up with everything the U.S. Army could throw at him, including Korea a couple years after that "police action" and Vietnam at the height of Ho Chi Minh's bloody Tet Offensive. Still, he wasn't sure he was ready for what his father had in mind when the call came through from West Texas.

"That was 1978, and he said I'd talked about retiring in 1978," Lee recalls. "Now I don't remember saying any such thing. In fact, I was an Army recruiter by then and I'd just gone up a grade, with a nice pay raise. I was thinking: Hey, I really wanna stick around and enjoy this for a while. But the more my father talked, the more I realized he was having trouble with this little convenience store he was running in Odessa. So I said, OK, give me 30 days. I'll get out and I'll get home."

Trouble was an understatement. The store employees weren't doing their jobs. The place was a mess, a fact taking its toll on customers. And there wasn't much of anything on the shelves to sell. As convenience stores go, Lee's father's place was sounding mighty inconvenient.

Son came dutifully home to father, however, retired from this man's Army. He looked things over at the store for a while, and finally asked anyone who'd listen: Where's the barbecue?

"When I was a kid, I had an uncle

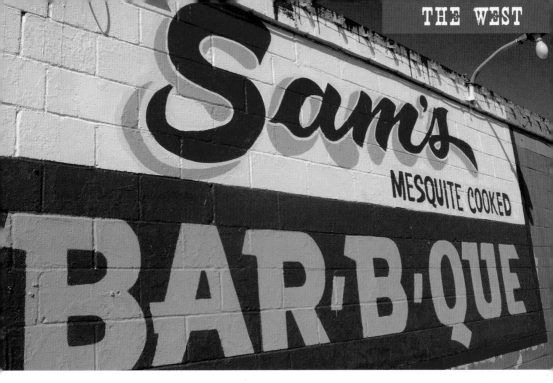

from East Texas," Lee says. "He would come out in the fall, up north of Abilene, and he was a real barbecue aficionado. He'd set up this little stand where people had come to gather the cotton. People would come from all over Texas back then, as there was a lotta work and a lotta money. My uncle had me as an assistant when I was 8 or 9 years old."

Before long, those childhood memories—and a lot of years of giving and following orders in the military—had turned the convenience store around. Employees had been nudged into compliance...the floors, walls and windows had been washed...and there was plenty of stuff to buy after Lee invested his savings. Best of all, he had mingled his own memories with those of older relatives to create something akin to his long-ago uncle's barbecue.

The customers loved it, and the revenue split quickly came to resemble that of a barbecue joint more than that of a convenience store. So when an old Laundromat came on the market in nearby Midland, Lee said, "Dad, I think it's time we thought about the restaurant business."

They did more than think about it, rebuilding and opening in 1983. The place got its name from a beloved cousin who had recently passed away.

Today, Lee is still tall, still fit, and still blessed with a glistening smile that no doubt made all things seem bright when he was an Army recruiter. He had exhorted a decade's worth of recruits to "be all you can be." Now it was Lee's turn, and he was ready—whether that meant long nights turning meat on the wood-fired pit or long days sticking flyers on windshields at local sporting events.

Lee relies on mesquite to cook his meats in an old-fashioned 10-foot-long barrel smoker, burning the wood down to white ashes on the side before spreading those around beneath the grate. In sales, brisket and ribs live in tight competition day to day—the beef getting nothing more than salt and pepper before going into the smoke for 8 to 12 hours, the ribs going in for only 2 to 3.

Chicken has always been a popular item here, even though it took Lee, his father and a cousin to beat that uncle's recipe out of their collective memories. Homemade sausage also sells well—90 percent beef, with just enough pork to give it moisture and flavor.

According to Lee, the goal each day is to keep things simple and perfect what they do. This applies to the mashed-up potato salad, the creamy pinto beans and, of course, the peach or cherry cobbler that joins banana pudding as dessert.

"Funny as it may sound," says Lee, "you just can't let nothing whip you. By rights, I should be gone after the oil bust and everybody around here filing for bankruptcy. I went through all that too. But you go and you borrow some money, and you just go on.

"I promised myself I'd give this business 10 or 15 years, and that would do me. That would be enough. Now I've been at it 25 years." Lee smiles, ever the recruiter. "I don't make any more promises to myself."

BAR-B-Q BARN ODESSA

ADDRESS: 3820 ANDREWS HIGHWAY, ODESSA
PHONE: (432) 362-7366
ESTABLISHED: 1991
OWNERS: DORLESE PERKINS AND PAULA CHAMBERS
BEST BITES: BEEF BRISKET, SAUSAGE, PORK RIBS, SMOKED TURKEY, GERMAN COLESLAW, PINTO BEANS, PEACH OR CHERRY COBBLER, BANANA PUDDING
PAYMENT: CREDIT CARDS

"You'll love those two ladies!"

That's what people tell you all over Odessa—even the ladies' competitors—when you ask about Bar-B-Q Barn. Some might tell you about the old-fashioned pit that the mentor of one of the ladies delivered by forklift. Others might describe the food, which ranges from traditional to, well, even more so. And still others might speak highly of the friendly, hyper-casual service.

But no matter what people in Odessa choose to tell you about Bar-B-Q Barn, it all adds up to the same thing: "You'll love those two ladies!"

Sitting with Dorlese Perkins and

Paula Chambers during a lull on a busy weekday serves to prove the prophecy. The two speak candidly about their opening of Bar-B-Q Barn in 1991 despite the fact that Dorlese knew nothing—"I mean *nothing*," she says more than once—about the business. To her credit, Dorlese recruited Paula, a friend of the family who had been working in another local barbecue joint for almost eight years.

"Dorlese kept driving by and driving by, and saying wouldn't that make a cute little barbecue place," Paula remembers. "It was a liquor store at the time. The possibilities were there, and here we are."

Despite the generous help of Paula's former boss, who found the ladies a pit and drove it over on a forklift, their best efforts at planning were in for a shock almost from the beginning. The place was tiny, and Dorlese envisioned the bare necessities for customers to walk in and order takeout—maybe even drive-thru without ever leaving their cars. The ladies put in only two tables, and those were for the family members and close friends who quickly got into the habit of visiting. Right? Wrong!

The first time a customer spotted one of the tables, he sat down to eat his barbecue. Before long there was no place for family and friends to sit. The ladies eventually succumbed to this change in their business plan and doubled their table count to four. They still do their share of takeout, and still pass a large amount of barbecue and sides out the drive-thru window. But within a few weeks of opening, they knew they were running a restaurant—albeit a *really* small one—with all the customer service issues running a restaurant entails.

First things first, though: Dorlese and Paula needed some barbecue.

Since Paula had cooked on a similar pit at her old job, that part came quickly. Inside the smoky metal shack she shows to a visitor, Paula does her best work on an old black barrel smoker, with three doors on top for meats and two smoke-stacks sticking up through the roof. Just outside, there's a firebox in which she burns nothing but mesquite wood for both heat and smoke. No electric heat is used, the ladies insist, and no gas either.

"It does the best meat," opines Dorlese, who describes herself as having had a "bunch of 29th birthdays." "I think the pit has a lot to do with it. And of course, the cook."

Each day that she's cooking brisket, Paula covers the meat with her own dry rub and puts it in the smoker for a minimum of 10 hours. At that point, each brisket is pulled and wrapped in plastic to wait in a holding oven at just under 150 degrees. Pork ribs get the same rub but naturally a much shorter smoking time.

"The hardest part is having to cook without knowing what's going to happen that day," says Paula. "You have to keep two steps ahead of everybody. Sometimes it's a rib day all day long."

Smoked sausage sells well, as does the smoked turkey breast the ladies manage to keep amazingly moist. Side dishes are limited: just potato salad and pinto beans, plus a light, vinegar-based "German coleslaw" that's a happy marriage of sweet and sour. Peach and cherry cobblers are made for Bar-B-Q Barn ("I'm not a baker," Paula says without regret), but the place makes its own banana pudding.

Over the years, Dorlese and Paula

have seen many changes in the restaurant business—too many, they might be tempted to say. Small, single-unit eateries such as theirs have disappeared regularly, almost always to be replaced by what they see through their windows: McDonald's, Wendy's, Arby's and Taco Villa. Still, business is good on this day at Bar-B-Q Barn, just the right amount for two ladies everybody loves.

If you ask Dorlese how she keeps such a positive attitude in such a negative world, she certainly has a story to tell you.

"One day we had people everywhere, out the door and lined up at both our windows," she says. "I was complaining just a little bit, and kinda under my breath I said, 'When I get to heaven, I'm gonna ask the good Lord why everybody always gets hungry at the same time.' Well, this sweet darling little lady heard me and she said, 'Dear, why don't you just say thank you?' Now that's just what I do."

JOHNNY'S BAR-B-Q ODESSA

ADDRESS: 2201 KERMIT HIGHWAY, ODESSA
PHONE: (432) 332-8941
ESTABLISHED: 1952, CURRENT OWNERSHIP 2007
OWNER: JOHN HERRIAGE
BEST BITES: BEEF BRISKET, PORK RIBS, HOT LINKS, COLESLAW, POTATO SALAD, MACARONI SALAD, LEMON MERINGUE PIE
PAYMENT: CREDIT CARDS

By the time John Herriage bought the half-century-old Johnny's Bar-B-Q in 2007, the place's signature neon sign hadn't lit up the night for close to 10 years. Only the occasional small catering job had emanated from this beloved old building, which was something of a supernatural occurrence, asserts John, since there was no water or electricity.

And that, it seems, was only the beginning.

"Johnny's was kind of an icon," says

John, who operated three other restaurants at the time he took over this one. "But driving by here, you could see the place looked like hell. In its day, Johnny's was known for the best barbecue. It was awesome. By the time it closed, it was known for OK food and cheap catering. It was known as that restaurant with the sticky tables, and you don't want to be known for that."

For all the bad reports on Johnny's in recent years, the legend did manage to remain. And it was that legend that John figured he was buying. Still, the total price kept going up each time he discovered another thing that didn't work. The renovation inside and out took three months. It also took, John says, about three times as much money.

"Every damn piece of equipment had to be replaced," he reports, still seeming to feel the pain. "They had an old pit that had fire after fire, 'til the fire marshal said that will not be used again. We have an electric pit now, using hickory for smoke just the way Johnny's did back in the '50s. If a customer does not know, they'll think it's the same thing. Our customers tell us all the time how glad they are we kept the old pits. We just say, 'Yeah.' "

One early stroke of luck was locating one of Johnny's longtime cooks. Though the guy at first bristled at using the new smoker, he came around big-time once he tasted the quality and experienced the consistency. No longer would a kitchen helper have to sleep on promises, getting up hour after hour to move the meat around the pit. Before that cook moved on, he had taught John enough of the old recipes to work his intended magic, a barbecue blast from the past.

John and his crew use a dry rub on their brisket and put it in the smoker overnight for about 10 hours. That means it's ready to come off and be served fresh as soon as Johnny's opens in the morning. The pork sausage, divided between "German" and spicier "hot links," has a following too, as do the pork ribs dusted with the same rub and smoked for about 6 hours.

Combining Johnny's tradition with his own ideas, John has developed terrific versions of mustard-yellow potato salad, celery-crunchy macaroni salad, thick-savory pinto beans and a coleslaw that's sweeter and lighter than most. His barbecue sauce, while certainly subject to customer preference, has got to be one of the best around for its balance of sweet, sour and peppery. There are peach and cherry cobblers for dessert, plus a host of meringue pies built around chocolate, lemon or coconut.

Though John has gone from project to project often in his years of restaurant-ing, going back to waiting tables at age 14 in tiny Levelland west of Lubbock, the rebirth of Johnny's looks like it's going to keep him busy for a while. After trouble getting a neighbor to clean up the overgrown lot next door, he purchased the rest of his block. On this land John plans to build a series of catering facilities, outdoor for casual barbecue events and indoor for weddings of up to 150 people.

All that will depend on Johnny's regaining its place in hearts and minds all around Odessa, on locals coming in regularly and sitting at the refurbished wooden tables in weird tilt-back chairs that seem to combine someplace to sit with someplace to turn around and get a massage. That's 75 seats in the dining room, plus 70 more in the banquet room. And filling them depends on Johnny's neon sign lighting up the night once again.

"It's working fine," offers John, "several thousand dollars later."

"Like just about everybody else in Odessa, I was in the oil field," says Maurice Hubbard, lifting his cigarette to his lips with long, lanky fingers. On the enclosed porch on a mild spring morning, heaters overhead whir and glow, too much for anyone not looking to get a tan. "I been in the booms and I been in the busts, and the last bust got me. I didn't so much get out of the oil business as it got outta me. So I needed a new way to make a living."

Just over a decade later, Bob is surrounded by the new way he found.

Rockin' Q Smokehouse grew out of a partnership with his sister's husband, Bob Barnes. Bob was a veteran of several restaurants, including the locally popular Taco Villa. In Odessa and neighboring Midland, you can drive from Taco Villa to Taco Villa without time to ever get hungry in between. The building in which they built their first (and so far only) Rockin' Q had been a Taco Villa.

According to Maurice, who served as the operation's hands-on partner, the learning curve just about killed him.

"The hardest part was learning it, let me tell you," he says, taking another drag and glancing at the account books that lie open on the table. "It was hit and miss for the first couple of years. Bob had lots of restaurant experience but no barbecue experience." He smiles. "I don't guess you get barbecue experience 'til you do it."

First, though, the partners had to take the former Taco Villa, filled as it was

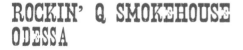

ROCKIN' Q SMOKEHOUSE ODESSA

ADDRESS: 3812 PENBROOK STREET, ODESSA
PHONE: (432) 552-7105
ESTABLISHED: 1998
OWNERS: MAURICE HUBBARD AND BOB BARNES
BEST BITES: BEEF BRISKET, PORK RIBS, SMOKED CHICKEN, JALAPEÑO SAUSAGE, PULLED PORK SANDWICH, COLESLAW, MACARONI AND CHEESE, GREEN BEANS, PEACH OR CHERRY COBBLER
PAYMENT: CREDIT CARDS

with the pastel colors that say Tex-Mex to generations of Texans, and turn it into a Western-themed barbecue joint. The décor went red, white and blue—the colors of the Texas flag, of course—with one huge flag taking the place of honor on a mural that covers one wall. The whimsical side of the Lone Star State came to be represented by the usual array of cowboy hats, oil gushers and happy armadillos.

Perhaps the biggest part of the reconstruction was adding this enclosed patio, once Maurice came to understand that with three bay doors that roll up like an auto mechanic's, Rockin' Q could turn indoor into outdoor whenever the weather was nice enough. Around Odessa, that meant whenever the wind wouldn't blow a pile of West Texas dirt into people's barbecue.

"You can have a good patio effect," Maurice explains.

Since a Taco Villa never needed a smoker, Maurice had to buy one; and after considerable research, he opted for the efficiency and consistency of a rotisserie. Wood also stumped him for a while, as he and Bob tried cooking with a lot of different types. Still, the decision came down to the only two woods readily available in West Texas, mesquite and oak. Maurice chose oak, because it cooks lower and slower than the mesquite favored by most other barbecue joints in the region.

Brisket is the big seller at Rockin' Q— it would almost have to be, considering that it turns up sliced for plates, chopped for sandwiches, rolled up in burritos, piled on salads ("for the wives," says Maurice) and hoisted atop 1-pound baked potatoes. Each brisket gets covered in dry rub before going into the smoke for 12 hours, turning slowly to receive the cooking juices given off by its brethren.

Ribs and chicken are the next most popular, but these never see the dry rub at all. Instead, Maurice and Co. coat them generously with a "wet rub" that resembles a marinade. The exact recipe is a secret, naturally, but Maurice lets on that

coarse ground black pepper and a little bit of cayenne are important components. And being a liquid, the marinade helps the ribs and chicken stay moist throughout their 4 hours on the rotisserie.

The biggest surprise on Rockin Q's menu is pulled pork—yes, served on a bun with a mound of coleslaw, just like they do in faraway Memphis. Bob encountered this style of barbecue during travels through Tennessee. Impressed, he encouraged Maurice to give it a try and give it time to develop a local following. He did, and it has.

"That's not something you see very much around here," Maurice says, chasing a swig from his coffee cup with an affectionate drag on his cigarette. "It took a while for it to catch on. Here in Odessa, for the longest time, people just didn't get the concept."

PACK SADDLE BAR-BQ SAN ANGELO

ADDRESS: 6007 KNICKERBOCKER AT RED BLUFF ROAD, SAN ANGELO
PHONE: (325) 949-0616
ESTABLISHED: 1987
OWNERS: MARSHAL AND SHERRI GRAY
BEST BITES: BEEF BRISKET, PORK RIBS, CHOPPED BEEF SANDWICH, HAMBURGER, FRIED CATFISH, COLESLAW, ONION RINGS, FRUIT COBBLERS
PAYMENT: CREDIT CARDS

"Let's go sit on the back porch," says Marshal Gray. And since the route past the kitchen passes remarkably close to a washtub full of bottled beer, he extricates one from the ice and invites a visitor to follow suit.

One must be sociable.

Settled at one of seven picnic tables Pack Saddle Bar-BQ uses when the dining room overflows and/or the weather's nice, Marshal looks back over the past 22 years of serving brisket, sausage and finally hamburgers and catfish to an ever-grow-

ing clientele. After earning an accounting degree and working in the oil field and in real estate, he had a pretty good idea what he was getting into.

"You have to pay attention to detail, and you have to listen to your customers," he says, drawing a long sip from his beer. "I mean, that's how we got into burgers and hand-cut fries. That's how we got into catfish and hush puppies, because some people just don't like barbecue. And once we were doing catfish, it wasn't hard to start doing chicken nuggets for the kids. If you make the little kids happy, mom and dad are coming back."

Clearly, Marshal didn't hail from one of those old Texas barbecue dynasties, one of those families that fill each new generation with more don'ts than dos. All he understood from opening day in 1987 was that he would go the extra mile to make people happy. He had barbecued for family and friends for years and, like so many Texas backyard pit guys, had received regular encouragement to turn pro. Still, he confesses some shock when it came time to cook barbecue as a business.

"It's day and night," says Marshal. "Quality is easy when you're doing small amounts. It's harder when you're doing 30 cases of brisket a week. But for all that, we've made a lot of friends."

For more than 15 years, Marshal and his pit guys used the old-fashioned wood smoker that came with the building, a simple and primitive heat source that required constant attention—and even then, was never the paragon of consistent cooking. But then (according to Marshal, you can insert the angel choir of your choice here) he switched over to a rotisserie smoker from Ole Hickory, one that kept a constant temperature and could be timed so no one had to stay all night moving the meat around.

"We did it the old way forever," he says. "All my cooks thought they'd died and gone to heaven when I bought the new smoker. Without it, there'd be no way to keep up with all the business we're doing." He thinks, hearing the criticism to come. "It's all about consistency. If you got a guy that has to keep running out there to put wood on, you're going to get highs and lows."

Pack Saddle's business includes plenty

of beef brisket, which is covered with a dry rub and put in the mesquite smoke for 13 to 14 hours. That means the staff can go home at night and come back rested to perfectly cooked meat. Marshal says his customers prefer lean brisket, so almost all fat is trimmed off for slicing as well as for chopping.

"We only put the pretty slices on the plate," he says, taking another swig of his beer. This is a sign for everyone else on the back porch to do the same. There are only two people on the back porch.

Pork ribs are popular, as is the slightly spicy smoked sausage. The ribs get the same rub as the brisket, but their time in the mesquite smoke is shorter, about 7 hours.

Potato salad, coleslaw and pinto beans are the favored side dishes, with peach, blackberry and cherry cobblers ruling the roost at dessert. Strangely, while the cobblers are baked elsewhere, Marshal has his waitresses make ice cream every day—eight gallons at a time, in a churn on the same porch that's so perfect for drinking beer.

Marshal predicts he'll hit at least 30 years in this, his final career. The job isn't hard as much as it's time-consuming, he says, explaining it was his wife, Sherri, who started making him close on Tuesdays: "She said I wasn't turning into a very nice person." He seems happier now, running Pack Saddle along with a KOA campground he can point to from the porch.

As for what comes after that, Marshal can do no better than shrug. It's a safe bet his three sons won't be interested, he says, since two-going-on-all-of-them are already committed to computers and other things that work very fast when barbecue works very slow. Perhaps someone will buy the place and keep it going, someone who's hungrier for the barbecue business than his sons.

"I don't encourage it," he says, sipping his beer and smiling wistfully, "and they don't encourage it."

OLD TIME PIT BAR-B-QUE, SAN ANGELO

ADDRESS: 1805 S. BRYANT BOULEVARD, SAN ANGELO
PHONE: (325) 655-2771
ESTABLISHED: 1993
OWNER: GARY ZESCH
BEST BITES: BEEF BRISKET, PORK CHOP, BEEF RIBS, JALAPEÑO SAUSAGE, POTATO SALAD, COLESLAW, GREEN BEANS, CORN ON THE COB, FRUIT COBBLERS
PAYMENT: CREDIT CARDS

Sometime in the early 1990s, Gary Zesch and his go-to guy, Gerald Pritchett, looked out at the pizza parlors and burger joints they were running and decided San Angelo needed barbecue. For the longest time, it looked like they'd open a franchise of Cooper's in Llano. But then, for one reason or another, the deal fell through.

Happily, the barbecue didn't.

Old Time Pit Bar-B-Que, as even the name suggests, is a virtual outpost of the Llano landmark—130 miles west of Llano. Cooking is done with direct coal heat (often referred to as the Llano Method), and meat is ordered right from the pit before you proceed inside for sides, desserts and drinks. The whole system, explains Gerald, was set up by the guys from Cooper's before negotiations broke down, and it just made the most sense to stick with the program.

"I wasn't here then, you understand," he says. "I was running a couple of Pizza Huts for Gary, and then at one point the burger place next door, before it became a Der Wienerschnitzel. But then he asked me if I wanted to run this place. Whatever he wants to start and wants to try, I'm kinda there for him."

Gerald confesses he wasn't sure if barbecue was for him. The process seemed to move so slowly, hours for this and hours for that, making him feel like he was moving through water compared to the fast-paced food he was used to. But once he fell into barbecue's own pace—yes, things can and do get very busy some-times, and people standing in line for meat at a pit can get quite impatient—he decided he liked working with barbecue after all.

In fact, Gerald has become something of an ambassador for the art form, and for its particular Llano iteration. This happens in volume each time Goodfellow Air Force Base gets a new crop of recruits, men and women from just about everywhere except Texas, it seems, each looking to experience the barbecue they've heard so much about back home in New Hampshire, Oregon or Illinois.

"The guys from up north are funny," Gerald says. "They keep asking me what brisket is, and I get a big kick out of that. And then, the ones from the Carolinas or Memphis, they all come in asking for pulled pork. Well, I tell them, we do pork loin, pork chop and pork ribs. But we don't do pulled pork."

Following the Gospel According to Llano, Old Time burns huge piles of mesquite down to coals in a firebox by the highway each night. "People passing by call the fire department more times than you'll ever guess," says Gerald, "and they have to come out even though they just drive by." These coals are shoveled into big, blockish brick pits with grates set right above the heat. Meats get nothing weird or secret as a dry rub; just coarse salt and plenty of black pepper.

Brisket, to the tune of 1,000 pounds or more per week, goes into the smoke about 4 hours for color and texture, then gets covered in foil and set back in the smoker until it's tender, about 3 hours more. A nonstop rotation process cooks 28 to 30 briskets per day, in an effort to keep something in the neighborhood of 100 ready for the warmer at all times. Gerald point outs without that supply, the pit guys could end up without meat to serve at the slightest whim of the fates.

Other top sellers at Old Time include the beef ribs and half chickens, the latter in close competition with chicken leg quarters. As at Cooper's in Llano, the sign out front sings the praises of the Big Chop, a pork chop that's 1 to $1\frac{1}{2}$ inches thick. This is sold by the pound, meaning that each Big Chop in the serving pit carries a little white flag with a price on it. A white flag, of course, means surrender, which is something a lot of people do trying to finish this.

An American lunchroom classic gets spun on its ear at Old Time, which combos its meats in a series of "blue tray specials" with a choice of two sides. It's always comforting to know you can add sausage to any special for $1.50. Or, in one of the few opportunities to do this in all Texas barbecue, Old Time offers an All-You-Can-Eat approach for $12.99. The visions that come to mind, staring down into the meats in the pit, are frightening.

Side dishes include all the classics from Cooper's and just about everywhere else, plus some surprisingly non-barbecue options like whole new potatoes, corn on the cob and green beans. If those sound healthful, however, you need to notice the amount of butter they're awash in on the serving line. And the green beans are simmered with bacon, as any green bean should demand to be. Peach cobbler is the default dessert, though cherry and blackberry also sell pretty well.

Asked what's the toughest part of running a barbecue restaurant, as opposed to pizzas or burgers, Gerald appears to be stumped for a moment. After all, he has come to love this life amid the smoke. But then he realizes what causes almost any problem that is one, day after day, year after year.

"Food cost control," he answers. "You don't want to run out of all the product before the night's over, and you can't afford to waste anything. With barbecue, no two days are ever alike."

SMOKEHOUSE BBQ
SAN ANGELO

ADDRESS: 2302 W. BEAUREGARD AVENUE, SAN ANGELO
PHONE: (325) 942-0868
ESTABLISHED: 1987
OWNER: SUE WHITAKER
BEST BITES: BEEF BRISKET, PORK RIBS, SAUSAGE, SPICY BARBECUE SAUCE, POTATO SALAD, MACARONI SALAD, FRUIT COBBLERS
PAYMENT: CASH

At one point, Sue Whitaker stayed home, enjoying the fruits of her husband's job selling electronics to the Oil Patch. But all that ended in the early 1980s, when oil prices plummeted, office corridors emptied and jobs like her husband's went up in smoke.

Sue had to do something.

"I wasn't going to just sit around the house," she recalls. "I looked in the paper for a service station, since I'd run a service station before. But all I saw was this barbecue place for sale. The guy selling it had had it only about three months, but he couldn't handle it…oh, I guess I shouldn't be saying that. My brother owned a barbecue place up in Salado. So he came down and looked it over with me." Sue smiles, remembering. "I'd never cooked a brisket in my life. I guess you could say I learned by experience."

Equally logical and pragmatic, with few deep statements about the artistry of it all, Sue the survivor is Sue the competitor. She says she made a point from the beginning of doing every little thing better than the other guy. In fact, a lot of those "other guys" she's faced over the years are no longer in business.

Hers is a small place, with just a dining room that feels like a closed-in porch, an ordering line, a small kitchen and a cobbled-together smoker out back. There's no room to play around in Sue's world, no room to dabble. She does only what she can do well, and she plays for keeps.

"People come here because we're always friendly and because of our food," she says. "We serve the best barbecue in Texas or anywhere else. We don't have room for a lot on our menu, but what we do have we try to make it the best."

This being a barbecue joint, the heart of the matter has to be her smoker. While covered outside in spotless silver sheets—Sue explains they'd had a fire and had to fix things—the smoker is all dark shadows within. There's no brand name on

the outside, and no standard mechanics inside either. The rotisserie resembles nothing more than a pair of Ferris wheels with eight oily racks hung between them, turned by a little motor that seems almost tacked to the outside above a bucket to catch the grease. There's a firebox for the mesquite Sue and the rest of West Texas use religiously, the smoke giving flavor while gas delivers the cooking power.

"The pit used to be inside," Sue says. "I mean, that was before I got the place. But they tell me it caught on fire all the time. I don't know who built the thing, but I think I have the best brisket anywhere."

That brisket gets a dry rub, then a few hours with mesquite smoke, then the rest of the cooking with gas, adding up to 16 to 18 hours in all. Sue's pork ribs get the same rub, going into the smoker for 5 to 6 hours. Her third most popular item is smoked sausage, which a lot of people in the dining room seem to be enjoying with at least one other meat.

Side dishes are simple and traditional, the excellent Big Three accompanied by a sweet macaroni salad imported from some best-day-ever church picnic. Peach and cherry cobblers are offered for dessert, though sometimes Sue feels like making apple too.

In a lot of Texas barbecue joints, your customer status ends once you pass through the ordering line and pay at the register. At Smokehouse, it keeps right on 'til you walk out the door. Sue and two waitresses pass regularly among the picnic tables, joking with regulars and almost begging for the chance to refill drinks. A lot of first names get used on both sides of the equation, with a visitor reduced to "honey." There are, of course, many worse names out there.

"It's not glitzy," explains Sue, something this side of breaking news. "It's an old building, but it certainly has done its job. I'll never get rich off this place, but I've made a good living."

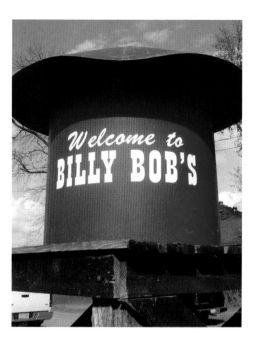

BILLY BOB'S BACKYARD BAR-B-QUE, HONDO

ADDRESS: 1905 19TH STREET (AT U.S. 90), HONDO
PHONE: (830) 426-3050
ESTABLISHED: 1999
OWNER: BOB HENDERSON
BEST BITES: BEEF BRISKET, HOGG SANDWICH, PORK SPARERIBS, POTATO SALAD, PINTO BEANS
PAYMENT: CREDIT CARDS

About 17 years ago, Bob Henderson opened a little white restaurant along-side U.S. 90 in Hondo and started selling fried catfish and hamburgers. He called his restaurant Billy Bob's and touted its handiwork as "Nothing But Excellent." Still, there are many who claim he deserved neither the faux-redneck moniker nor the high praise until he opened a barbecue shack out back in 1999.

At a glance, you might confuse the two places as you're turning in off the highway. You might even stroll into the white restaurant by accident—or on purpose, if you're looking for a restroom. But if you drive around past the first eatery and the menu sign for its drive-thru, you find yourself in front of a tiny unpainted wooden shack with a smoker just to the left of it. Most times you're likely to pull into Billy Bob's Backyard Bar-B-Que, smoke curling from that ancient-looking device will convince you you've come to the right place.

"The reason people come here?" repeats store manager Albert Maldonado, as though no one had ever asked him in the seven years he's taken orders through this window. "There's much advertising and stuff out there, of course, and other barbecue places in town. I guess the people who come here just spread the word." He smiles, as though a light has snapped on. "Plus, the mesquite smoke brings them in when they drive by."

According to Albert, beef brisket is Billy Bob's No. 1 seller, even though it's served farther down the highway to San Antonio at McBee's and JB's. Billy Bob's is simply better, he says, or at least people seem to like it better—a function of the secret dry rub and a cooking process that smokes each brisket for 3 hours with plenty of mesquite, then covers it in foil and slow-cooks it for another 6 to 7 hours. Pork spareribs are a big hit as well, first dusted with the same dry rub and then smoked for at least 4 hours.

"The meat falls right off the bone," enthuses Albert.

One of the quirkier items on Billy Bob's briefest of menus, displayed on the outside of the shack but unavailable on paper, is billed as a Hogg sandwich. Perhaps a reference to the famed Texas family of that name, or perhaps not, this is essentially a traditional pulled pork sandwich. The difference, says Albert, is that it has a "wild game" taste that everybody seems to love. Questions about whether it *is* wild hog are met with a shrug, as are other inquiries about what is done to it during smoking to make it taste that way.

"Everything else is smoked here, but the pork comes to us already cooked," he says. "We really can't sell wild game, but that's how it tastes." He shrugs one more time for good measure. "I don't know how they do it."

Side dishes are limited, as befits a kitchen no bigger than what a lot of Texans store their riding mowers in: just some tangy potato salad and some nicely spiced pinto beans. Desserts are even more limited: peach cobbler that shows up at Billy Bob's frozen. Still, the overall effect can be quite pleasant, especially when you grab your order from Albert at the window and carry it over to a closed-in patio beneath the sign inviting you to "Chow Down Here." By this point in the process, no less of a plan has any significant appeal.

"The hardest thing," Albert says, "is making sure the meat and stuff is consistent. You want it to always have the same taste, the same tenderness that the customers pull off the highway for."

EVETT'S BAR-B-QUE UVALDE

ADDRESS: 301 E. MAIN STREET (U.S. 90), UVALDE
PHONE: (830) 278-6204
ESTABLISHED: 1964, CURRENT OWNERSHIP 1995
OWNERS: BOB AND JAN GAGLIARDI
BEST BITES: BEEF BRISKET, PORK RIBS, POTATO SALAD, PINTO BEANS
PAYMENT: CASH, DEBIT CARD WITH PIN

When Bob Evett built his barbecue joint in 1964, he obviously was seeking the restaurant industry's fabled Triple Crown: location, location, location. Yet so, in arched-crowned-and-pigtailed testimonial to Bob's impressive intuition, has the largest collection of fast food in the 155 miles between San Antonio and Del Rio.

Evett's is, as Elton John used to sing, still standin'.

"Barbecue doesn't sometimes go along with the young kids as much as those other places, but I don't see a problem,"

says Angie Gagliardi, whose parents bought Evett's from Bob in 1995. "We don't really compete with them. People know exactly what we have. There's more than 40 years of history here."

Asked what she did to help her parents with the place starting when she was 10, Angie merely smiles and rolls her eyes, as though struck silent by the memory. But by this point, you know exactly what she means: after-school afternoons and evenings clearing tables, taking out the bagged trash, racing across the parking lot to catch napkins blown off the shaded front porch. Angie is clearly proud of her parents, Bob and Jan, and equally clearly can't imagine them with any other kind of job.

"They specialized from the beginning in just brisket, beans and potato salad, always cooked the same way, over and over and over," Angie says. "You don't have to worry about us having an off day. It's always the great stuff."

From a customer standpoint, Evett's belongs to the most highly focused tradition of Texas barbecue, offering a menu that virtually isn't one. The place serves no fried catfish and no cheese enchiladas, no burgers and no stuffed jalapeños. Every other restaurant along their well-trafficked strip of U.S. 90 dishes up those sorts of things. What Evett's serves,

going back to the days of Bob Evett himself, is barbecue.

Brisket is the best-selling meat here, helped along no doubt by being the Gagliardis' *only* meat a good deal of the time. Bob handles the smoking on the restaurant's two original concrete pits out back—utterly unromantic gray blocks that more closely resemble World War II bunkers than smoke-filled wonderlands with racks inside. The wood, always mesquite, gets positioned directly under the 20 or 21 briskets Bob cooks each day, with flare-ups prevented by a "grease tray" that clearly has seen better days.

According to Angie, Bob doesn't use any seasoning, preferring to let the smoke paint his briskets with color and flavor during the 12 to 14 hours he leaves them on the smudge-black pit.

"All the time I was growing up, this took a lot of work," Angie observes, pausing briefly to help her little nephew color a picture with his crayons spread across the worn wood. "It still does. It's the long hours, I guess, and there's no way around it. It's the briskets. If they're not done, then you gotta stay. Even though we're only open five days a week, it's a seven-day job."

Despite techniques going back to Bob Evett, the Gagliardis wouldn't want you to think they haven't innovated at all.

Over the years, they've added pork ribs, sausage and coleslaw to the menu. At first, the ribs were only served as a special on Thursdays. Cooked over mesquite on the smoker 4 to 5 hours, these proved so popular that now they're offered Thursdays, Fridays and Saturdays.

These are excellent days to go to Evett's for barbecue, load up your tray and, if the weather's decent, head outside to a picnic table on the front porch. Thanks to the Gagliardis' hard work, the food is good. And you have such a terrific view of all the traffic you're not in and the fast food you're not eating.

HOT PIT BAR-B-QUE DEL RIO

ADDRESS: 309 AVENUE F (U.S. 90), DEL RIO
PHONE: (830) 775-3883
ESTABLISHED: 1963
OWNERS: JERRY AND MARILYN COTTLE
BEST BITES: BEEF BRISKET, SAUSAGE, POTATO SALAD, PINTO BEANS
PAYMENT: CASH AND LOCAL CHECKS

Presented with the news that most barbecue joints close to the Mexican border serve fajitas, enchiladas, refried beans, guacamole and pico de gallo right along with their brisket, Marilyn Cottle seems surprised, confused and perhaps a little miffed.

"There are so many Mexican places in Del Rio," she says, as though confirming

the fact to herself. "Not that all of them are any good, but there sure are a lot of them. We never had any of that stuff here. The locals know what they're wanting when they come in. We don't have a very big menu, but it's what we do."

Hot Pit Bar-B-Que, which was a barbecue place on U.S. 90 as far back as anyone can remember, became a kind of Cottle family project in 1963. That was the year Jerry Cottle's brother Bob took it over while stationed nearby in the military. Bob ran it for more than six years, until it was time for another posting. His father-in-law ran it for a handful of years, then Bob returned and operated Hot Pit until he could sell it to Jerry and his wife, who moved to Del Rio from the very different terrain of northeast Arkansas.

Happily for Jerry, his brother was able to stick around for several months and show him the ropes. After all, barbecue in Texas is very different from anything that passes for barbecue in Arkansas, which would surely be the pork-centric affair of African-Americans across the Deep South. Jerry apparently was an excellent student, since the only pork on Hot Pit's menu sneaks in by way of the sausage.

There are no ribs offered, explains Marilyn, since the couple discovered years ago they could get stuck by purveyors with old meat, dry meat, tough meat, and never know for sure until they'd invested hours in smoking it. The main meat everybody wants here is brisket anyway, and the Cottles see no reason to change that.

"It's just a lot of things to learn," she says of Jerry's apprenticeship. "But you get into a routine. By the time Bob went out of it, Jerry knew everything to do."

While simplified somewhat by this briefest of menus, anyone who's ever smoked a brisket knows that one of those alone can consume your life, with all the possible combinations of rub, sauce, wood, time and temperature. Generally, Jerry has ignored the Rubik's Cube of variations: no rub at all, no sauce until the meat is served, local mesquite for wood, and a mainstream temp that smokes the brisket a mainstream 12 to 14 hours. Jerry relies on a gas-powered rotisserie to do the hard work—"You know, it turns," explains Marilyn—letting the mesquite kick in its signature tangy smoke flavor.

All three of their traditional side dishes are popular, and all are good in a traditional sort of way. The potato salad, with just a hint of yellow mustard, is most days the top-selling accompaniment, yet the pinto beans have their fans as well. It would be a shame to be this close to Mexico—Ciudad Acuña is right across the border from Del Rio—and not dish up a decent bowl of beans. The only dessert is one of those mini pecan pies from one of Hot Pit's suppliers.

"Other than those little pies and our potato chips, everything else is cooked here from scratch," says Marilyn. "We don't have any other prepared foods." Her favorite menu item? "Hmm, I don't know. I don't eat a lot of it anymore, but I could probably eat any of it."

Hot Pit gets its share of passersby on U.S. 90, though from the looks of traffic on this day, most folks traveling far have found another way to get from here to there. Big-time east-west travel is clearly a function of Interstate 10 to the north, so people driving through Del Rio have a specific reason for being here. That, of course, doesn't mean they don't stop for barbecue—just that there aren't as many of them anymore. As a result, the couple estimates their business as 90 to 95 percent local. People with memories going back to 1963, and beyond. People who know what they want before they walk in the door.

"It's been in the family all the years," says Jerry. "The same recipes and everything." He smiles with his own version of satisfaction. "If you ate here 45 years ago and came back and ate here today, I'm pretty sure you'd know you're in the same place."

LUM'S BAR-B-QUE JUNCTION

ADDRESS: 2031 N. MAIN STREET, JUNCTION
PHONE: (325) 446-3541
ESTABLISHED: 1978
OWNERS: LOUIS AND RICK LUMBLY
BEST BITES: BEEF BRISKET, PORK SPARERIBS, SMOKED TURKEY BREAST, COLESLAW, SPICY SPAGHETTI, BANANA PUDDING, CHOCOLATE PIE, PEACH COBBLER
PAYMENT: CREDIT CARDS

In most barbecue joints, if you put the briskets on at 8 a.m. and cook them 12 hours or more, your place will be closed before they're cooked. At Lum's, however, there are still 5 or 6 hours before quitting time.

According to manager Umberto Vidal, staying open until 11 on weeknights and as late as 1 a.m. on weekends is all part of earning and keeping the customer loyalty that has made Junction a stop on the barbecue trail for three decades. People have come into Lum's from Las Vegas, others after hearing about the place on a Caribbean cruise. Still others have phoned from the highway hours away, putting in their order and promising to make it in before closing time.

"This is a nice little place to come in and enjoy yourself," Umberto says simply, sitting at one of the colorful picnic tables. "Some places you come in and they just want to move you on down the line."

He thinks about all those phone calls, most from people afraid that Lum's will run out of their favorite foods. "We'll save whatever they need. And if they run a little late, we'll stay open for them. I mean, people drive 4 or 5 hours to eat here. We need to make sure it's good for them."

Lum's is just over a mile off Interstate 10, connecting the Atlantic to the Pacific but more specifically East Texas at Orange to West Texas at El Paso. Over 30 years, the place has become a popular lunch or dinner stop for Texans traveling across their state. And since Lum's sells

gasoline out front, it's easy enough to make it a cross-country pit stop.

Umberto is happy to show anyone who asks the trio of black iron pits under a shed where all the magic is made. Mesquite is the wood of choice—100 percent when they can get their hands on enough of it—with brisket getting the merest sprinkling of salt and black pepper before going into the smoke for 12 to 15 hours. While beef is popular sliced or chopped, so are the pork spareribs and, in recent years, the smoked turkey breast. Turkey, in fact, is usually the first meat to sell out, lasting little more than an hour after Lum's opens its doors at 7.

It's important, says Umberto, that nearly all meats are sold on the day they're smoked. Any leftover pork ribs or sausage links are definitely thrown out because they'll dry out in the refrigerator. Occasionally, a bit of brisket is wrapped carefully and held over, becoming the first beef sold the next day. And at Lum's, the "next day" is never more than a few hours away.

Over the years, owner Louis Lumbly and his son Rick, who now runs the place, have mastered traditional sides like potato salad and coleslaw, but they've also branched out in some unexpected directions. Pinto beans, for instance, blend the cowboy style of chili powder with the baked-bean style of brown sugar. And how many barbecue places offer "spicy spaghetti" as a side—thin vermicelli to be precise, given zip by tomatoes, green onions, garlic, cayenne pepper and jalapeños? Possibly none, other than Lum's.

Still, as best Umberto can tell after working here during high school and coming back later for real, Lum's is more than the sum of its parts—and definitely more than the sum of its foods. As much as guests love the barbecue on the buffet line, and as much as they love carrying it outside to eat in all but the worst weather, he's convinced it's the human touch that turns them into regulars. And he goes the extra mile as manager to teach his employees to, well, go the extra mile. It's the least they can do, Umberto emphasizes, considering how many miles people drive to get here.

"We always say: 'How you're doing, where you going and how long you here for?' " he says. "If you talk to people for two or three minutes, they can tell you a lot. If you have a place with good friends and good food, then that's a place you'll come back to."

CURLY'S BBQ SIERRA BLANCA

ADDRESS: 405 E. EL PASO STREET, SIERRA BLANCA
PHONE: (915) 369-9999
ESTABLISHED: 2005
OWNERS: PATRICK AND TERESA BROWN
BEST BITES: BEEF BRISKET, SMOKED SAUSAGE,
PULLED PORK, BARBECUE PIZZA, CURLY'S SPECIAL,
FRIED OKRA, FRIED MUSHROOMS, HAND-CUT FRENCH
FRIES, MILK SHAKES
PAYMENT: CREDIT CARDS

More mornings than not, Teresa Brown and her husband—Patrick by name, Curly by fame—are serving barbecue before they've flipped the sign in the window from CLOSED to OPEN. And more evenings than not, they're serving barbecue long after the sign has reverted from OPEN to CLOSED, if it bothers to revert at all.

Working just 30 minutes west of where Mountain Time meets Central Time on a remote stretch of Interstate 10, the Browns have discovered what Einstein discovered about time: the pesky stuff can be relative.

"Our 11 o'clock is their 12 o'clock, so it's lunchtime," Teresa reports. "People come in and ask what time do we close. I just tell 'em, 'When you leave.' " Teresa pauses, as though seeking a deeper, more tangible truth. "If my truck is here, we'll fix you something."

Teresa and Curly have spent most of their lives in some variation on law enforcement, which makes them totally at home with a clientele heavily weighted toward state troopers, with the occasional sheriff's deputy or border patrol for variety. The different uniforms are strewn about their dining room—perhaps even some that Curly taught to use firearms— joking across jurisdictions and sometimes engaging in a quick game of cards before their plates turn up from the kitchen. Time is finite for these men, a clock and a two-way radio ever ready to send them

back out on the highway.

Running a barbecue joint is a new twist for Teresa and Curly, but one that (as did so many things that get people into the restaurant business) seemed to make sense at the time. Curly's first barbecue gig had been within law enforcement, catering a fellow officer's wedding. Many requests followed, 'til before long cooking barbecue had become Curly's second job. A trip to Georgia to visit their son at Fort Benning convinced the Browns this hobby might become a career.

"We stopped at this barbecue place, and it was just horrible," Teresa remembers, making a face to match her words. "And all my husband and I could talk about or think about was: If they can make money serving *that* stuff, then we oughta be able to make a whole lot more."

They found a location in remote Sierra Blanca, just a turn off the interstate for those traveling to or from El Paso. Before long, they'd secured bank financing, stripped and repainted every inch that could be, and covered the walls with memorabilia. Some décor came from eBay,

but a lot of it was stuff Curly spotted along the West Texas backroads during his patrols.

As for the serious end of barbecue, Curly got a large rotisserie that he kept on a trailer out back, never truly permanent in case he got a big catering job. Mesquite became his wood of choice since this was West Texas, a far cry from the hickory, pecan or post oak preferred by pit bosses in his native East Texas. With mesquite, though, he quickly became a master, using only salt and pepper to season his meats and letting "low and slow" smoke do the rest of the work.

His briskets cook for 14 to 16 hours, becoming not only his best-selling meat but also a wonder to behold. The meat is fork-tender and chunky, sliced a little thicker than most, stained a deep red by the smoke and crusted with the sweet-tasting, almost blackened beauty that barbecue guys call the "bark." You'd swear Curly sprinkles his briskets with brown sugar—but no, he insists, just salt and pepper.

Though Curly makes no pretense of being a chef in the French sense of that word, he has over the years come up with dishes that many trained chefs would shy away from introducing. Terrific flavor has turned Curly's barbecue pizza into a huge hit—with homemade barbecue sauce where the marinara might be, plus brisket and sausage as the chosen meats. Another fascination is Curly's Special: a fire-roasted poblano pepper not batter-fried here as Tex-Mex chiles rellenos, but topped with chopped brisket and molten cheese. Another of Curly's food fetishes, barbecue nachos, never really caught on with customers...but he loves the dish so much that he'll try to make it for you if you ask.

Any and all of these wildly personal interpolations are enjoyed regularly by those in uniform or street clothes, along with superb homemade side dishes ranging from potato salad and coleslaw to Curly's favorite, fried okra, and "whatever chips we can find in the back." Desserts are limited but good, a couple of cakes on the counter under glass, pecan pie and, perhaps the most popular finale, a milk shake available in one of 20-plus flavors.

"We don't believe in a whole lot of things," offers Curly, wiping his hands from the kitchen and seeming to speak culinarily, rather than politically or theologically. "People who eat here never complain, so we just keep it simple."

KATHY'S KOSMIC KOWGIRL KAFE TERLINGUA

ADDRESS: JUNCTION OF HIGHWAYS 118 AND 170, TERLINGUA
PHONE: (432) 371-2164
ESTABLISHED: 2006
OWNER: KATHY WISDOM
BEST BITES: BEEF BRISKET, PULLED PORK SANDWICH, POTATO SALAD, HAMBURGER, FRENCH FRIES, KOSMIC CHIPS, KOSMIC BURRITO, FRITO PIE
PAYMENT: CASH

In Texas, there are many barbecue places that are big and many barbecue places that are small. But, by all logic and anecdotal evidence, there's only one barbecue place that's pink.

On the winding, crumbling, rising and falling snatch of highway from Big Bend (the nation's least visited national park) to the hyper-quirky Terlingua, Kathy Wisdom has staked out her roadside legacy. She's lived in Terlingua for most of 28 years, after arriving from Kansas City in a van with a 9-month-old son. After several futile attempts to escape—to Houston and Austin, to Utah and Alaska—Kathy customized a trailer to be her kitchen, crafted a covered outside dining area and connected a simple rack smoker in a shed.

As a flourishing final touch, she pulled a sawed-off bus up to her trailer and filled it with tables, especially for locals who want to sip coffee beginning at 6 a.m. and

check their e-mails on her Wi-Fi. And just about anything that could hold paint, Kathy painted pink.

"My least favorite color is pink, but it draws a lot of attention," says Kathy, grinning beneath her pink cowboy hat and above her pink T-shirt. "I did it for marketing strategy. This is a pink oasis in the middle of a green-brown desert. You come around that bend in the road, and here I am!"

Kathy's Kosmic Kowgirl Kafe is more than a barbecue joint. It's more like the unofficial Terlingua community center, the unconventional gathering place for some extremely unconventional people. During one recent visit late in a spring-time lunch period, most of the locals who stopped by didn't even order food. They did, on the other hand, discuss buying and selling used kitchen appliances, post flyers on the message board about need-ing a ride to San Antonio, pick up pack-ages dropped off by FedEx and UPS, and otherwise inquire about relatives, friends and neighbors. In a remote world virtual-ly without cell phone service, getting together seemed the best way to make some kind of human contact.

"I look at this place as the mystery dinner party," Kathy says. "You never know who's going to show up."

The idea for Kathy's Kosmic Kowgirl struck its namesake during one of her

moves back to Terlingua, when she realized that two things she truly loved were cooking for people and visiting with people. She'd done a bit of catering here and there, and she certainly remembered the taste of barbecue from her native Kansas City. But getting serious about Texas barbecue was a lot like going back to school. Kathy experimented with time and temperature, with different kinds of wood and different recipes for dry rub. Before long she'd chosen local mesquite to power her smoker and had perfected two different rubs, one for beef brisket and one for the pork shoulder that became her wildly popular pulled pork sandwiches.

Kathy wanted her roadside place to be about barbecue. But she knew the tourists, bikers, aging hippies and bona fide cowboys who drove by would want some variety. Sandwiches were born, both traditional and innovative, along with some of the best burgers served any-where: a half-pound hand-formed patty cooked on Kathy's flat grill. Chili also has a huge following, as do chili dogs and the closely related Frito pie. Even this Frito pie gets another generation, its compo-nents being rolled inside a tortilla to find new life as the Kosmic burrito.

Kathy has traveled a long road to arrive at this bend in the highway, which one day might funnel her a steady stream of cars and another day a rally with 150 motorcycles. There's usually a fire out front for sharing gossip around and always some meat on the smoker. Most of all, there's the moonscape beauty of Big Bend every direction you look, along with the quirky anti-establishment charm of one of America's strangest little towns.

"It's laid back here in Terlingua," Kathy says, hitting understatement out of the park. "Nobody's judging people here. And nobody's trying to keep up with the Joneses."

ADOBE MOON BBQ
MARFA

ADDRESS: 200 S. ABBOT STREET, MARFA
PHONE: (432) 729-3030
ESTABLISHED: 2007
OWNER: MARK DAVENPORT
BEST BITES: BEEF BRISKET, SMOKED CHICKEN, SAUSAGE, COLESLAW, PINTO BEANS, CHOCOLATE CAKE
PAYMENT: CREDIT CARDS

Mark Davenport spent 18 years teaching science at a college in San Antonio before a different form of science captured his attention. It's the kind of science that experiments with what happens to a beef brisket when it's dusted with seasoning and subjected to smoke from a 225-degree fire for 12 to 14 hours.

Such experimentation hasn't produced any universal theories in the style of Newton or Einstein, at least not yet. But it has produced a whole new life and a whole new career for Mark in a Texas town outrageous for the number of Hollywood stars, visual artists and literary figures who swell its posted population of 2,121.

For decades, the 1956 movie *Giant*—starring Elizabeth Taylor, Rock Hudson and the doomed James Dean—was a major part of Marfa's legend, right along with the mysterious nighttime glimmers known as the Marfa Lights. In 2007, the same year Adobe Moon opened its doors, Marfa served as the setting to both of the hottest Oscar-winning films: *No Country for Old Men* and *There Will Be Blood*.

"I get some famous people here, giving our barbecue a try," Mark says of the clever, colorful tangle of tables inside and outside, some resembling a beach bar minus the beach and others spread around the inside of a tepee. "But my main customers are the locals. There are several rich people who have bought up a lot of land here, but it's the ordinary folks that keep me alive."

Mark was invited by friend Jon Johnson to move to Marfa and create a barbecue joint at the heart of Johnson's corner property where Highway 90

curves into town, only blocks from the courthouse and other historic buildings now surrounded by design studios, fashion boutiques and gift shops. Plans call for the restaurant to anchor an event space, a live music venue with a dance floor, and a bicycle tour company that will bus rugged visitors high into the mountains and let them ride down.

Like many Texas pit masters, Mark got into cooking barbecue as an amateur invited to cater this or that party out of his home kitchen. Obviously, he was considered good at it; he kept getting hired until his friend whisked him off to West Texas.

"The hard part is that it's hard to get the stuff you need here," says Mark. "There's only one supplier that delivers here, and if I wanted to go get stuff myself, it's like 3 hours in one direction or the other. And January and February are the dreary months, when we barely have any business at all. On the bright side, even in the summer you're high and the air's dry, so you don't swelter like you do in San Antonio and Houston. And I don't think I've been in a single traffic jam since I've been here."

In the Adobe Moon kitchen, Mark cooks meat on a smallish Ole Hickory steel pit, filling the firebox for indirect heat with oak rather than regional mesquite. Science type that he is, he has organized his daily smoking into three "loads": brisket that goes on at 8 p.m. for lunch the next day, more brisket at 5 a.m. for that night's dinner, and pork ribs and chicken that go in around noon for that night.

"It was wild," Mark says of his early barbecue regimen. "When I was just getting started, I had to keep looking at my notes."

Adobe Moon keeps things simple, serving its sliced brisket, smoked sausage, pork ribs and pulled pork sandwiches on a piece of butcher paper spread over a colorful plastic tray. Side dishes, including homemade (and delightfully rough-cut) coleslaw and spicier-than-

usual pinto beans with pork trimmings, onions and jalapeños, show up in small Styrofoam cups. Desserts are close to nonexistent in this old adobe dining room beneath a ceiling of woven reeds, most days limited to a slice of chocolate cake.

"In a barbecue place, you have to cook up to 14 hours in advance," says Mark, pondering all he's learned from his barbecue experiment. "If you have a slow lunch, there's nothing you can do about it, and barbecue doesn't keep very well. And if you're busy, you might run out of food. That's the hardest part, guessing each day how busy you'll be."

SMITTY'S PIT BAR-B-Q EL PASO

ADDRESS: 6219 AIRPORT ROAD, EL PASO
PHONE: (915) 772-5876
ESTABLISHED: 1955, CURRENT OWNERSHIP 1976
OWNER: HERIBERTO "EDDIE" PAYAN JR.
BEST BITES: BEEF BRISKET, PORK RIBS, SMOKED TURKEY, JALAPEÑO SAUSAGE, CALDILLO, POTATO SALAD, COLESLAW, PINTO BEANS, RUM CAKE
PAYMENT: CREDIT CARDS

Like a person after a serious health scare, Heriberto "Eddie" Payan counts his blessings each day he gets to open for business.

Unlike a person after a brush with death, however, Eddie has a brush every single day with the icy realities of the restaurant business. Glancing across the crowd at a busy lunch, he understands that many of these customers' parents virtually never ate in a chain restaurant ...and that their children eat virtually nowhere else. It's only a matter of time, he fears, before beloved half-century-old landmarks like Smitty's are replaced by glitzy eateries with national TV advertising and little actual cooking in their kitchens.

"Here's a place famous for barbecued ribs," he laments, giving the place's name. "The ribs are cooked in some commissary, vacuum-packed and shipped to be reheated in the oven. They pour sauce all over them and say, 'This is barbecue.' But this *isn't* barbecue."

Eddie pauses, thinking of another chain. "And what about baby back ribs? They're just little pieces they were cutting off and didn't want to throw away. They're nothing but bones. They're a rip-off, and people pay a premium for them. They're garbage." He smiles, not without resignation. "You should put that in that book of yours."

Eddie is nobody's idea of an old guy, but he has an old guy's sense of history. He knows that somewhere on his desk, for instance, is a photo from the 1940s of the area where his restaurant now resides: just a small airfield left over from World War II and desert as far as the eye can see. El Paso's airport has grown many times over since G.S. Smith first looked at this space, as has the now-typical airport sprawl of hotels, restaurants and shopping strips. It's hard to see what Smitty saw in the place, really, except the chance to have a real barbecue joint after years of selling smoked meats from the back of a saloon and later at a local farmers market.

"This was the outskirts of El Paso back then," Eddie says. "There was just this building and the old airport—that was it. Somehow Smitty pulled together some funding and opened in 1955."

Several good reputations followed the crusty Army cook, including one for sharing a cold beer with his best customers, or with anyone who happened in when he was wanting a cold beer. Some customers followed him from his previous incarnations, and others found him fresh. He ran Smitty's for just over 20 years, making it the kind of place parents and even grandparents take the younger generation to show them how things used to be. It's unclear how many of a younger generation agree with their elders that things used to be better.

Eddie's father, a butcher by trade, bought Smitty's in 1976, opening in the midst of the patriotic Bicentennial cele-

bration. His father had owned a restaurant in New Mexico, and besides, nobody ever suffered in the barbecue business for knowing a lot about meat. In fact, Eddie says while showing off hooks in the walk-in cooler, meats used to come in larger cuts and be "broken down" on the spot.

"Mr. Smith stuck around for a year," Eddie remembers from his childhood. "He didn't want to see his business go down."

If anything, thanks to the labors of the Payan family, Smitty's has done just the opposite. While sticking to some of Smitty's famous recipes, Eddie has played bob and weave with the times, introducing many more menu choices and even items like smoked chicken and turkey for that health-minded crowd invariably referred to by barbecue men as "the ladies."

Still, the core of Smitty's remains the same meats Smitty himself mastered in the same brick pit more than half a century ago. Unlike most of his neighbors in West Texas, Eddie relies on the same oak Smitty always preferred, adding bits of apple wood and soaked hickory chips for additional smoke and sweetness. He uses two secret-recipe dry rubs to season his meats, letting them marinate for a full 48 hours, and then cooks them slowly over indirect heat. It's more the smoke than the heat that cooks them, he says.

Beyond the lovely brisket, other popular meats within these walls include pork ribs, beef ribs and some amazing jalapeño sausage. Surely the most surprising item is corned beef—a local taste, Eddie theorizes, going back to long-departed Jewish delicatessens downtown. With the curing and then slow-smoking on Smitty's pit, the savory result is something between deli corned beef and pepper-crusty hot pastrami.

Like Smitty and his father, Eddie makes each day's batches of barbecue sauce and beans by placing the pot right inside the pit. It makes complete sense, says the kid who grew up to earn an economics and accounting degree from UT, considering the high cost of fuel these days.

Despite the traditionalism of Smitty's barbecue, there are other rich traditions on every street corner in El Paso—most from the long-colonial Hispanic world. There's an appetizer here, for instance, called Rio Grande. It's a slice of smoked sausage covered with cheese and green Anaheim chiles. And there's an unbelievably delicious stew called caldillo (chunks of beef and potato floating in a high-octane green chile broth) that seems ready to cure almost anything. If it doesn't, Melanie's rum cake sprinkled with Texas pecans seems certain to do the trick.

"And," adds Eddie, "we do smoked turkeys for Thanksgiving and honey-glazed hams for Christmas. We do smoked lamb for Easter and Passover. Have you ever had that? It's amazing!" He grins. "And, of course, we do salmon every Friday, cuz I'm a good Catholic."

THE STATE LINE EL PASO

ADDRESS: 1222 SUNLAND PARK DRIVE, EL PASO
PHONE: (915) 581-3371
ESTABLISHED: 1977
OWNERS: SKEETER MILLER, ED NORTON, RANDY GOSS
BEST BITES: BEEF BRISKET, BABY BACK PORK RIBS, GARLIC MASHED RED-SKIN POTATOES, BREAD PUDDING, BROWNIE
PAYMENT: CREDIT CARDS

Almost suddenly, the sun drops into the desert, with no clouds to paint a Jackson Pollock in the sky. The fiery paintball draws a winter-blue shade behind it, a chill grabbing hold of the evening air, as it so often does here in the desert. Yet close by the blazing fire in the stone courtyard, the air is as warm as the margaritas are icy. It's just another sunset to be toasted while waiting for a table at The State Line.

There's something valedictory about this courtyard straddling the Texas-New Mexico line, about these margaritas and the barbecue that's to come...not least because our journey began months earlier at its sibling, The County Line, on a lovely hillside in Austin. Nearly 15,000 miles have been logged between that festive meal and this one, each mile now registered by our car, our life and our waistline. There may be something touted as "barbecue" beyond this state line. But it *won't* be Texas barbecue.

"This is a little bit of an oasis for us desert rats here," general manager Mike Shahan is explaining, drawing us back from our reverie. "We look at this courtyard as a relaxing place, a place for people to unwind and get ready for dinner. We, fortunately, are a very busy place, so people often need to wait. They relax and wait for their table." Mike shares a knowing laugh, nodding toward the frosty drinks on the table. "There have definitely been a few margaritas put away out here."

If you think of The State Line as a corporate afterthought, a place to grow the brand after all the more logical places had been taken, you'd be badly mistaken. Back in 1977, there was only The County Line on that hillside in Austin, with locations like the River Walk in San Antonio barely even a capitalist fantasy. One of the founders of the company, however, had studied at the University of Texas at El Paso (never expressed here except as UTEP) and thought it would be cool to have an excuse to hang out there a few more years. Among the guys who started The County Line, as we learned at the beginning of this barbecue journey, something being cool is all the motivation that's ever required.

From the start, perhaps the single *coolest* thing about The State Line is that it is exactly what it says it is. It sits on the state line, with that fabled designation running right through the margarita-splashed courtyard. Legally, part of the

courtyard and all the vast parking lot are in Texas, with the dining room in New Mexico. Sales taxes collected for barbecue here, Mike explains, go to New Mexico…so the world is lucky there's no such thing as a parking tax. For Texas barbecue, this is literally the end of the line.

Over the years, The State Line has adhered with considerable force to the *party* line—the menu and techniques at the Austin locale and other locations. Still, says Mike, there have been local evolutions that owe their existence to the unique melting pot of cultures that is El Paso. There are, for instance, brisket tacos served at lunch. And while the menus in Austin and elsewhere years ago responded to health concerns by adding salads and other light items, the issue never came up in El Paso.

"We want to cater to the local taste buds," Mike says, "but it's the barbecue they want. It's amazing how many people from Mexico and New Mexico we get, and they just love the food. It's been great from Day 1."

Mike, who has worked at The State Line since almost that day, explains that the only secret to all this success is doing things right. That means, in many cases, buying better (more expensive) ingredients, starting with the meat, and treating all with care throughout the traditional, drawn-out cooking process. It also means passing up the local mesquite to bring in oak from East Texas 800-plus miles away, a decision that adds to the cost of everything smoked here as well.

Still, since 1977, the taste profiles set by The State Line in El Paso have been formative to a whole new generation of Texas (and yes, New Mexico) barbecue lovers: people who love few things better in this world than knocking back a margarita or three while enjoying ribs, brisket, sausage and chicken, with side orders of potato salad, coleslaw and beans.

As we've learned through so many meals and so many miles, there are so many worse things in this world to love.

THE
RECIPES

THE MEATS

CLASSIC TEXAS SMOKED BRISKET

Brisket is the Holy Grail of Texas barbecue, reflecting the only significant barbecue tradition in America based on beef instead of pork. There are as many brisket recipes as there are brisket cooks, and each cook is convinced everybody else is dead-wrong. At the risk of being precisely that, here's our way to make a terrific beef brisket, complete with both a dry rub and a bit of mop sauce.

2 teaspoons paprika
1 teaspoon black pepper
1 teaspoon onion powder
1 teaspoon garlic powder
1 boneless beef brisket (6 to 8 pounds), trimmed
$^{1}/_{2}$ cup water
1 bottle (12 ounces) Shiner Bock beer, *divided*
2 cups steak sauce, *divided*
$^{1}/_{2}$ cup finely chopped onion
2 tablespoons butter
1 cup ketchup
2 tablespoons prepared mustard
1 tablespoon brown sugar
1 tablespoon hot pepper sauce

Combine the paprika, pepper, onion powder and garlic powder; rub evenly over the surface of the brisket. Place with fat side up in a large disposable pan. Add water and about half of the beer to pan. Seal tightly with foil. Place pan in the middle of a grill rack over hot coals. Close grill cover; cook for 5 hours, turning brisket in the pan juices about every 90 minutes. Add additional water to pan as needed.

Remove foil from pan. Transfer brisket directly onto the grill rack over very low coals. Combine 1 cup pan drippings with 1 cup steak sauce and remaining beer; brush some of this sauce over meat. Set remaining drippings aside. Close grill cover; cook for 1 hour, brushing meat occasionally with remaining sauce.

Allow brisket to rest for 20 minutes. Meanwhile, in a saucepan, saute onion in butter until transparent. Stir in the ketchup, mustard, brown sugar, hot pepper sauce, remaining steak sauce and reserved drippings. Simmer for about 10 minutes. Slice meat $^{1}/_{4}$ to $^{1}/_{2}$ inch thick across the grain. Serve with warm sauce on the side. Serves 8-10.

BRISKET-STUFFED
1015 ONIONS

If you think brisket is only for slicing and eating, or perhaps for chopping and mixing with sauce to make a sandwich, think again. This variation uses the Texas sweet onions that are named after their recommended planting date of October 15 (10-15). These large super-sweet onions are commonly available from mid-April through May. During other times of year, you can use another mild, sweet onion.

10 large Texas 1015 onions *or* other
    sweet onions
1 pound smoked beef brisket, shredded
1 teaspoon rubbed sage
$^{1}/_{2}$ teaspoon minced garlic
$^{1}/_{2}$ teaspoon ground red pepper
$^{1}/_{2}$ teaspoon ground cumin
$^{1}/_{2}$ teaspoon salt
$^{1}/_{2}$ teaspoon black pepper
1 cup unseasoned bread crumbs

Peel the onions and boil in salted water for 10 minutes; drain, reserving water. Cut out the centers from the onions to create shells; set aside. In a sauté pan, combine the shredded brisket, sage, garlic, red pepper, cumin, salt and black pepper. Cook and stir over medium heat for 2 minutes. Remove from the heat; stir in bread crumbs.

Preheat oven to 350°. Spoon stuffing into onion shells. Place in a shallow baking dish. Add enough of the reserved onion water to cover the bottom of the dish. Bake, uncovered, for 45 minutes or until onions are tender. Serves 10.

OPEN-FACED
BRISKET SANDWICHES

Though "chopped beef" is the most common form for brisket destined for a bun, we also like this shredded version. We think the meat is more tender this way, and it helps us not confuse it with a Sloppy Joe.

1 beef brisket (6 to 7 pounds), smoked
    (see recipe on page 211)
1 large onion, diced
1 tablespoon minced garlic
$^{1}/_{4}$ cup olive oil
2 tablespoons all-purpose flour
4 cups canned onion soup
2 loaves French bread (15 inches)

Shred the brisket and set aside. In a large skillet, caramelize onion and garlic in oil. Stir in the flour; cook until browned. Add brisket and onion soup; stir to thicken into gravy. Cut each loaf of French bread into four sections; slice open. Spoon brisket and plenty of gravy over bread. Excellent topped with coleslaw (see recipes on page 224). Serves 8.

WEST TEXAS STRIP

Beef is king in West Texas, and if you're more in the mood for a grilled steak than for slow-smoked barbecue, here's a simple but super way to dress it up with a wine, mushroom and tarragon cream sauce.

4 boneless New York strip steaks (about 1 inch thick and 8 ounces *each*)
2 tablespoons black peppercorns, crushed
1 cup sliced fresh mushrooms
3 tablespoons finely chopped shallots
2 tablespoons unsalted butter
3 cups dry red Texas wine
$^1/_2$ cup heavy cream
1 teaspoon dried tarragon
Salt to taste

Roll steaks in crushed peppercorns; set aside. In a large skillet, sauté mushrooms and shallots in butter until softened. Add wine; reduce over high heat until about $^1/_3$ cup remains, about 5 minutes. Add cream and tarragon; reduce until sauce is thickened and about $^1/_2$ cup remains. Grill the steaks until meat reaches desired doneness. Season with salt and top with sauce. Serves 4.

RASPBERRY CHIPOTLE BBQ MEATBALLS

To some, barbecue is a process...to others, it's a flavor. Here's a treat for any party, inspired by the ridiculously wonderful roasted raspberry chipotle sauce created by our friends Fischer & Wieser in Fredericksburg.

5 pounds ground beef
2 teaspoons black pepper
1 teaspoon onion powder
1 teaspoon garlic powder
1 teaspoon salt
$1^1/_2$ cups roasted raspberry chipotle sauce
1 cup barbecue sauce
3 tablespoons ketchup
2 tablespoons cider vinegar
1 tablespoon yellow mustard

Combine the beef with pepper, onion powder, garlic powder and salt. Form into 40-50 small cocktail meatballs. Broil or bake until meat is no longer pink. Cool. In a large bowl, combine the remaining ingredients. Add meatballs, stirring gently to coat completely. Cover and refrigerate for 3 hours.

Just before serving, transfer meatballs and sauce to a saucepan to reheat; serve with toothpicks. Serves 8-10.

THUNDER HEART BISON FAJITAS

We'll never forget the road trip we took deep into South Texas to visit Hugh Fitzsimmons on the ranch where he raises his Thunder Heart Bison. Yes, it's where the "buffalo roam," except they're really bison. Cooking with Hugh at the ranch inspired us to come up with these fajitas.

1 pound Texas bison skirt *or* flank steak
Juice of 3 limes
$^1/_2$ teaspoon garlic powder
$^1/_2$ teaspoon chili powder
$^1/_2$ teaspoon salt
$^1/_2$ teaspoon black pepper
1 large onion, sliced
1 large green bell pepper, sliced
$^1/_4$ cup olive oil
1 large tomato, chopped
Guacamole, sour cream and salsa
6 to 8 corn *or* flour tortillas, warmed

Using a mallet, pound the meat to about $^1/_2$ inch thick; place in a resealable plastic bag. Add lime juice, garlic powder, chili powder, salt and pepper; seal bag. Marinate in the refrigerator for 8 hours, turning occasionally.

In a skillet, caramelize the onion and bell pepper in oil; keep warm. Remove meat from marinade. Grill over mesquite coals to medium-rare, 2-3 minutes on each side. Thinly slice the meat; serve atop caramelized onion and bell pepper, with tomato, guacamole, sour cream, salsa and warm tortillas on the side. Serves 6-8.

JUNETEENTH PORK SPARERIBS

Especially in East Texas, barbecue remains an African-American thing, as it tends to be throughout the South. These ribs are meant to celebrate Juneteenth— the annual remembrance of June 19, 1865, when the slaves of Texas learned they were free.

6 pounds pork spareribs
$3^1/_2$ cups water
$^1/_2$ cup sherry
1 cup ketchup
$^1/_2$ cup packed brown sugar
$^1/_2$ cup diced onion
$^1/_4$ cup white vinegar
$^1/_4$ cup Worcestershire sauce
$^1/_4$ lemon, thinly sliced
1 teaspoon chili powder
1 teaspoon celery seed
1 teaspoon salt
$^1/_8$ teaspoon black pepper

In a large pan, brown the ribs. Add water and sherry. Cover and simmer for 1 hour. Meanwhile, in a saucepan, combine the remaining ingredients; cook until ribs finish simmering. Remove ribs from cooking liquid; cover with the sauce. Finish cooking over low indirect heat on the grill until meat is tender, about 1 hour more. Serves 8-10.

MARGARITA PORK CHOPS

*Historians aren't 100% sure, but it
seems today's frozen margarita is more
a creation of modern Texas than ancient
Mexico. Still, Mexico has loved tequila
grown in the state of Jalisco for centuries
and, in many cases, mixed it with lime
juice and other things. Here's a dish that
will remind you of that popular cocktail.*

$^1/_3$ cup orange marmalade
2 tablespoons lime juice
2 tablespoons tequila
1 jalapeño pepper, seeded and chopped
1 teaspoon freshly grated ginger
4 boneless pork loin chops (1 inch thick),
   trimmed
Lime wedges and chopped fresh cilantro

To prepare glaze, combine the marmalade, lime juice, tequila, jalapeño
and ginger in a small bowl. Grill the
pork chops over medium heat for 10-15
minutes or until a meat thermometer
reads 160°, brushing with glaze during
the last 5 minutes. Garnish with lime
wedges and cilantro. Serves 4.

LAMBSHEAD RANCH
BARBECUED WILD PIG

*There is a tradition around Lambshead
Ranch near Abilene, as there is around
many Texas ranches, of hunting the wild
pigs that gather along rivers, streams or
any source of water. Not everybody will
want to "go whole hog" as we do in this
recipe, but if you're ready for a Hawaiian
luau, you're ready for its Texas kin.*

1 wild *or* domestic pig (20 to 25 pounds),
   thoroughly cleaned
1 cup bacon grease
2 tablespoons minced garlic
1 tablespoon chopped fresh rosemary
2 teaspoons cumin seeds
2 bay leaves
2 teaspoons salt
2 teaspoons black pepper
2 onions, sliced
1 carrot, chopped
4 ribs celery, chopped
1 apple, quartered

Insert an empty coffee can into the cavity
of the pig to help hold the shape during
cooking. Prop open the mouth using a
stick. Combine the bacon grease, garlic,
rosemary, cumin, bay leaves, salt and
pepper; spread over the outside of the pig
and inside the cavity. Stuff the cavity with
onions, carrots, celery and apple. Cover
the ears with foil. Tie the pig's feet under
the belly with string.

Prepare the grill for indirect cooking,
using soaked mesquite chips for smoke.
Grill the pig far above the coals for even
heat. Remove the string after the first
hour. Cook until the internal temperature
reaches 170°, about 4-5 hours. Place
whole pig on a large serving tray and
insert an apple or large pepper into the
mouth. Carve and serve immediately.
Serves about 20.

DR. PEPPER BARBECUED CHICKEN

The original recipe for Dr. Pepper was for-
mulated in Waco, and to this day, Texans
are the first to ask, "Wouldn't you like to
be a pepper, too?" Whatever your feelings
about the quirky soft drink, we think
you'll like what it brings to the table in
this version of barbecued chicken.

$^3/_4$ cup water
$^1/_2$ cup Worcestershire sauce
$^1/_2$ cup Dr. Pepper
$^2/_3$ cup white vinegar
Grated peel of $^1/_2$ lemon
3 slices bacon, chopped
2 tablespoons butter
$^1/_2$ tablespoon prepared mustard
1 teaspoon minced garlic
$^1/_2$ teaspoon celery salt
$^1/_2$ teaspoon salt
$^1/_2$ teaspoon black pepper
$^1/_4$ teaspoon hot pepper sauce
4 chickens (about $1^1/_2$ pounds *each*), cut
    in half
Additional salt and black pepper

In a saucepan, combine the first 13 ingredients. Bring just to a boil; reduce heat
and simmer for 30 minutes. Meanwhile,
season the chicken halves with salt and
pepper. Place skin side down on a hot
grill. Brown on both sides, turning occasionally, for about 15 minutes. Continue
to grill, brushing regularly with sauce,
until a meat thermometer reads 180°,
about 45 minutes. Serves 8.

SMOKED SAUSAGE WITH HONEY-MUSTARD SAUCE

Of course, you can simply buy good
smoked sausage almost anywhere, but
we like to give ours a little extra smoke—
maybe just on principle. And although
barbecue sauce makes a fine dip for
smoked sausage, so does this simple
blend of honey and coarse-ground
mustard.

1 pound smoked sausage (pork, beef *or* a
    combination)
$1^1/_2$ cups Creole, Dijon *or* other coarse-
    ground mustard
2 teaspoons honey

Place the sausage over indirect heat with
a low fire on a smoker, 145-165°. Close off
all ventilation to keep the fire from burning too hot. We recommend smoking the
sausage for 4-6 hours, stopping before
the meat dries out. When ready to serve,
combine the mustard and honey in a
small saucepan; heat until bubbling. Slice
sausage; serve with sauce for dipping.
Serves 6-8.

APPLE-BRINED SMOKED TURKEY

Chefs will tell you that the only true way to assure a turkey that's full of flavor and not dried out is the old-time but rediscovered process known as brining. To paraphrase brining as a slogan: the flavor goes in before the heat goes on.

7 cups apple juice
2 cups packed brown sugar
1 cup kosher salt
3 quarts water
3 Texas oranges, quartered
15 whole cloves
6 slices fresh ginger
5 bay leaves
2 tablespoons minced garlic
1 turkey (14 pounds), cleaned
$1/4$ cup olive oil

In a large saucepan, bring the apple juice, brown sugar and salt to a boil. Cook until sugar is dissolved; remove from the heat. Cool to room temperature. In a large (5-gallon) container, combine the water, oranges, cloves, ginger, bay leaves and garlic. Stir in the apple juice mixture. Submerge the turkey in this brine; cover and refrigerate for 24 hours. (Use a heavy weight to keep turkey submerged if necessary.)

Prepare the grill for indirect cooking, using soaked wood chips for smoke. Remove turkey from the brine and pat dry. Tie legs together with kitchen string. Lightly brush with olive oil. Set on a rack inside a heavy-duty foil pan. Grill over indirect medium heat until wings are golden brown, about 45 minutes.

Wrap the wings in foil to prevent them from burning. Grill until turkey breasts are golden brown, about 1 hour. Cover entire turkey with foil; continue to cook until a meat thermometer reads 180°, about 2 hours. Transfer turkey to a cutting board and let rest for 20 minutes before carving. Use the pan drippings to make gravy if desired. Serves 8-10.

SHINER BOCK
BARBECUED CABRITO

Shiner Bock is just about our favorite beer anywhere, rain or shine. And that's not bad for a brewery whose employee roll is just about as big as the population of its town. The folks who live in Shiner, though, take special pride in this bock beer and its several siblings, whether they work at the brewery or not. In this recipe, it becomes a magical ingredient in a marinade for roast goat. By the way, there's a whole Texas cook-off devoted to the art of barbecuing goat—it's held in the town of Brady each year.

1 goat hindquarter (5 to 6 pounds),
   cleaned
$1/2$ cup prepared mustard
2 jalapeño peppers, seeded and chopped
$1/2$ cup chopped fresh cilantro
$1/2$ cup lemon-pepper seasoning
$1/2$ cup chili powder
2 tablespoons garlic powder
1 teaspoon ground red pepper
1 cup butter
1 large onion, sliced
1 tablespoon minced garlic
2 lemons, quartered
2 limes, quartered
1 bottle (12 ounces) Shiner Bock beer
2 cups vegetable oil
$1/2$ cup Worcestershire sauce
Barbecue sauce

Rub the goat with mustard. In a gallon-size resealable plastic bag, combine the jalapeños, cilantro, lemon-pepper, chili powder, garlic powder and red pepper. Place meat in the bag, turning to cover with seasonings. Seal and refrigerate overnight.

To prepare the sauce, the next day, melt butter in a large saucepan. Cook the onion and garlic until caramelized. Add the lemons, limes and beer. When the foam subsides, stir in the oil and Worcestershire sauce. Simmer for about 25 minutes.

Prepare the grill for indirect cooking, using soaked mesquite chips for smoke. Remove meat from marinade and place directly on the grill. Smoke for 2-3 hours, basting regularly with the sauce. When a meat thermometer reads 155°, wrap meat in foil. Return to the grill; continue to cook until the thermometer reads 185°. Remove from the grill and let rest for 20 meats before carving. Serve with barbecue sauce on the side. Serves 6-8.

THE SIDES

CLASSIC POTATO SALAD

Of the Holy Trinity of barbecue side dishes—potato salad, coleslaw and beans—this one tends to be the ultimate must-have. In Texas, the balancing act in potato salad is generally between the mayo that makes it sweet and the mustard that makes it tangy. This just in: You don't need a Ph.D. in chemistry to adjust this recipe according to your personal preference.

2 pounds russet potatoes, peeled and
    cut into cubes
1 cup diced pickles
1 cup diced celery
2 tablespoons diced red bell pepper
$^2/_3$ cup mayonnaise
3 tablespoons yellow mustard
1 teaspoon salt
1 teaspoon black pepper

Boil the potatoes in salted water until tender, about 15-20 minutes; drain. In a large bowl, combine the pickles, celery and bell pepper; add warm potatoes. In a small bowl, combine the mayonnaise, mustard, salt and pepper. Pour over salad and gently toss to coat, being careful not to break up the potato cubes. Cover and refrigerate for at least 2 hours. Serves 8-10.

WARM GERMAN POTATO SALAD

Germans were important to the development of Texas barbecue, opening those butcher shops and meat markets in central Texas that, lacking refrigeration, started making sausage with what was left of their fresh meats. From there, it was a short (and frugal) journey to the smoker—and one entire wing of the Texas barbecue tradition. In central Texas, you'll sometimes see this warm, vinegary potato salad instead of the standard mayo-mustard kind.

2 pounds russet potatoes
$^1/_2$ pound bacon, chopped
1 large onion, chopped
2 ribs celery, chopped
1 teaspoon chopped fresh tarragon
$^1/_2$ teaspoon chopped fresh basil
$^1/_2$ cup cider vinegar
$^1/_2$ cup water
3 tablespoons sugar
1 tablespoon cornstarch
1 teaspoon celery seed
1 teaspoon salt
$^1/_4$ teaspoon black pepper

Boil the potatoes in salted water until tender, about 35-40 minutes. Meanwhile, in a large skillet, cook the bacon until crisp and fat is rendered. Using a slotted spoon, remove bacon to paper towels. In the drippings, saute the onion, celery, tarragon and basil for 5 minutes. Stir in vinegar and water; bring to a boil. Add the sugar, cornstarch, celery seed, salt and pepper.

Drain potatoes; peel and slice while still warm. Place in a large bowl; add dressing and stir to coat. Sprinkle with bacon. Serve warm. Serves 8.

SWEET 'N' CREAMY COLESLAW

It's possible to make coleslaw without mayonnaise, as we imagine you might for dietary reasons. For our money and mouth, though, the taste of traditional Texas coleslaw is more than worth the caloric price of admission.

1 head green cabbage, shredded
$^2/_3$ cup chopped green onions
$^1/_2$ cup shredded carrots
1 $^1/_2$ cups mayonnaise
1 cup heavy cream
$^1/_4$ cup honey
2 $^1/_2$ tablespoons sugar
1 tablespoon minced seeded jalapeño
    peppers
1 teaspoon salt
$^1/_2$ teaspoon Worcestershire sauce
$^1/_2$ teaspoon white pepper
$^1/_2$ teaspoon black pepper

In a large bowl, combine the cabbage, green onions and carrots. In a small bowl, whisk the remaining ingredients until blended. Pour over cabbage mixture and toss until thoroughly combined. Cover and refrigerate for at least 1 hour. Serves 6-8.

NO-MAYO VINEGAR COLESLAW

Though Texas, like most of the Deep South, loves its mayonnaise in almost anything, some barbecue places logically prefer a lighter, tangier side dish. Arguably, this coleslaw is less redundant with the potato salad than the mayo-based, plus it can have a little kick of its own.

1 head green cabbage, shredded
2 large carrots, thinly shredded
1 large onion, chopped
1 green bell pepper, chopped
1 cup sugar
1 cup white vinegar
1 tablespoon grated horseradish
1 teaspoon mustard seed
1 teaspoon celery seed
1 teaspoon ground turmeric
1 teaspoon salt

In a large bowl, combine the cabbage, carrots, onion and bell pepper. In a saucepan, combine the remaining ingredients. Bring to a boil just until blended. Pour over cabbage mixture and toss until combined. Refrigerate for several hours before serving. Serves 6-8.

CHUCK WAGON PINTO BEANS

The more south and west you go in Texas, the more an eastern fixation on sweet baked beans gives way to this taste of the Old West. In all those movies when Gabby Hayes served cowboys from a chuck wagon (named after Charles Goodnight, of Goodnight-Loving Trail fame), it's a safe bet they tasted a lot like this.

2 cups dried pinto beans, sorted
 and rinsed
Water
1 ham hock
$^1/_2$ cup chopped onion
1 tablespoon sugar
1 tablespoon chili powder
1 teaspoon paprika
$^1/_2$ teaspoon minced garlic
$^1/_2$ teaspoon salt
$^1/_2$ teaspoon black pepper
$^1/_3$ cup heavy cream

Place the beans in a large pot or Dutch oven. Add enough water to cover beans by 3 inches. Add the ham hock, onion, sugar, chili powder, paprika, garlic, salt and pepper. Bring to a boil; reduce heat. Cover and simmer until beans are tender, about 3 hours. Add cream after about 2 hours of cooking. Add water if more liquid is needed. Do not stir to avoid breaking the beans. Serves 6-8.

BROWN SUGAR BAKED BEANS

Though chili powdered pinto beans are preferred in some Texas barbecue joints, many opt to serve a sweeter version made by juicing up canned pork and beans. It's all pretty easy, really, and the flavors are phenomenal. Here's a recipe that borrows the best from several places we've visited.

2 cans (15 ounces *each*) pork and beans
$^2/_3$ cup packed brown sugar
$^1/_2$ cup chopped onion
$^1/_2$ cup ketchup
1 tablespoon yellow mustard
1 teaspoon Worcestershire sauce
1 teaspoon red wine vinegar
$^1/_2$ teaspoon salt
$^1/_2$ teaspoon black pepper
2 slices bacon, chopped

Preheat oven to 350°. In a baking dish, combine the pork and beans, brown sugar, onion, ketchup, mustard, Worcestershire sauce, vinegar, salt and pepper. Stir in the bacon. Bake for 1 hour or until sauce is thickened. (Or you can set the dish in the smoker, as many barbecue places do, and cook until thickened.) Serves 8.

BLACK-EYED PEAS

*In addition to the good luck they suppos-
edly bring if devoured on New Year's Day,
black-eyed peas smothered the Texas way
are simply one of the best bean dishes
you'll ever taste. They're terrific as a
side dish, or spoon them over steamed
rice and serve as the centerpiece of a
light meal.*

4 slices bacon, diced
1 large carrot, diced
2 ribs celery, diced
1 yellow onion, diced
2 cups dried black-eyed peas, sorted
    and rinsed
2 cups chicken stock
1 bay leaf
2 tablespoons chopped fresh thyme
2 tablespoons chopped fresh oregano

In a skillet or saucepan, sauté the bacon
until it starts to turn crisp. Add the
carrot, celery, onion and black-eyed peas;
cook and stir over medium-high heat
until vegetables are softened. Add the
stock, bay leaf, thyme and oregano.
Simmer over medium heat until the beans
are cooked through and the stock has
evaporated, about 45 minutes. Discard
bay leaf before serving. Serves 4.

PEPPER JACK
POTATO CASSEROLE

*Texans love casseroles. You wouldn't find
something like this on a cattle drive, of
course, but you certainly would find it
served by the lady of the house at many a
social on the ranch. And if you go to a
church supper, look out...you might have
to vote on which of several versions you
like best!*

6 medium potatoes, peeled and quartered
$1/2$ cup sour cream
$1/2$ teaspoon salt
3 to 4 tablespoons whole milk
1 cup (4 ounces) shredded pepper Jack
    cheese

Boil the potatoes in salted water until
tender, about 25 minutes; drain. Mash by
hand or with an electric mixer set on low.
Add the sour cream and salt, along with
just enough milk to make a fluffy consistency. Stir in the shredded cheese.

Preheat oven to 350°. Transfer potato
mixture to a greased $1 1/2$-quart baking
dish. Bake, uncovered, for 45 minutes or
until heated through and golden on top.
Serves 6.

COWBOY POTATOES

This is one of those dishes that everybody in Texas makes a little differently, but nobody makes less than well. Here's our version that's great with barbecue.

2 medium potatoes, peeled and cut into
   $1/2$-inch cubes
2 tablespoons vegetable oil
1 yellow onion, thinly sliced
$1/2$ teaspoon salt
$1/2$ teaspoon black pepper
1 tablespoon minced garlic
$1/2$ cup chopped green onions
2 tablespoons chopped fresh parsley
1 tablespoon Worcestershire sauce

Partially cook the potatoes in just enough water to cover for about 5 minutes; drain and cool slightly. In a skillet, heat oil; add the potatoes, onion, salt and pepper. Cook until golden brown, 10-12 minutes, stirring in the garlic halfway through cooking time. Add the green onions, parsley and Worcestershire sauce; cook 1-2 minutes more. Serves 4-6.

CANDIED SWEET POTATOES

In East Texas especially, where barbecue is so strongly associated with the African-American community, it's a given that you need these candied sweet potatoes to serve to guests with just about anything. Also, considering the geographic proximity to Louisiana, a lot of folks mistakenly call this dish "candied yams," just as they do over in New Orleans.

4 large sweet potatoes, peeled and sliced
2 cups sugar
$1/2$ cup packed light brown sugar
$1/2$ cup butter, melted
2 teaspoons vanilla extract
$1/8$ teaspoon ground cinnamon
$1/8$ teaspoon ground nutmeg

Preheat oven to 375°. Rinse the potato slices and pat dry; place in a baking dish. Add the remaining ingredients; stir until combined. Cover tightly and bake for 45 minutes or until potatoes are tender. Serves 8.

FRIED GREEN TOMATOES

Long before this dish figured in a popular book and movie, the batter-frying of green tomatoes was a Deep South favorite. Though these sometimes turn up with very fancy touches in the hands of very fancy chefs, we prefer our down-home foods—well, down-home.

2 cups all-purpose flour
1$^{1}/_{2}$ cups water
2 teaspoons black pepper
$^{3}/_{4}$ teaspoon salt
2$^{1}/_{2}$ cups unseasoned bread crumbs
6 medium green tomatoes, cut into
   $^{1}/_{4}$-inch slices
Vegetable oil for frying

In a shallow bowl, whisk the flour, water, pepper and salt to form a smooth batter. Pour the bread crumbs onto a plate. Dip tomato slices into batter and then into the bread crumbs, shaking off any excess.

In a skillet, heat about $^{1}/_{4}$ inch of oil; fry the tomatoes in batches until golden, about 2 minutes on each side. Excellent with Honey-Jalapeño Party Dip (recipe on page 240). Serves 8.

FRIED OKRA

A fair number of Texas barbecue joints don't have fryers at all...meaning no fried chicken or catfish, no french fries, and none of this wonderful fried okra. But if there is a fryer in the kitchen, it's a safe bet this favorite will be one of the choices of sides.

2 cups all-purpose flour
1$^{1}/_{2}$ cups water
2 teaspoons black pepper
$^{3}/_{4}$ teaspoon salt
2 to 3 cups unseasoned bread crumbs
$^{3}/_{4}$ pound fresh *or* frozen whole okra pods
   or sliced okra
Vegetable oil for frying

In a shallow bowl, whisk the flour, water, pepper and salt to form a smooth batter. Pour the bread crumbs into a separate bowl. Toss the okra with batter until evenly coated, then cover with bread crumbs. Place on a plate in the freezer while the oil is heating.

In a deep-fat fryer, heat about 3 inches of oil to 350°. Using a basket, fry the okra in batches until golden brown, 5-6 minutes, shaking the basket occasionally to keep okra from sticking together. Drain thoroughly. Serve hot. Serves 8.

SMOTHERED GREENS

We love leftovers, especially when they're "left over" from the rich African-American traditions some people like to call soul food. We have no trouble making these greens part of our or anybody else's religion, since they sure do speak to our soul.

$^3/_4$ pound bacon, chopped
1 cup finely chopped onion
$^3/_4$ cup chopped green bell pepper
$^1/_2$ cup chopped celery
7 pounds tender greens (one variety *or* mixed), torn into 2-inch pieces
2 small ham hocks
2 tablespoons vinegar
$1^1/_2$ teaspoons salt
$1^1/_2$ teaspoons black pepper
1 teaspoon hot pepper sauce
2 cups chicken stock

In a heavy pot, cook the bacon until the fat is rendered. Add onion, bell pepper and celery; cook until caramelized. Add the greens; cover and cook until wilted, about 15 minutes. Add the ham hocks, vinegar, salt, pepper and hot pepper sauce, cover and cook for another 15 minutes.

Add stock; cover and simmer for about 1 hour. Serve with a bottle of hot peppered vinegar. Excellent spooned over squares of Jalapeño-Cheddar Cornbread (recipe on page 232). Serves 10.

CREAMED SPINACH

Barbecue joints with side dishes on a buffet line—which means a lot of barbecue joints—love few things better than this down-home creamed spinach. And besides, it holds up really well on a steam table.

$^1/_2$ cup all-purpose flour
3 cups half-and-half cream, *divided*
3 packages (10 ounces *each*) frozen chopped spinach, thawed and drained
$^1/_2$ cup butter, cubed
3 teaspoons salt
$1^1/_2$ teaspoons black pepper

In a large saucepan over medium heat, mix the flour and 1 cup cream to form a paste. Add the spinach; blend well. Stir in the butter and remaining cream. Season with salt and pepper. Reduce heat; simmer until thickened, about 20 minutes. Serves 6-8.

SMOTHERED SNAP BEANS

It's a shame so many kids these days presume green beans grow in a can. When you get your hands on the fresh ones—especially the kind your Texas grandparents sat around a big bowl breaking, or "snapping"—don't you dare cook them without bacon and onion. Your Texas grandparents would never forgive you.

2 pounds fresh snap beans
1$^{1}/_{2}$ pounds bacon, finely chopped
1 large onion, finely chopped
2 cups water
$^{1}/_{2}$ teaspoon salt

Snap off the ends of the beans and chop each into two to three segments; set aside. In a saucepan, stir the bacon and onion until bacon begins to get crisp. Add the beans, water and salt. Cover and cook until beans are tender, about 30 minutes. Serves 4-6.

HUSH PUPPIES

Often associated with fried Gulf fish near the Texas coast (and fried catfish almost anywhere), these fried cornmeal delights turn up as a side in barbecue joint after barbecue joint. Somebody out there must be eating 'em!

1 cup yellow cornmeal
$^{1}/_{2}$ cup all-purpose flour
1 teaspoon sugar
$^{3}/_{4}$ teaspoon coarsely ground black pepper
$^{1}/_{2}$ teaspoon baking powder
$^{1}/_{2}$ teaspoon baking soda
$^{1}/_{2}$ teaspoon garlic powder
$^{1}/_{2}$ teaspoon salt
1 tablespoon finely minced onion
$^{1}/_{2}$ tablespoon finely minced red bell
    pepper
$^{1}/_{2}$ tablespoon finely minced jalapeño
    pepper
1 egg, lightly beaten
1 cup milk
2 cups vegetable oil

In a large bowl, combine the dry ingredients with onion, bell pepper and jalapeño. Stir in the egg. Add milk slowly until the batter is thick but still pourable. In a large skillet, heat oil; drop teaspoonfuls of batter into oil; cook until golden brown. Drain on paper towels. Serves 6-8.

JALAPEÑO-CHEDDAR CORNBREAD

What could be better than cornbread? Well, actually, this could. We're not sure who first thought of mixing cheese and jalapeños into this Old South favorite, but we sure would like to give him or her a medal.

$1^1/_2$ cups all-purpose flour
$1^1/_8$ cups yellow cornmeal
$2/_3$ cup sugar
3 teaspoons baking powder
$1/_2$ teaspoon salt
2 eggs
$1^1/_3$ cups milk
5 tablespoons unsalted butter, melted
1 cup (4 ounces) shredded cheddar cheese
3 tablespoons chopped seeded jalapeño
    peppers

Preheat oven to 350°. In a bowl, combine the flour, cornmeal, sugar, baking powder and salt. In a separate bowl, lightly beat the eggs, then whisk in milk and butter. Stir into dry ingredients just until moistened. Blend in the cheese and jalapeños.

Pour into a greased 8-inch square baking pan. Bake for 50 minutes or until golden brown. Serve warm or at room temperature. Serves 6-8.

GRILLED VEGETABLES

In the past, cowboys worked hard enough all day that they never had to order grilled vegetables to lose a few pounds. But when you have wood or coals glowing hot on a grill, it seems a shame not to whip up a batch of these wonders. They're about as much fun as you can have with vegetables without recourse to bacon.

$3/_4$ cup olive oil
$1/_3$ cup dry white Texas wine
2 tablespoons minced onion
2 tablespoons minced garlic
1 cup chopped fresh basil
2 tablespoons chopped fresh rosemary
2 teaspoons black pepper
1 teaspoon salt
5 zucchini, sliced lengthwise
5 yellow squash, sliced lengthwise
5 small eggplant, sliced crosswise
5 red bell peppers, sliced

In a large bowl, combine the oil, wine, onion, garlic, basil, rosemary, pepper and salt; let stand for about 1 hour. Add the vegetables and toss to coat; marinate for 1 hour.

Preheat the grill to medium. Oil the cooking surface to prevent sticking. Grill the vegetables in a single layer until marked and tender, turning occasionally, about 5 minutes for the squash and 10 minutes for the eggplant and peppers. Serve arranged on a platter. Serves 8-10.

BLACK BEAN AND RICE SALAD

For those outdoor gatherings in spring and fall, when the weather is neither too hot nor too cold and the skies tend to be deep blue, there isn't much better than a heaping bowl of this colorful, nutritious salad for the crowd that's certain to gather 'round it.

3 tablespoons olive oil
2 tablespoons freshly squeezed lime juice
$1/4$ teaspoon ground cumin
$1/4$ teaspoon black pepper
1 cup cold cooked rice
1 cup cooked *or* canned black beans,
    rinsed and drained
1 cup cooked corn kernels
1 cup chopped tomato
$1/4$ cup thinly sliced red bell pepper
2 green onions, chopped
3 tablespoons chopped fresh cilantro
2 tablespoons chopped fresh parsley
$1/3$ cup toasted pecan halves
Lettuce leaves for garnish

In a large bowl, whisk the oil, lime juice, cumin and pepper. Stir in the rice, black beans, corn, tomato, bell pepper, green onions, cilantro and parsley. Stir in the pecans. Serve at room temperature or chill for 30 minutes before serving atop lettuce leaves. Serves 4-6.

SUMMERTIME FRUIT SALAD

Make no mistake: It gets hot in Texas. Some parts get hotter than others, but we can't think of any square inch that doesn't mean it when it says "summer." For those hottest of summer days, even when you're more likely to spend them splashing in the pool than working in the barn, here's a treat to help cool you down.

$3/4$ cup sour cream
$1/4$ cup orange juice
1 tablespoon honey
2 teaspoons fresh mint, crushed
4 cups mixed fresh fruit (such as berries,
    sliced peaches and cubed melon)

To prepare the dressing, combine the sour cream, orange juice, honey and mint in a small bowl. Refrigerate for at least 1 hour. Just before serving, pour over mixed fruit and gently blend to coat. Or, for individual servings, arrange the fruit on lettuce leaves and drizzle with dressing. Serves 6-8.

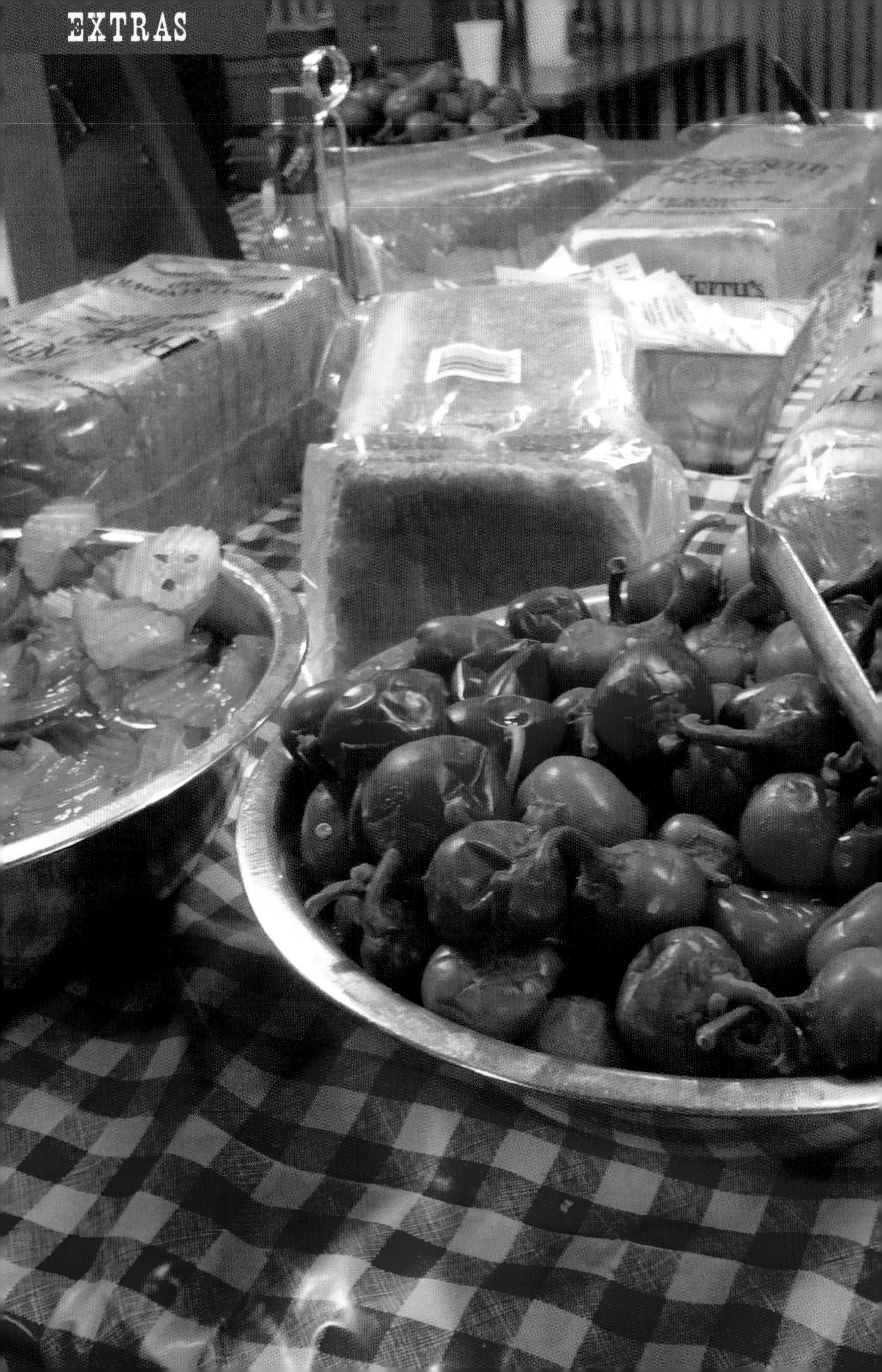

THE EXTRAS

VENISON CHILI

The moment the fall temperature drops a few degrees, many Texas barbecue joints consider it a sign that it's chili season. In such a setting, chili is nearly always made with leftover beef. But in homes across Texas, once deer season has begun, chili can be made with one thing and one thing alone.

4 thick slices bacon, diced
2 pounds Texas venison, cleaned and
  cut into $1/4$-inch cubes
2 large onions, diced
2 ribs celery, diced
$1/2$ cup minced garlic
1 to 2 poblano or jalapeño peppers,
  seeded and diced
2 cups diced tomatoes
2 cups beef stock
Juice and zest of 1 lemon
6 tablespoons chili powder
4 tablespoons cumin
2 tablespoons brown sugar
6 ancho chiles, seeded and puréed
Salt and black pepper to taste

In a soup pot, cook the bacon until fat is rendered; using a slotted spoon, remove and set aside. In the drippings, brown the meat in batches over high heat; set meat aside. In the same pot, sauté the onions, celery, garlic and poblanos.

Add the bacon, tomatoes, stock, lemon juice and zest, chili powder, cumin, brown sugar and puréed anchos. Bring to a boil; reduce heat. Return meat to the pan. Simmer slowly for 2 hours, adding a little beer or water if chili becomes too thick. Serves 10-12.

SAGEBRUSH CHICKEN SOUP

Every culture needs a great chicken soup...something your mother or grand-mother can give you (or prescribe over the phone) when you feel the slightest cold coming on. While some of these can be pretty basic, here's one that will please even when there's no cold in sight.

2 quarts chicken stock
$3/4$ pound boiling potatoes, peeled and
  finely chopped
2 ribs celery with leaves, finely chopped
2 carrots, finely chopped
1 large onion, finely chopped
1 tablespoon minced garlic
$3/4$ teaspoon rubbed sage
$1/2$ teaspoon dried thyme
$1/3$ cup Texas Chardonnay
Salt and black pepper to taste
2 cups cubed smoked *or* roasted chicken
Sour cream and chopped fresh parsley
  for garnish

In a soup pot, bring stock just to a boil. Add the potatoes, celery, carrots, onion, garlic, sage and thyme. Cook until vegetables are tender, about 30 minutes. Stir in the wine; season with salt and pepper. Add the chicken; heat through. Ladle into soup bowls; garnish with a dollop of sour cream and sprinkling of parsley. Serves 6-8.

ALL POTATOES
NEW RED POTATOES
SM/LRG. and SWT
POTATOES
89¢ A #

ound

GRILLED SNAPPER TACOS WITH PEACH SALSA

As Texas has learned to "think outside the bun," in the popular advertising parlance, it thinks more often than not inside the taco. Here's a variation on the fish tacos that came here from that other piece of Mexico—California. The salsa is a great use for Hill Country peaches when they're at their peak of seasonal sweetness.

1 pound red snapper fillets, skin removed
$^1/_4$ cup freshly squeezed lime juice
1 tablespoon minced fresh cilantro
1 teaspoon minced garlic
1 teaspoon chopped seeded Serrano
    pepper
$^1/_2$ teaspoon salt
$^1/_2$ teaspoon black pepper

Salsa:
2 cups chopped peeled peaches
1 cup chopped tomato
1 cup diced red onion
$^1/_4$ cup freshly squeezed lime juice
3 tablespoons minced fresh cilantro
2 tablespoons minced green onions
1 teaspoon chopped seeded Serrano
    pepper
1 teaspoon honey
$^1/_4$ teaspoon salt

16 corn *or* flour tortillas, warmed
2 cups shredded green cabbage
Additional minced cilantro for garnish

Place snapper fillets in a glass bowl or plastic bag; add lime juice, cilantro, garlic, Serrano, salt and pepper. Marinate in the refrigerator for 2 hours.

To prepare the salsa, combine the peaches, tomato, onion, lime juice, cilantro, green onions, Serrano, honey and salt in a bowl. Toss gently so peaches and tomatoes are not damaged. Let stand for 10-15 minutes for flavors to combine.

Preheat grill to high. Drain marinade. Grill fillets for 3-4 minutes on each side or until fish flakes easily with a fork. Cut fish into small chunks; wrap in two warm tortillas for each taco. Garnish with peach salsa, shredded cabbage and a little more cilantro. Serves 4.

FRIED CATFISH WITH SWEET JALAPEÑO TARTAR SAUCE

As more and more Texas barbecue joints have fryers in their kitchens—as some have from Day 1—more and more are offering fried farm-raised catfish, at least as a special on Fridays. By the way, there are quite a few catfish farms springing up in the Lone Star State, including several in Palacios near Matagorda Bay.

Tartar Sauce:
$^2/_3$ cup mayonnaise
4 teaspoons diced Spanish olives
3 teaspoons diced sweet pickled jalapeño
   peppers
2 teaspoons minced green onion
$^1/_2$ teaspoon minced fresh parsley
$^1/_2$ teaspoon freshly squeezed lemon juice
$^1/_8$ teaspoon Worcestershire sauce
$^1/_8$ teaspoon hot pepper sauce
$^1/_8$ teaspoon dill weed
$^1/_8$ teaspoon ground red pepper
$^1/_8$ teaspoon salt
$^1/_8$ teaspoon black pepper

Catfish:
4 catfish fillets (8 ounces *each*)
1 teaspoon salt
1 teaspoon black pepper
Yellow cornmeal seasoned with salt and
   pepper
2 eggs, beaten
1 teaspoon water
Vegetable oil for frying

In a bowl, combine the tartar sauce ingredients. Cover and refrigerate for at least 1 hour.

Cut each catfish fillet into two to three long slices; season with salt and pepper. Place the seasoned cornmeal in a shallow bowl. Combine eggs and water in another bowl. Dredge catfish pieces in cornmeal, then dip into the egg wash, then dredge again in cornmeal.

In a skillet or deep-fat fryer, heat oil to 350°. Fry catfish until golden brown, 3-4 minutes. Drain on paper towels. Serve with tartar sauce. Serves 6.

PANHANDLE CHICKEN FRICASSEE

Every Texas country cook should have chicken fricassee ("chicken stew," if you're not in the mood for French) in his or her bag of tricks. It's a wonderful destiny for a whole chicken, and it makes use of one of our other favorite ingredients, bacon. In that Dutch oven, you can even make this recipe in the ground with hot coals, the way cowboys on cattle drives used to.

3 tablespoons vegetable oil
2 slices bacon, diced
1 chicken (6 to 7 pounds), cut into
    serving-size pieces
3 yellow onions, finely chopped
4 cloves garlic, minced
2 tablespoons all-purpose flour
2 cups chicken stock
2 bay leaves
2 sprigs fresh thyme
2 tablespoons minced fresh parsley
1 tablespoon Worcestershire sauce
2 teaspoons salt
$1/2$ teaspoon black pepper
Hot cooked white rice

Heat the oil in a Dutch oven; cook bacon until crisp and fat is rendered. Add chicken pieces; cook until browned on all sides, about 10 minutes. Remove the chicken. In the drippings, sauté the onions and garlic until golden. Stir in the flour to create a roux, letting it cook until dark golden brown.

Return chicken to the pot. Add the stock, bay leaves, thyme, parsley, Worcestershire sauce, salt and pepper. Cover and cook over medium heat until chicken is tender, about 1 hour. Discard bay leaves and thyme sprigs. Serve chicken with gravy in a bowl or tureen with plenty of rice. Serves 6-8.

SMOKED SAUSAGE QUESO

Along with fajitas, queso must be considered the national dish of Tex-Mex. To look at the entrées when they come out at a "Mexican" meal, it's hard to understand why anybody really needs more cheese. But that never stops us from grabbing a tortilla chip or seven and digging in.

$3/4$ pound Texas smoked sausage
2 tablespoons olive oil
$1/2$ cup finely chopped red onion
$1/2$ cup finely chopped green bell pepper
3 cups heavy cream
$2 1/2$ cups (10 ounces) shredded Monterey
    Jack cheese
$2 1/2$ cups (10 ounces) shredded pepper
    Jack cheese
2 teaspoons cornstarch
2 teaspoons cold water
$1/2$ cup chopped green onions
Tortilla chips

In a food processor, pulse sausage into a fine crumble. Heat oil in a skillet; brown the sausage over medium-high heat. Add the onion and green pepper; cook and stir until caramelized, 4-5 minutes.

Stir in cream. Reduce heat to medium and whisk to incorporate. Gradually add the cheeses, stirring until melted and incorporated. Dissolve cornstarch in water; add to cheese mixture and cook until thickened. Garnish with green onions. Serve in a bowl with tortilla chips. Serves 10-12.

TEXAS PECAN CHEESE BALL

Texans love to throw parties, especially around the holidays. We've found this cheese ball to be quite a hit. And remember: Both the wine and the pecans, like all those ex-es in the song, should live in Texas.

1 package (8 ounces) cream cheese, softened
2 ounces crumbled Gorgonzola cheese
$1/4$ cup shredded sharp cheddar cheese
2 tablespoons Texas Riesling
$1/2$ cup finely chopped Texas pecans
2 tablespoons paprika

In a mixing bowl, blend the cheeses and wine. Shape into a ball. Sprinkle pecans and paprika onto a sheet of waxed paper; roll the cheese ball over pecans and paprika until coated. Wrap in waxed paper. Refrigerate for at least 6 hours or overnight before serving. Serves 8-10.

HONEY-JALAPEÑO PARTY DIP

When the party table needs one more thing, after you've whipped up the queso and the cheese ball, go for this appetizer that doesn't even include cheese. To the naked eye, here's a dip that looks nice and cooling...but it definitely can pack a punch. How much punch is totally up to you. Vary the amount of jalapeños, hot pepper sauce or red pepper.

1 cup mayonnaise
4 teaspoons honey
$1/3$ cup thinly sliced green onions
$1^{1}/_{2}$ teaspoons minced seeded jalapeño pepper
$1/4$ teaspoon Worcestershire sauce
$1/4$ teaspoon hot pepper sauce
$1/8$ teaspoon black pepper
$1/8$ teaspoon white pepper
$1/8$ teaspoon ground red pepper
Tortilla chips

In a bowl, whisk the mayonnaise, honey, green onions, jalapeño, Worcestershire sauce, hot pepper sauce and seasonings. Cover and refrigerate for 1 hour. Serve with tortilla chips. Serves 6-8.

THE SWEETS

BBQ JOINT BANANA PUDDING

*To lovers of old-fashioned Texas barbe-
cue, a meal pretty much isn't over if it
doesn't end with a scoop or three of
banana pudding. These days, more and
more of the stuff in restaurants is store-
bought, or else it's made from a mix.
Come on, guys, banana pudding isn't
hard to make. Here's our toast to the
old-fashioned way.*

$^3/_4$ cup sugar
$^1/_4$ cup all-purpose flour
$^1/_8$ teaspoon salt
3 egg yolks, beaten
$^1/_2$ teaspoon vanilla extract
$^1/_2$ teaspoon banana extract
2 cups milk
3 bananas, sliced
14 vanilla wafers
Whipped cream and additional vanilla
    wafers for garnish

In a mixing bowl, combine the sugar,
flour and salt. Whisk in the egg yolks and
extracts. In a saucepan, heat milk; gradually stir in egg yolk mixture. Cook until
thickened. Layer the bananas and vanilla
wafers in a $1^1/_2$-quart dish. Pour pudding
over the top. Refrigerate until chilled.
Garnish with whipped cream and additional vanilla wafers. Serves 8.

DEWBERRY COBBLER WITH PORT WHIPPED CREAM

*You just don't see Texas dewberries as
much as you used to, though their season
has always been pretty short anyway.
If need be, you can make this cobbler
with blackberries (as a lot of barbecue
joints do). But a basket of the real deal
means you must make it, no questions
asked, no prisoners taken.*

2 sheets refrigerated pie pastry
1 quart Texas dewberries *or* blackberries
2 cups sugar
$^3/_4$ pound butter, cubed
1 cup heavy cream
2 tablespoons Texas Port

Preheat oven to 325°. Line the sides of
a 2-quart baking dish with half of one
sheet of pastry. Place half of the berries,
sugar and butter in baking dish. Cut the
remaining half sheet of pastry into small
pieces; scatter over berry layer. Top with
remaining berries, sugar and butter.
Cover with second sheet of pastry. Cut
holes in pastry. Bake for 1 hour or until
golden brown.

In a small bowl, whip the cream and wine
until light and fluffy. Cut cobbler into
squares; serve warm with a dollop of
whipped cream. Serves 6-8.

SWEETS

HILL COUNTRY PEACH BREAD PUDDING

Good years and bad, Texas Hill Country remains one of America's greatest destinations for peaches in the summertime. And when the peaches come in, juicy and sweet, it is every Texas cook's moral responsibility to use them as many ways as possible. Thus this delicious (and very timely) bread pudding.

2 cups milk
1 cup heavy cream
1 cup peach juice
1 loaf French bread, torn into pieces
3 eggs, beaten
2 cups sugar
2 tablespoons vanilla extract
$1^1/_2$ cups chopped Texas peaches
$^1/_4$ cup unsalted butter, melted
Whipped cream

In a large mixing bowl, combine the milk, cream and peach juice. Add bread pieces; soak for 45 minutes. In a separate bowl, combine the eggs, sugar, vanilla and peaches. Using your hands, combine the peach mixture with the milk and bread mixture.

Preheat oven to 300°. Pour melted butter into an 11-inch x 7-inch x 2-inch baking pan; pour batter evenly into pan. Bake for 1 hour or until a knife inserted in the center comes out clean. Serve warm with whipped cream. Serves 8.

GRILLED BANANA SUNDAES

It's not every day you make dessert outside on the grill. But the next time you have the grill all heated up, you might consider making these grilled bananas with sauce, ice cream and almonds your meal's grand finale.

3 large firm bananas
1 tablespoon melted butter
1 tablespoon orange juice, *divided*
$^1/_2$ cup caramel ice cream topping
$^1/_4$ teaspoon ground cinnamon
4 scoops vanilla ice cream
Flaked coconut and toasted sliced almonds

Slice bananas in half lengthwise, then cut across, making 12 segments in all. Combine the butter and $^1/_2$ tablespoon orange juice; brush over all sides of bananas. Grill over low heat for 2 minutes; turn and grill 2 minutes more.

In a large saucepan, heat the caramel topping and remaining orange juice. Stir in cinnamon. Add grilled bananas, stirring gently to coat. Scoop the ice cream into dessert dishes and top with bananas and sauce. Sprinkle with coconut and almonds. Serve immediately. Serves 4.

PECAN PIE

Texas is one of our largest pecan-producing states, with pecans grown in the vast majority of its counties. Each year, as soon as fall comes around, pickups proliferate beside country roads, each with a hand-lettered sign announcing PECANS, by one spelling or another. If we have our way, nearly every pecan grown in Texas will end up as pecan pie.

1 1/2 cups all-purpose flour
1/2 cup shortening
2 tablespoons water
1/2 cup packed brown sugar
1 tablespoon cornstarch
3 eggs, beaten
1 cup dark corn syrup
1 cup light corn syrup
2 tablespoons vanilla extract
1 1/2 cups pecan pieces
Pecan halves for garnish

Place flour in a bowl; cut in shortening until crumbly. Add water, tossing with a fork. Cover and let stand for 30 minutes.

Preheat oven to 350°. On a lightly floured surface, roll out dough; transfer to an 8-inch pie pan. In a mixing bowl, blend the brown sugar, cornstarch and eggs. Add corn syrups and vanilla; mix until thoroughly combined. Sprinkle pecan pieces evenly into crust; top with filling.

Bake for 40 minutes or until a knife inserted in the center comes out clean. Garnish with pecan halves. Cool before slicing. Serves 8.

PRALINES AND CREAM

Ice cream is a huge deal in Texas, at least partially because of the state's loyalty to the Blue Bell brand originating in Brenham. Since Blue Bell is now available in many states far from Texas, no one can say we're not willing to share.

2 cups firmly packed brown sugar
1 cup sugar
1 cup heavy cream
1 cup water
1 teaspoon vanilla extract
3 cups chopped pecans
Blue Bell vanilla ice cream

In a large saucepan, combine the sugars, cream, water and vanilla. Cook and stir until thickened and bubbly. Remove from the heat; beat with a whisk until smooth. Stir in the pecans. Spoon over bowls of ice cream. Serves 10.

TRES LECHES

Rumor has it this recipe first made the rounds by way of condensed milk cans distributed throughout Latin America. What we do know is that Latin Americans fell in love with the super-rich cake called "three milks," and that Americans have followed suit since the first time we got the chance.

$^1/_2$ cup unsalted butter, softened
1 cup sugar
5 eggs
$^1/_2$ teaspoon vanilla extract
$1^1/_2$ cups all-purpose flour
1 teaspoon baking powder
1 cup whole milk
7 ounces sweetened condensed milk
6 ounces evaporated milk

Topping:
1 cup sugar
$^3/_4$ cup evaporated milk
1 teaspoon vanilla extract

Preheat oven to 350°. In a mixing bowl, cream the butter and sugar until fluffy. Add eggs and vanilla, beating well. Combine the flour and baking powder; gradually add to creamed mixture, mixing until incorporated. Pour into a greased and floured 13-inch x 9-inch x 2-inch baking pan. Bake for 30 minutes or until a toothpick inserted in the center comes out clean. Cool on a wire rack.

With a fork, pierce the cake in about 10 places. Combine the three milks; pour over cake. Refrigerate for 2 hours before serving. In a small bowl, whip the topping ingredients until thick. Spread over chilled cake. Serves 8-10.

INDEX OF BBQ JOINTS

INDEX OF RECIPES